Children and Drama

Also by Nellie McCaslin

COLLEGE TEXTS
Creative Drama in the Classroom
Theatre for Young Audiences
Children's Theatre in the United States:
a History

JUVENILES
Shows on a Shoestring
Puppet Fun
Act Now!

PLAYS
Pioneers in Petticoats
Tall Tales and Tall Men
Legends in Action
More Legends in Action

Children and Drama

SECOND EDITION

Edited by
Nellie McCaslin

The Program in Educational Theatre
New York University

Longman
New York & London

Children and Drama, Second edition

Longman Inc., New York, 19 West 44th St., New York, N.Y. 10036
Associated companies, branches, and representatives throughout the world.

Developmental Editor: Gordon T. R. Anderson
Editorial and Design Supervisor: Judith Hirsch
Interior Design: Patricia Smythe
Cover Design: Angela Foote
Manufacturing and Production Supervisor: Maria Chiarino
Composition: A & S Graphics, Inc.
Printing and Binding: Fairfield Graphics

Manufactured in the United States of America

Printing: 10 9 8 7 6 5 4 3 2 1

Library of Congress Cataloging in Publication Data
Main entry under title:

Children and drama.

   Bibliography: p.
   Includes index.
   1. Drama in education — Addresses, essays, lectures.   I. McCaslin, Nellie.
PN3171.C49   1981   792'.0226   80-20266
ISBN 0-582-28250-0

To Nancy and Lowell Swortzell, colleagues and friends, with whom it is a continuing pleasure to work; and whose work brings continuing strength to our field.

Contents

Foreword

Kenneth L. Graham

Kenneth L. Graham, professor emeritus of the Department of Theatre Arts at the University of Minnesota, is a past president of the American Theatre Association and the Children's Theatre Association. His involvement in both college and children's theatre has taken him to various campuses in the United States and abroad. He has conducted institutes for teachers in creative drama and has been a research consultant for the Arts and Humanities Branch of the U.S. Office of Education. Dr. Graham has received numerous awards and honors, including the American College Theatre Festival Award of Excellence in 1973. His wide experience makes him one of the most knowledgable leaders in the educational theatre field.

In this second edition of *Children and Drama*, Nellie McCaslin has expanded her earlier version by including the current thinking of six leading practitioners in the field, five British and one American, as well as retaining the fourteen previous essays, most of which have been substantially revised or updated. Geraldine Siks has written a new article wherein she presents an excellent summary of the major developments in the field during the past six years and predicts possible future thrusts. As before, writers have been given free rein to express individual philosophies in their distinctive writing styles, which range from the pragmatic to the sheer poetry of Agnes Haaga's "Reflections on a Spring Day."

The editor has called on such early innovators as Winifred Ward, Gerald Tyler, and Peter Slade, as well as current leaders in the United States, Britain, and Canada. Among the new British contributions, three must be mentioned here: Donald Baker's informative views on the importance of play for the very young (he speaks of the "under-sevens"); Ian Bowater's incisive exploration of why drama has not yet become central to the curriculum in Britain; and Gavin Bolton's superb analysis of the "myths" that have grown up around drama education. All three are most applicable to the American scene. Indeed, Bolton's article should be required reading for all students in teacher-training institutions as well as for established drama teachers.

Evident throughout the book is a clear theme: The creativity of the individual leader is what makes for exciting results in drama by and for children. In these chapters one may enjoy insights into new directions that reflect viewpoints of the individual writers, but one may also recognize a unifying concept: the power of drama to stimulate in young people meaningful aesthetic experiences.

The important panel report published in 1977, *Coming to Our Senses—The Significance of Arts in American Education*, contains evidence that education in the arts, although still all too often considered peripheral, is in many instances moving toward a more central position in the curriculum. It also indicates, however, that many American educators are reluctant to place drama centrally in teacher-training programs. One hopes that this stimulating book will be a strong incentive toward the further accomplishment of those worthy goals.

Children and Drama is highly recommended for all students and practitioners in drama and theatre — and most especially for administrators involved in teacher-training at the elementary and secondary levels.

Acknowledgment

I should like to take this opportunity to express my great appreciation to all the contributors to *Children and Drama* for their cooperation and generosity in taking the time to discuss their work. Their willingness to be a part of this project has helped create a whole that is larger than the sum of its parts. My thanks would not be complete without also acknowledging the constant help of Gordon T. R. Anderson, executive editor at Longman. His confidence in this book and his guidance throughout the preparation of the manuscript have made my task a pleasure. The resulting text, I hope, will be a unique resource.

Introduction

Nellie McCaslin

Nellie McCaslin, editor of Children and Drama, *teaches in the Program in Educational Theatre at New York University. Dr. McCaslin is the author of the college text* Creative Drama in the Classroom *and the editor of* Theatre for Young Audiences. *She has written three books for young people and four collections of plays for children based on folklore. She is also the author of* Children's Theatre in the United States: a History *and numerous articles and book reviews. She received her B.A. and M.A. degrees from Western Reserve University and her Ph.D. from New York University. She studied with Maria Ouspenskaya in California.*

Dr. McCaslin has taught at National College of Education, Mills College of Education, and Teachers College of Columbia University; she has lectured and led workshops throughout the United States and in England and Canada. She is a past president of the Children's Theatre Association of America, the recipient of the 1967 Jennie Heiden Award, and a fellow of the American Theatre Association.

In my introduction to the first edition of this book I described it as having originated in postconference reflection. Challenged by questions raised in discussion and stimulated by workshops and demonstrations, I found myself periodically attempting to sort out ideas and recall opinions I had heard expressed and contested. Because I felt that others must share this experience of fragmented recollection, I decided to assemble the views of a number of well-known leaders. The result was *Children and Drama.*

Much has been written and said about the place, practice, value, definition, role, and scope of drama in education. Many leaders have demonstrated ways in which the theatre arts can be incorporated into the curriculum and used to enrich community service. Various programs have been introduced over the years. Some of them are still in existence, although most have been altered; others have been discarded in favor of new ideas or changing interests and needs. Aesthetic education versus the arts as teaching tools is an ongoing argument, along with the question, "Who makes the best teacher — generalist, specialist, or artist?" Despite the fact that no consensus has been reached, drama, as means or end, under one kind of leadership or another, has found its place in education on all levels and is now recognized as a subject worthy of inclusion in the curricula of hundreds of schools and colleges. Realistic objectives have been stated, and content appropriate to different age levels and circumstances has been suggested and used. Drama has finally moved from the periphery of the curriculum to a more central, if still insecure, position.

As for children's theatre, it is now generally understood to mean theatre *for* children, not *by* children. Though some may take exception to this definition, the term implies focus on product rather than process. It is process with which this book is primarily concerned.

Education for teachers of drama is today a carefully designed curriculum, though there are few of us who would not like to see both quantitative and qualitative improvements. Effective classroom teaching requires education in the arts, and this means a program that offers more than one course or unit in drama. Ideally, it should be a sequential program including both theory and laboratory experience. There should be an opportunity for the education of both specialist and generalist in a program that recognizes the idiosyncratic needs of each.

Aesthetic education is a relative newcomer to American schools; the concept of drama as a specific teaching tool is even newer. Theory and practice in the arts in our country have been shaped by the social, political, economic, and scientific climate of the period. Within this century we have seen evidence of that shaping. Interest in skill development for vocational use was followed by an emphasis on behavioral goals. This was replaced by a concern for the creative process and its transference to other subject areas. Current interest in cognitive skills and full development of intellectual capacities is accompanied by a concern for humanistic goals. All these interests are evident today in statements of our objectives. Though we are far from unified in our attitude toward the arts, the 1977 Rockefeller report *Coming to Our Senses* reported that the majority of Americans are in favor of arts education. Yet, widespread implementation of this positive expression does not exist.

By the end of the 1970s the use of drama as a therapeutic technique was officially recognized through the formation of a professional association for practitioners, the National Association for Drama Therapy. Programs for special groups, such as the physically handicapped, the emotionally disturbed, the gifted, the retarded, and the culturally and economically deprived, are funded throughout the nation. *The Little Theatre of the Deaf*, established in the 1960s, not only brought quality entertainment to the nonhearing child but stimulated an interest in the further use of drama/theatre with this heretofore neglected population. The latest group to receive attention is the senior adult. It is interesting to note that some of the most successful techniques used on this level have come from teachers of children's creative drama.

Since the turn of the century, social workers in urban areas have been aware of the value of theatre in working with children of immigrants. Today many teachers of the language arts use creative drama as one of the more effective ways of helping children express themselves. Whether used as means or end, drama has gradually gained acceptance and may now be found in school and after-school programs.

Through the structure of the American Theatre Association, divisional organizations representing major areas of interest have been established. One of the largest of these is the Children's Theatre Association of America. Its members are drawn from faculties of elementary schools and university theatre departments; from staffs of community centers, civic theatres, and libraries; and from professional theatre companies. This spread of membership offers an extraordinary opportunity to see beyond the walls of one's own classroom into new avenues of experimentation. The professional journals and conferences of the C.T.A.A. provide further opportunities for sharing ideas. Members are constantly examining the relationship of theatre to education and education to theatre. Many excellent books and articles on various aspects of the subject have been published in the United States, Canada, and England in recent years, but no collection has, as its single purpose, the presentation of current thought and practice by leading authorities in these three countries. Thus the rationale for this text.

In preparing the first edition of this book, I consulted a number of colleagues to find out whether they shared my enthusiasm for such a collection. The results of my questionnaire were encouraging and helpful concerning authors and format. The selection of the contributors was a more difficult task than I had anticipated. There were many outstanding teachers of drama, and choices had to be made. An arbitrary number, necessary as it was, would eliminate many leaders whose reputations and work qualified them for inclusion in any book purporting to represent significant contributions to the field. I regretted the need for selectivity, though I understood it.

The following criteria for selection were finally established: a clearly defined point of view, a demonstrated position of leadership, and contribution to the field. The enthusiastic reception accorded the first edition of *Children and Drama* was gratifying; the request for a new edition six years later proved that it had filled a need. I was particularly pleased that a larger book would allow me to include additional contributors for the second edition. Once more, however, I was to be faced with the problem of selection; the field had grown in six years' time, and there were now even more educators whose methods were attracting attention. Because of the innovative work being done in England, I decided to include more British leaders in this new edition. The presentation of their programs and philosophy, in my opinion, enhances and strengthens the text. The six new authors include Donald Baker, Gavin Bolton, Ian Bowater, John Hodgson, Peter Slade, and Nancy King. The work of the first five has attracted attention in the United States as well as England, while Nancy King's books and workshops in movement and drama surely identify her as an important new American voice.

In both editions of *Children and Drama* I have made an effort to avoid superficiality through the use of a single focus. One topic, discussed by a number of educators, seemed to me to have greater value than a variety of topics dealing with different aspects of the subject. Although the word *children* is used in the title of the book, there are implications for all age levels, including secondary school and college. The book is philosophical rather than practical by intent. It does not aim to tell the reader how to teach by giving lesson plans and exercises; rather, it presents each leader's point of view and the base from which he or she works. In many instances procedures are described as an integral part of the presentation.

Some leaders give the highest priority to drama as a way of learning; others stress aesthetic education; and still others the social and personal growth of the participants. Yet throughout the text I am conscious of an underlying basis of agreement. This may be described simply as their belief in a common goal: experience in the arts for every child. The differing means of reaching that goal distinguishes one author from another.

It is obvious from the varying views expressed that no one approach is always right. Methods must be used, tested, modified, altered, discarded. There is, moreover, the constant reality of the changing times. No situation remains static. Shifting populations, social issues, needs, staff, and budget affect all of us. We have witnessed the popular methods, the gimmicks, the shortcuts to showy results; but we have also seen the slow evolution of concepts that in the end proved sound.

This last observation brings up another point. In our eagerness to "sell" drama to those in power — administrators, parents, school boards — we risk denying what we are trying to promote. To argue the importance of the arts solely on their merit as teaching aids may be giving tacit endorsement of the view that the arts are a "frill." In attempting to assess their worth in practical terms, we ignore their humanizing qualities. This is not to minimize the fact that learning takes place; rather, it is to voice a concern that in stressing one value, we may be obscuring others of equal importance.

Similarly, in an effort to win a class by presenting drama as "fun," we may be implying that substance is dull. The most entertaining works in dramatic literature have content, whereas a thoughtful or provocative play must entertain in order to communicate its message. Describing drama as fun, therefore, stresses only one aspect. Fun means enjoyment and relaxation to many, but it can mean a lack of seriousness to others. Hence to employ the term *fun* as persuasion not only misleads but denies the importance of drama.

Perhaps it is also time to review our curriculum instead of giving it unqualified support through the arts. Does it still meet our needs? Is a new curriculum in order? What about a curriculum in which the arts have a place equal to the so-called basic subjects? Budget cuts have already eliminated arts programs that were acknowledged to be popular and successful. Is it possible to evaluate the effectiveness of the arts without also examining the curriculum in which they are placed?

My own views toward drama and theatre education are well known. In expressing them, I must acknowledge my indebtedness both to those colleagues who have preceded me and to those currently engaged in work that I know and respect. Their influence and my own years of teaching have led me to certain convictions: all children should be given the opportunity of experiencing both drama and theatre, and each should be of the highest quality. Whereas children's theatre engages the child as spectator, creative drama involves the child as participant. Only participatory theatre, under skilled leadership, succeeds in blending the two so as to create a form that is new and different. With the exception of participatory theatre, however, which serves in a special way, I am convinced that creative drama is better than public performance for children of elementary school age. Performance for an audience must, by its nature, stress product and the technical skills with which to display it. Young children enjoy the process of creating and only occasionally wish to share their work with outsiders. The pressures of rehearsal more often than not bore the child and dampen the spirit, particularly when the decision to produce a play comes from the teacher.

Committed as I am to this point of view, I am willing to concede that sharing a play with an audience is at times a valid and worthwhile experience. When a play is produced, the teacher should avoid long rehearsals, pressures for perfection, and rote memorization of movement and lines. Avoided also should be the featuring of a few children at the expense of the others. Often the ones not cast are those who most need the experience. I do not mean to imply by this statement that the gifted and talented should be denied opportunities, but I believe that after-school and enrichment classes are a better way of meeting their needs than preferential treatment in class.

Outside audiences for plays should be composed of students from other classes and understanding adults rather than strangers. I should hope that such occasions were rare and that the performances were regarded as "work in progress" or the culmination of a project rather than a planned and finished production. Often far more interesting to outsiders is the demonstration, which shows both process and product. Despite certain inherent drawbacks, the demonstration is an excellent way to share work if the audience is clear from the beginning that it is witnessing a process, not a finished production. Viewed as the former, a good demonstration can help the observer (parent or administrator) better understand the nature and value of drama. Viewed as a product, however, drama is invariably confused with theatre and assessed as such. If a project develops to a point where the players want to share it with others, the wise teacher will cooperate. She will give help and encouragement, thus enabling the class to achieve success. Conversely, she will not deny a performance on the grounds that she disapproves of it. She must keep in mind that a performance is the exception and not the usual expectation of a drama class. Personally, I have no objection to shows per se, only to the exploitation that so often takes place when children are used to meet the goals of adults. The expectations of the adult differ from those of the child; when an attempt is made to create a perfect product, the standards of formal theatre are suddenly imposed on young and inexperienced players who lack the necessary performance skills and are therefore not ready for public performance.

The harm, it seems to me, lies not in the performance itself but in the exploitation of the players. The good teacher stimulates and inspires, respecting all honest efforts and making sure that learning takes place. She does not order, test, or pass judgment on young players as to the right or wrong way to perform. Therefore, when work is shared with others, she handles it as an extension of the original experience. To be sure, it must be as good as the group can make it, thus satisfying the players. Older children, on the other hand, enjoy the discipline of the directed play and are stretched by its demands. This is not creative drama, however; it is mentioned here only because of the misunderstandings that so often occur when the subject of performance comes up.

To recapitulate, the most frequently cited purposes of child drama are to educate, to offer an opportunity for experience in the arts, and to aid the social growth of the participants. To these I should like to add two others, though they lie outside the purview of this book: to serve as a therapeutic medium and to provide recreation.

Regardless of purpose, drama must first capture and hold the interest of the participants. It must stimulate their imagination to further activity. If it does not, it will fail as an experience in the performing arts. There must be substance, but the form and the substance must be closely interlocked. Otherwise, we shall be guilty of sugarcoating curricular material in order to make it palatable rather than expressing it in dramatic terms. Trivial entertainment soon bores; but so also does teaching when the medium is *abused*, rather than *used*, to illuminate.

Regarding material for drama, I believe the resources are infinite. Curricular subject matter, recommended by some of the authors, can be highly rewarding when used properly. A good working relationship between the school and a first-rate professional theatre company (e.g., Theatre-in-

Education, or T.I.E.) provides a special kind of experience and stimulates further exploration. Their "programmes" (a word preferred by the British to "plays") challenge the thinking and arouse the emotions of the audience. In this way children and young people not only learn from exposure to ideas presented in dramatic form but are pushed to critical thinking, research, and participation in dramas of their own creation.

I must at this point express a concern. I suspect that "educational theatre" has become a popular term in the United States because of its marketability. Unfortunately, what goes by this name is often little more than entertainment bearing some superficial relationship to the curriculum, for which study guides are prepared and given to classroom teachers. This is not Theatre-in-Education any more than are the countless plays advertised for "children of all ages" children's theatre. It is incumbent on the concerned adult, teacher, and parent to check programs and producing companies carefully in advance of booking for the promised content and quality of the performance. In all fairness, it must be said that many producers do not understand what is meant by "educational theatre," but their companies receive grants to perform a special job, and it is our responsibility to withhold patronage from the unqualified as well as to support the efforts of the well prepared and serious artist/teacher.

A further word is in order regarding other kinds of plays and programs. To exclude literary material (myths, fables, legends, folktales, poetry, and contemporary stories), as some advocate, is to deprive children of a rich source of drama. Good literature offers values and absorbing plots that original plays frequently lack. Moreover, this source can serve as examples of literary structure, with which young players struggle. Personal human experience, on the other hand, when suggested by the group, is the essence of drama and can be used with richly satisfying results. Content that embraces all these things—curricular material, literature, social issues, and personal problems—serves to expand the experience on many levels.

Finally, I believe that a good teacher avoids a rigid adherence to the practices of any one authority or text. The effective teacher becomes familiar with a variety of views and methods, but eschews imitation of a single one. My concern is not for the leaders but for the followers, those who lack confidence in their own abilities. It is true that imitation offers a sense of security in the beginning, and for that reason it has value; but the imaginative teacher will find his or her own way in time, and that way will be better because it was created to meet the teacher's specific needs. In the final analysis, the individual teacher must determine emphases according to the situation. Regardless of personal bias and skills, each of us, given a different set of circumstances, well might realign our priorities and adopt new methods and goals.

The acceptance of a philosophy of education is a different matter. In order to teach effectively, we must know where we are going, and why. The authors who have contributed to this book inspire us because they present a clear philosophical basis for their work, showing how their individual techniques were formed from their philosophies.

There is general agreement that the three major components of an ideal program in drama/theatre are:

aesthetic education (drama/theatre as an art)

art in education (the integration of drama/theatre in the curriculum)

use of community resources for enrichment (theatre brought to the schools and/or children to the theatre).

In the following essays these three components are examined from the standpoint of the authors' particular expertise and experience. Not only are the values of each component revealed but we perceive the added dimension that accrues when all three are included and interrelated.

A Retrospect

Winifred Ward

Winifred Ward's distinguished contributions to the field of child drama are well known. In articulating the principles and demonstrating the effectiveness of creative dramatics as opposed to formal theatre for children, she was instrumental in changing the direction of education in the dramatic arts in this country. She was the author of four texts, Creative Dramatics, Playmaking with Children, Stories to Dramatize, *and* Theatre for Children. *Her convictions about the improvisational approach developed during her early years as a public school teacher and culminated in the establishment of the famous Evanston Program. Perhaps her most lasting accomplishment was the founding of the Children's Theatre Association of America, the national professional organization and a division of the American Theatre Association, devoted to the promotion of drama for and with children.*

In this retrospect, her last piece of writing, Winifred Ward shared some of her personal reminiscences rather than repeating her philosophy, which as she said, had already been written. Her death in 1975 saddened drama/theatre educators throughout the United States.

Do you consider creative dramatics important enough in a child's education to be included in the curriculum of every public school along with music and art? Do you who believe in its value enough to practice it, write books about it, give workshops for teachers — feel satisfied with its present status?

Shortly after I had published my first book, *Creative Dramatics*, in 1930, I was shocked when I came upon this statement by a widely experienced educator: "Whenever a new idea in education is proposed, it is at least fifty years before it becomes common practice."

How do new subjects get into the public schools? Because a need is strongly felt. And in the case of creative dramatics, the need was felt by Mr. Skiles, superintendent of the Evanston, Illinois schools. He had come to Evanston in 1918, had visited all the grade schools, and had recognized that the middle grades were lacking in interest. He talked with a school board member, Ralph Dennis, who was also dean of the School of Speech at Northwestern University, asking him to recommend a teacher. Mr. Dennis came to my office, hoping I would be interested. Since I had begun to teach a course in drama for teachers, and this would open the door for my students to gain experience, I knew it was a wonderful opportunity. But I was not sure that I wanted to undertake it myself, so I hesitated, and he said, "Think it over and I'll talk with you in a day or two."

I was torn as to whether or not I should accept, especially as it was likely to become a larger responsibility than I wanted to add to my already full program. When Mr. Dennis came back, I decided I must tell him the reason why I hesitated. "I'm very much afraid," I said, "that this offer will develop into a full-time job and I would have to leave Northwestern, in which my roots go very deep." The dean stood up from where he was sitting by my desk, put his hand gently on my shoulder, and said, "It will *never* take you away from here." Then, as if embarrassed by his show of sentiment, he strode to the window and stood looking out at the lake.

Of course, I then agreed to undertake the position, even though I was not at all sure how I could find time to do all that I was sure it would involve. Soon afterward I met Mr. Skiles and we had a long talk in his office. I knew at once that he would be wonderful to work with.

During our first conversation he had discussed the lack of interest in the fifth- and sixth-grade courses of study; they needed the liveliness that drama would supply. It was not long before the idea spread and other grades were added. Both Mr. Skiles and I had been retired for some years, however, before all the grades had dramatics.

I have begun with a short history of the drama department in the Evanston elementary schools, which is almost unique in our country. Is it because the Evanston schools were rich? Not at all. The superintendent who established the department was known as a very careful man concerning finances. The answer is simple and clear: He believed in the importance of dramatics. That was sufficient.

In recent years, with high taxes and new superintendents unsympathetic to this art, the whole department has been threatened. So strong, however, have been the protests of parents and children that, as of now, Evanston still has a fairly large dramatic staff, ten teachers in all. And I thought we might have to settle for a home with the language arts!

Few people start at the top of their careers. I was not one of them, in spite of what my opening story might indicate. I had graduated from the two-year course at the School of Speech at Northwestern, and until I could find a teaching position, I had to be content with coaching high school students for oratorical contests and senior plays. The first real offer came in the middle of the year from the public schools in Adrian, Michigan, where I was to have the following assignments: coaching students for high school contests in public speaking, directing the senior play, teaching reading in the upper grades, coaching girls' basketball, dancing, and conducting calisthenics once a week with the primary grades.

The declamation contests were easy; my student won the state contest the first year. My reading classes were successful, especially when, occasionally, they could read stories in "parts." And the senior play "went over" best. My basketball girls rarely won an intercity game; however, they were always good friends.

I met with some surprises in my many duties with physical exercise in the lower grades. I found that if I could add a dramatic element, the children would have enjoyed physical training all morning. For instance, one exercise designed to give the first grade a change was as simple as this: As the children stood alongside their desks, I told them about a snowman standing in front with arms stretched out at his sides like sticks. One child at a time took this part. Then all the other children at their seats were to pick up some snow, pat it into balls, and on a signal throw it with all their might at one of the arms of the snowman. They always aimed accurately and the arm was knocked off, of course. Then, on a signal, the other arm met the same fate; next the snowman's head fell forward; and finally, the big climax — the last snowballs knocked the snowman down and he crumpled to the floor!

I had no idea how popular that game was going to be! Every child in the room had to have his chance to be the snowman; after a while we had several snowmen at once lined up along the front of the room. By that time all the children had had plenty of exercise and fun for the morning and were content to sit at their desks.

Creative dramatics! Why didn't I think of it then? The children and I could have had the joy of it several years sooner.

For the next two years after my experience in Adrian, I was finishing my master's degree at the University of Chicago and making ready to move to Evanston. Here I was to teach for the next thirty-two years, until my retirement.

I had come to teach at Northwestern at the end of World War I. No other invitation could have made me so happy as the one that came from Agness Law who, with Professor Hardy, had been heading the speech department during the absence of Dean Dennis, then filling a wartime post as vice-consul in Russia.

I am sure that my years of teaching in Michigan, coming to know and work with children of all ages, had much to do with my invitation; for my future at

Northwestern was quite sure to involve the preparation of students who would be teachers of children.

Almost as soon as I came to live in Evanston, I began to hear the names of John Dewey and his followers. I had heard of him before, but it was different now. I was close to a center where many of his devoted followers lived and worked. As I read in a book published in 1964 by the Southern Illinois University Press called *John Dewey and the World View*, edited by Douglas Lawson and Arthur Lean,

> No other professor in American history has had so powerful, so lasting and so widespread an influence in the whole field of education as had this shy, simple, gangling son of Vermont.
>
> He had his own school in Chicago for seven-and-a-half years, but his real career was at Columbia University where he influenced educational practice in his role as teacher of professors of educational theory. They in turn profoundly affected the course of educational development through the many thousands of teachers and administrators they helped to prepare for service in the schools. A philosopher of growth, change and experimentation, John Dewey may long remain one of the world's most frequently misunderstood and misinterpreted scholars.

One of the earliest schools I visited was the Francis Parker School in Chicago. I thoroughly liked what I saw. The attitude of both teachers and pupils was unlike any I had ever seen. There was no lifeless response to teachers' questions, no looking at the clock to see if it was almost time for the class to be over. There seemed to be a feeling of responsibility on the part of the young people. If this was the "new education," I approved most heartily.

In those first years I wanted to find out more about these schools and their philosophy. I read several of Dewey's books, including *The School and Society*, one of his most popular works. From Kilpatrick's works, I read *Foundations of Method*; I liked especially Rugg and Shumaker's *The Child-Centered School* with its interesting chapter on the Children's Theatre. But when I read Hughes Mearns' three books, *Creative Youth*, *Creative Power*, and *The Creative Adult*, I knew that, for me, these were the best!

All Mearns' books were acclaimed, but *Creative Power* carries on its jacket such kudos as, "Here's the great book of intellectual adventure and psychological experiment that burst upon the world of ideas like a bombshell and has been hailed as a step forward in education — praised by such people as Louis Untermeyer, Carl Sandburg, Angelo Patri, Dorothy Canfield Fisher, and a host of famous men and women of distinction and success — 'A new force in the field of creative education,' says the *New York Herald Tribune*."

By this time I was enthusiastic about creating a new course which I would call *Creative Dramatics*. It was based on the philosophy of Hughes Mearns and the "new education." So began what turned out to be a far-reaching plan for spreading ideas whose time had come.

The three books written by Mr. Mearns became classics in their field. I was to use *Creative Power* as required reading in my course. My students were always so enthusiastic after reading it that their reports were glowing. One girl was so fascinated that she stayed up practically all night to finish the book. Any author, it seemed to me, would be happy to know that young people were thinking about his book, and so I occasionally sent Mr. Mearns one or two of the best of these written reactions.

To my surprise and delight he responded with notes so gracious and clever, expressing his appreciation for the comment, that I saved all of them. Here is one he wrote after receiving a report from Margie Owens, one of my students.

Dear Winifred Ward:

Your contagious spirit always sets me up and makes me feel worthy of good deeds ahead. And you knew that Margie Owens' honest and sincere critique of *Creative Power* would do the same. What delights me so much, and assures me, is that she has told very simply what I intended by the writing of that book but could not be certain that I had really done it until some intelligent person like herself came along and said, "It's here!" I wanted the inexperienced — inexperienced professionally, I mean — reader to feel stirred to interest in the possibilities of finding hidden powers, generally unnoticed gifts; and I wanted the professional teacher to get from the book practical help in finding them in herself and in her charges. Well, I must have done just that, or Margery Owens would not have announced it as true.

I have so many other things that I hoped readers would sense in the motive and the method I have used in this trilogy on creative education; and verification has come from so many discoverers that I am made most happy. Professors have scolded me for being colloquial, for telling stories of real children, for making my material out of human endeavor instead of translating it into cold abstractions, for deliberately avoiding, in short, the method of the learned for the sake of helping others to see and to perform in a region, the creative arts, where learning without feeling, precept without illustrative example, is useless if not fatal. Every common illustration I used out of my own experience was placed with a deliberate teaching purpose, never merely for entertainment, and I have proof that the plan has worked into the heart as well as into the mind of others.

Thanks for the assurance you have always given me and for this added one from Margie Owens.

Fifty years of teaching and the three volume report, seem to me to make a completed thing. I have nothing more to add, and I do want to finish some belated creative work of my own. It is taking the form of light verse, an avocation of a life time. Some of it is pure nonsense—the Carolyn Wells' forthcoming Anthology will contain some of that. David McCord will be the editor. But nonsense with always a foundation in truth, as this one:

Live and Learn

By clever planning I contrived
To come before I had arrived,
But uselessly my time was spent—
I should have gone before I went.

Isn't it the truth for all of us!

For you and Margie I am enclosing another type of verse. Don't ask when the whole shall be published. Sometime, no doubt, but we'll have to find an insane publisher first.

Here is an excerpt from a later letter:

You are right about the effect of the recent attacks on "progressive educa-tion." I predicted long ago that that would happen after Dewey's death. None of them would have dared to speak up while he was alive. They are hashing over the same old stuff of fifty years ago, "putting the screws on 'em"—stuffing 'em with irrelevant "facts," and that old phantom, liberal arts, concerning which, the last named, I could never get anyone to give me a clear definition.

Well, cheerio! Good things do not die. Reactionaries do not take the trouble to investigate what they are attacking. This is my contribution to the subject:

The Perfect Reactionary

As I was sitting in my chair
I *knew* the bottom wasn't there,
Nor *legs* nor *back*, but I just sat,
Ignoring little things like that.

When Hughes Mearns died, newspapers all over the country, instead of noting his three remarkable books, printed his best-known nonsense rhyme:

As I was going up the stair,
I met a man who wasn't there.
He wasn't there again today
I wish, I wish, he'd stay away.

Volume 9 of the *Encyclopedia of Education* contains this statement:

The Soviet launching of Sputnik [an artificial satellite] in 1957 intensified both popular and professional doubt concerning the quality of American education. We had obviously fallen behind in the science curriculum. Where else were we inferior? Education suddenly took on international overtones, and because of the climate of opinion, it was suddenly possible to enact in the National Defense Education Act 1958 all the ideas which had been brewing for almost a century.

In addition to Sputnik what had brought about this strong reaction to Progressive Education? Why had so many of the best minds, influenced by the outstanding scholar of the century in the field of education—John Dewey—failed? The answer is clear: Too many teachers in the country at-tempted to use Dewey's methods with little or no understanding of them. An illustration of the kind of teaching carried on with little or no judgment is that of one such teacher who asked her pupils to choose what they would like to study for the coming year; and their choice turned out to be "Shells!"

Some years ago, I was introduced to the head of the School of Education of a large university whose two teachers of creative dramatics I had trained.

Minutes after speaking of them with genuine admiration for the quality of their work, he voiced his scorn for Progressive Education. I smiled inwardly. I knew that his teachers had been using the very creative approach he had been condemning.

Years after the downgrading of Progressive Education, the effect of it was felt in many ways. A sudden move toward education in science sent young men into that study in such numbers that soon the country had educated more scientists than we needed. The arts were slighted for years. Washington had only one theatre of any note, and we never heard of government grants for projects at home or for foreigners wishing to study here. In recent years, worthy ventures in the arts, both for native American groups and for foreign visitors, are more and more common. Washington itself has become a cultural city with the completion of Kennedy Center and its program of performing arts.

When the schools in Evanston began offering electives to the students of seventh and eighth grades, I had saved time for two classes I would teach and had one or two very capable seniors who had taken the course and were ready to do student teaching. But the registration was so much larger than we expected that we had to increase the number of students in each section.

We found the children eager to participate, and the classes went well. During those first years I wanted to find out what the children felt they were getting from the course. Some said, "It gets a person over being afraid to speak out." But many of them just enjoyed dramatics. As with all electives, it gave them more time to spend on what they especially liked. In later years, instead of electives, every child has spent a certain amount of time in various fields.

To be convinced that creative dramatics should have a place in the public school curriculum you should observe it in action with a good teacher. You may not see anything spectacular in one visit, though a single visit will give you a very good idea of the respect in which it is held. At other times, something happens which is inspiring.

There was the second-grade class, for instance, which was playing out a barnyard story. One little boy, well liked by the class, but who never had anything to contribute, surprised the other children by volunteering to be the rooster.

In the midst of the playing, at precisely the right moment when the animals were in high dispute, Jimmy came forth with a tremendous "cock-a-doodle-do," so loud that the whole action stopped and the barnyard fowls forgot their playing and looked at Jimmy, amazed and delighted. They crowded around him, full of praise. After the class, Jimmy said almost unbelievingly to his teacher, "Gosh, Miss Taylor, wasn't I wonderful?" The teacher's comment to me was, "If Jimmy never does anything else, he has had one real triumph."

If we are accustomed to praise ourselves, we can't know how important it is to a slow child to have the joy of success now and then. But I have seen evidences enough of what success does to a child to wish that even the slowest boys and girls might have praise once in a while. But a wise teacher will be wary of praising an overconfident child.

Another child I remember from dramatic class I shall call Mary. Mary was a quiet, timid little girl who spoke so softly in class she could hardly be heard. In an assembly program she played one of the three witches in *Macbeth*. No trouble to hear her there! Her eighth-grade teacher exclaimed afterwards, "I couldn't believe it was Mary! In the classroom I can hardly hear her!"

I do not often know the future of children who have been in our public school dramatic classes, but Mary has kept in touch with me during all the years since. In a holiday note when she was in high school, she told me how much easier dramatics had made it for her to adjust there. Later she wrote me about college and how much more assurance she had now because of her dramatic work. Nowadays, married and with two children, she cannot come to see me, but she writes at Christmas about her Boy Scout group and her work in PTA where she is unafraid to speak.

On opening night at the Civic Opera in Chicago a few years ago, a young man came up to me and said, "You don't know me, but I was in your *Rumpelstiltskin* when I was a boy and that experience opened up a whole new world to me. If it were not for that, I wouldn't be here tonight shouting my lungs out for Joan Sutherland."

I trust there have been many Marys and Jims and Bills whose lives have been made more effective because of their participation in creative drama. But I am perhaps just as grateful for the implication of the boy who wrote, "I like dramatics because I'm right more times."

I have reserved for the last the most remarkable teacher of creative drama we ever had in Evanston: Ann Flagg.

Ann was black. I met her in Cleveland at Karamu House, a center for teaching arts and crafts. Ann was teaching creative dramatics and was all excited because I, "who had written a book on creative dramatics," was there to see her! She needn't have worried. She was exceptionally gifted and I could truthfully praise her work. Ann was especially concerned, I think, because she was hoping to win a scholarship to Northwestern the following year. I could enthusiastically write a letter of recommendation for her.

Ann was a college graduate and came to Northwestern the next year for her graduate work. While there she took a course in play writing from Professor Walter Scott and wrote a play titled *The Great Gittin' Up Mornin'* which told of a little black boy sent to school for the first time. Dr. Scott considered it good enough to enter in a Samuel French play contest where it won first prize; later that year, Ann was flown to California to oversee its production for television. With her delightful sense of humor, she told us later that during rehearsals she sat in a *chair with her name on the back!*

We kept her in Evanston doing part-time teaching until she had her master's degree; from then on, she taught a full schedule for several years. Nearly all her time was spent at Foster, a black school in Evanston. She found that most of the children there felt inferior, and she did magnificent work in building real pride in being black.

"What country did our race come from?" she asked one class.

They named every continent except Africa.

"Where else?" she prodded.

Finally a timid little girl said, almost in a whisper, "Africa?"

"Yes," she echoed in a strong voice, "Africa!"

In every way possible she emphasized dignity in their cultural background. Ann felt deep pride in her race and taught it to her students. She saw to it that the school library had the best books from which the children could learn about their people, and they sang songs which fostered this love and pride. Ann was interested in children as individuals. When a child was lacking in confidence, she gave him parts to play to bolster his courage. And he never let her down.

Though I had retired from teaching, Hazel Easton and I always went to Ann's plays which were built up in classwork. One such, which was remarkably effective but was never recorded or photographed, grew out of what the children had studied concerning their race. The children had learned about many black leaders of whom they could be proud. They had read poetry by Paul Lawrence Dunbar and James Weldon Johnson, among others; they knew the historical fact that the first man in the Revolutionary War to die for his country was black; they knew the accomplishments of George Washington Carver, a revered name to them.

This production, I recall, had both a singing and a speaking choir. The singing choir sat in the front rows of the auditorium; the speaking choir was grouped on the steps leading up to the stage, some of them sitting, some standing. On the stage itself, scenes were enacted depicting historical events such as the Underground Railroad and the dedicated work of Harriet Tubman. As a climax, the speaking choir on the steps called the names of people of note in their race of whom they could be proud: "Marian Anderson! Ralph Bunche! Martin Luther King!" Sometimes one strong voice would call a name, at other times two or several voices; but all of them ringing loud and clear and building with intensity of feeling — a spine-tingling effect. It was a thrilling performance. When it was over, the audience, visibly moved, gave a standing ovation. I remember it as one of my most moving experiences in the theatre.

It would be profoundly interesting to know how much those years of Ann's teaching influenced the children of Foster School. There were not many years — her health was never good, and at a teachers' meeting after school one afternoon she suddenly died. It was a sad loss and a very great one.

A memorial service was held in the school auditorium, and the room was packed with parents and teachers. The service was as unique as Ann. A children's choir sat on one side of the stage, and there was a lectern on the other side with one large jar of flowers in front of it. Each of Evanston's drama teachers paid a short tribute to Ann, many of them simply repeating lines Ann had spoken to her classes. Simultaneously pictures of Ann teaching her classes were thrown on a screen. And finally the principal of the school came to the podium with a letter he had directed to Ann. It called to mind anecdotes, some of them very humorous. Among them was a little ritual that he and Ann spoke when they met in the hall. Mr. Hill would say, "How's your behavior?" And Ann would respond, "You've stopped talking and gone to meddling." Mr. Hill finished his letter simply, "See you later." It was the most moving aspect of a ceremony which ended with the choir coming down from the stage and walking out, singing the song that had given the title to her play — "The Great Gittin' Up Mornin'."

Drama in Education—
A Changing Scene

Geraldine Brain Siks

Time is a sort of river of passing events,
and strong is its current.
—Marcus Aurelius, *Meditations*

Geraldine Brain Siks is an international leader in the field of children's drama. She is a fellow of the American Theatre Association and has served on its board of directors; currently she is a commissioner of the association's Commission on Theatre Education. Mrs. Siks is the author or editor of six textbooks in the creative drama field including Drama With Children, *which is soon to be published in a second edition. This text and her* Creative Drama: An Art for Children *are published in Japanese editions. With her sister Hazel Dunnington, she edited* Children's Theatre and Creative Dramatics, *a monograph requested by the American Theatre Association. Geraldine Siks is the author of several published plays for children's theatre and more than thirty articles and essays in professional journals. Her degrees are in education and theatre, her M.A. degree having being granted by the Northwestern University School of Speech. She has served as lecturer and creative drama workshop leader at several universities in the United States and in other countries.*

Mrs. Siks was the recipient of a contract with the U.S. Office of Education to research Theatre Arts Materials for Use in Children's Drama in seventeen European countries. For many years a professor of drama at the University of Washington, Seattle, she recently retired as professor emeritus. Geraldine Siks has received numerous honors and awards, among them the 1979 Medallion of Honor of Theta Alpha Phi, National Theatre Honors Fraternity.

The flow of educational events in our country, which have shaped the children's drama movement thus far in the twentieth century, appears strong as it moves into the last two decades. This essay examines major events and looks ahead to identify thrusts for the possible future of drama in the education of children and youth.

Historical Overview

Creative Dramatics Movement

Traditionally, public school education has focused on the three Rs. During the first quarter of the twentieth century, the educational philosophy of John Dewey and others led to a concern for education that utilized children's natural interests in "learning by doing." The creative dramatics movement emerged out of this educational trend.

Winifred Ward is recognized as the pioneer of creative dramatics, the person who developed and advanced creative dramatics at all educational levels for almost fifty years. Among her many accomplishments were the introduction in 1925 of a course in creative dramatics at the School of Speech at Northwestern University and, later, classes in creative dramatics for children in the Evanston public schools; the publication in 1930 of *Creative Dramatics* and the continuing publication of textbooks, articles, and a government bulletin; the founding in 1944 of the Children's Theatre Conference; and, collaborating with Rita Criste, the production in 1960 of a teaching film, *Creative Drama: The First Steps*.[1] Miss Ward's influence on her students was far-reaching. Many went on to become leaders in the field, introducing creative dramatics courses into college curriculums and children's programs. Several Ward students published creative drama texts.

Support for the Arts in Education

The entrance of the federal government into the arts was a most significant educational event in the 1960s for the cultural community in the United States. Several milestones led to key developments in the 1970s. A comprehensive panel report, *Coming to Our Senses*,[2] affirmed: "As we trace today the cultural history of America, we are forced to pursue two parallel lines: one of education, strong and straight; the other of the arts, wavering and uncertain."[3] The report added: "not until the last thirty of the three hundred years do we see sure signs of the two lines converging, of a conscious effort to move the study, practice, and appreciation of the arts from the periphery of the educational experience toward its center."[4]

Arts and Humanities Program   In 1962 the Cultural Affairs Branch within the U.S. Office of Education (USOE) was established to develop programs and activities aimed at improving arts education at all educational levels. This branch, renamed the Arts and Humanities Program in 1963, continues to pursue its objectives. At present a chief function is to work with the Alliance for Arts Education (AAE).

AAE   The Alliance for Arts Education is a joint project of the John F. Kennedy Center for the Performing Arts and the USOE. Created by the Kennedy Center's board of trustees in 1973 in response to Public Law 85-874, the AAE sponsored a series of regional meetings to identify common national concerns in the arts and education. Recommendations from these meetings were used to develop specific program directions to meet the broad congressional mandate. In 1974 the AAE began establishing its basic substructure of state AAE organizations, and in 1975 it awarded small grants to these organizations for projects designed to increase the effectiveness of this national network. By 1980 the AAE was a network of fifty-five committees, one in each state plus the District of Columbia, Puerto Rico, Samoa, the Virgin Islands, and the Bureau of Indian Affairs. Each committee sets its own goals, objectives, and activities. To strengthen the state or organization, the AAE in 1979, established regional networks aimed at intensifying communication among the states to effect improved arts' education programs throughout the country. Regional networks are within the same geographic area with each network having a regional chairperson.[5]

Federal Legislation   Two laws passed in 1965 recognized the need for support of the arts. First, the Elementary and Secondary Education Act (ESEA), initiated a partnership between the arts and education. This act was meant primarily to assist state and local education agencies in providing compensatory programs for disadvantaged children, innovative educational programs, and support for educational research. Over a five-year period the act resulted in the funding of approximately $80 million for innovative and exemplary arts projects.[6]

The second important legislation created the National Endowment for the Arts (NEA) and the National Endowment for the Humanities. The USOE transferred considerable funds to the NEA to support and develop the nationwide Artists-in-Schools program. By the mid-1970s, endowment expenditures for the program had grown to approximately $4 million.[7]

National Institute of Education (NIE)   The NIE was established in 1972 with a specific research-oriented mandate including arts education research. NIE supports research in the Aesthetic Education Program of the Central Midwest Regional Educational Laboratory (CEMREL) in St. Louis, Missouri.

CEMREL   Formed in 1965 to improve the quality of education for the nation's children by relating sound educational research to actual practice in schools, CEMREL in 1967 launched the development of an aesthetic education curriculum program in grades K–6. Working cooperatively with individuals in many educational agencies and institutions, CEMREL's Aesthetic Education was developed over an eight-year period. It is designed as a solid general education program on which separate arts programs can be based; it is a systematic attempt to enrich arts education for all youngsters in all the major art forms. Curricular objectives and emphases of the forty-four multimedia instructional units are described in *Through the Arts to the Aesthetic*.[8]

To assist classroom teachers in the use of the curriculum, CEMREL has developed a comprehensive teacher education program with eleven Aesthetic Education Learning Centers, which offer training nationwide. CEMREL's intensive research program is reflected in three yearbooks; *The Teaching Process and Arts and Aesthetics*,[9] the third in the series, describes how research in the arts and aesthetic education may be applied to classroom teaching and learning.

The Southwestern Regional Educational Laboratory SWIRL, in Los Alamitos, California, is also involved in curriculum development in the arts. The government-supported SWIRL focuses on the development of materials in art criticism that aim at training elementary and secondary teachers to discuss art objects with students, thereby enabling the students to become more perceptive and appreciative of works of art.

The JDR 3rd Fund—Arts in Education Program In 1967 the JDR 3rd Fund, a private foundation established by John D. Rockefeller III, introduced the Arts in Education Program. "All the arts for every child" was their stated aim with development centering on the inclusion of the arts as part of the total curriculum rather than as separate and specialized subjects. Under the direction of Kathryn Bloom, this program hopes to make the arts an integral part of the general education of every child. During its development over a ten-year period, it created an arts project model that involved little outside funding but required local support; established a national network composed of a League of Cities for the Arts in Education; and identified the political forces operating within school power struggles.

International Conference on the Teaching of English

An Anglo-American conference on the teaching of English, held at Dartmouth College in 1966, convened under the auspices of the American Modern Language Association, the American National Council of Teachers of English, and the British National Association for the Teaching of English. A major outcome of the month-long seminar was the realization of the dynamics of drama for fostering children's learning of language and communication skills. Direct results that utilized drama included the publication of *A Student-Centered Language Arts Curriculum, Grades K–13*;[10] *Spectrum of English*,[11] a basic language arts program (K–6) that emphasizes dramatic expression as one of its three content areas; the adoption by many colleges of a text from England, *Development Through Drama*;[12] and workshops at Northwestern University and other American universities by Dorothy Heathcote, one of England's outstanding drama educators.

Current Status of Drama in Education

The "back to basics" educational trend continues. Because a large percentage of the states have enacted laws requiring tests that measure a child's

Perceiving emotions.
Courtesy of Geraldine Brain
Siks.

learning of basic skills in the three Rs, the arts tend to receive limited time and limited resources in public school education. Drama in the elementary schools is included in a few states in much the same manner as music and art. For the most part, however, if drama is included, it is integrated in language arts and reading curricula and is taught by classroom teachers who are convinced of its value in children's education.

Although no policy guides the inclusion of drama and theatre arts in the nation's schools, there is evidence of developments that point in this direction. This is apparent in actions taken by the American Theatre Association (ATA) and its divisions, particularly the Children's Theatre Association of America (CTAA), by institutions of higher learning, and by actions at state and local levels.

ATA and CTAA Actions

The ATA and the CTAA continue to exert an influence for the inclusion of drama and theatre in education at all levels. Among their significant actions are (1) a redefinition of terminology of drama/theatre with and for children, (2) a national CTAA conference on Theatre Education for Public Schools, (3) the organization of the ATA Special Committee on Drama/Theatre and the

Handicapped, (4) CTAA's Winifred Ward scholarship program, (5) ATA's Commission on Theatre Education, and (6) CTAA's Committee on Research.

Creative Drama Defined A CTAA Committee to Redefine Terminology in Creative Dramatics was appointed in 1975.[13] After two years of deliberations, the governing board of CTAA approved the following definition of creative drama:

> "Creative Drama" is an improvisational, non-exhibitional process-centered form of drama in which participants are guided by a leader to imagine, enact, and reflect upon human experiences. Although creative drama traditionally has been thought of in relation to children and young people, the process is appropriate to all ages.
>
> The creative drama process is dynamic. The leader guides the group to explore, develop, express and communicate ideas, concepts, and feelings through dramatic enactment. In creative drama the group improvises action and dialogue appropriate to the content it is exploring, using elements of drama to give form and meaning to the experience. The primary purpose of creative drama is to foster personality growth and to facilitate learning of the participants rather than to train actors for the stage. Creative drama may be used to teach the art of drama and/or motivate and extend learning in other content areas. Participation in creative drama has the potential to develop language and communication abilities; problem solving skills, and creativity; to promote a positive self concept, social awareness, empathy, a clarification of values and attitudes, and an understanding of the art of theatre.
>
> Built on the human impulse and ability to act out perceptions of the world in order to understand it, creative drama requires both logical and intuitive thinking, personalizes knowledge, and yields aesthetic pleasure.[14]

Conference on Theatre Education for Public Schools At the request of the ATA for a theatre education conference, and with some government support, a CTAA conference convened in August 1977 at the Johnson Foundation Wingspread Center in Racine, Wisconsin. Thirty-five selected specialists in creative drama and children's theatre met for three days to consider these questions: How can children's theatre and creative drama enhance education as a unique discipline and as a process/tool within today's school curriculum? How can the generalist and specialist meet the needs of education through drama and theatre in schools today? How can CTAA and other concerned national associations implement recommendations made by the conference participants? Position papers, recommendations, and ideas generated from the conference are being used to initiate action at state and local levels.[15]

Drama/Theatre and the Handicapped Federal legislation, funding for the arts, and a growing awareness on the part of the public concerning the potential and actual needs of the handicapped led to the organization in 1978 of a Special ATA Committee on Drama, Theatre, and the Handicapped. The committee hopes to increase the knowledge and activity in drama and theatre with, by, and for the handicapped. A direct outcome of a special-project program grant from the National Committee, Arts for the Handicapped, was the 1979 publication of *Drama, Theatre, and the Handicapped*.[16] A national invitational conference in 1979 resulted in the formulation of broad, flexible guidelines for committee action.

Winifred Ward Scholarship   A chief mission of the CTAA as a division of the ATA is to enhance the quality of experience for all children who participate in children's theatre and creative drama. In view of this mission, and to pay special tribute to Winifred Ward, the CTAA launched in 1978 a major scholarship program to recognize and support future leaders in the children's drama field. An annual award of at least $2,000 is presented to a graduate student who has demonstrated intellectual and artistic ability in the area of children's drama. The recipient is selected by the Winifred Ward Scholarship Committee.

ATA Commission on Theatre Education   In accordance with the by-laws of the association, ATA commissions were established to facilitate an exchange of ideas, deal with issues related to the field, recommend policies related to various aspects of the field, articulate cross-divisional concerns, establish effective liaison with related organizations, and join with related organizations in developing advocacy positions. The Commission on Theatre Education is charged with establishing criteria and developing methods and strategies for the uses of theatre in education and humanistic studies at all levels of education.

CTAA Committee on Research   In 1980 a research committee was appointed to assist the CTAA vice-president for policy and research in the promotion and coordination of all CTAA research programs. The committee aims at promoting research in all areas of children's drama in several ways including: (1) describing the nature and emphases of current research in the field; (2) revealing areas in which no research is currently under way; and (3) facilitating communication between researchers, the CTAA, and interested persons. The committee plans to update a listing of current research in children's drama by publishing annually in the *Children's Theatre Review* brief descriptions of research in progress or recently completed.

Drama in Education at State Levels

The National Center for Education Statistics, in its "Fast Response Survey System," reports on Arts Education and Needs at the Elementary and Secondary Level:

> 1. 31 State Boards of Education have adopted an official resolution or policy statement specifically supporting the arts in elementary and secondary schools. 20 reported that they had *not* adopted such a statement.

2. 48 reported they had supported the arts with funding during the last year.

3. If there were new funds available to support arts education, the two activities which would first be implemented would be (a) in-service training and (b) integration of arts into the curriculum.[17]

Drama and theatre programs in public school education have increased during the past decade. This has resulted from three chief factors: (1) federal support, (2) support by state arts councils and commissions; and (3) support by state boards of education. Since the creation of the NEA in 1965, every state in the nation has established an arts council or commission. These agencies have been effective in developing Arts Education support. Twenty states now have Theatre-in-the-Schools programs. Fourteen of these programs are funded by the NEA through the state art agencies, while six programs are funded entirely by state arts agencies.

Four drama programs at state levels are described briefly here to indicate how policy, practices, and emphases vary from state to state. These programs are from Texas, North Carolina, Pennsylvania, and California.

Texas Educational Theatre Continuum   The Texas Education Agency is made up of the state's board of education, Commission of Education, and Department of Education.[18] The Educational Theatre Continuum is a sequential and cumulative learning continuum. Drama (creative dramatics) is part of a balanced elementary curriculum and is required to be taught in kindergarten and grades 1–6.[19] The Theatre Arts Framework approved in 1979 for grades 7–12, offers theatre courses as electives that provide a continuity of involvement from the elementary school curriculum. The program philosophy is as follows: "The learning processes of perceiving, creating, and evaluating begun in the creative dramatics curriculum expand in scope and complexity through grade 12. . . . In grades 7 and 8, the theatre arts curriculum begins to focus on interpretation and performance as students develop their communication skills. In grades 9–12 these processes are refined and utilized in theatrical productions."[20] The curriculum provides comprehensive guidelines for kindergarten through grade 7; guidelines for grades 9–12 are in the process of development.

North Carolina Drama Program   To be accredited by the state's Department of Public Instruction in this state, each local school system (some 140) must meet the drama guidelines for grades K–12. The drama program serves "as a key to the ideas and beliefs of humankind as communicated through literature and theatre and as a technique for teaching and learning in a vital manner."[21] At the elementary level the program focuses on the unfolding of the child's creative capacities, the development of knowledge and skills relating to drama, and the evolution of aesthetic awareness. At the middle school/junior high level the program builds on and refines the creative capacity, skill, and aesthetic development of previous years. At the high school level these emphases are realized within individual courses and across a broad range of varied course offerings.

A second part of the drama program involves sending professional drama groups into schools across the state to present theatre performances. Money for these performances is funded directly by the North Carolina Assembly. Funding has grown from $52,000 in 1972 to $129,000 in 1980. Theatre productions are chosen in an open bid process by a committee of school and theatre personnel and college and university professors. In 1979 the committee selected eleven productions out of eighty-one bids.[22]

Children's Theatre Ensemble in Pennsylvania   Several theatre companies have developed programs for children in the elementary schools under the federally supported Arts in Education Project. However, the Children's Theatre Ensemble is the only company performing for children and interacting with them that has developed institutional roots in the state. In addition, it is the only ensemble that provides continuing assistance to teachers in making drama an intrinsic element of instruction and curriculum design.[23]

The Children's Theatre Ensemble, under the leadership of Helen Manfull, is in its tenth year as a component of the Department of Theatre and Film of the Pennsylvania State University and its fourth year in conjunction with the Arts in Education Project. The ensemble, a year's course in children's theatre, develops an informal production with two companies (of 8–10 members each) during the fall and tours during the winter and spring. Material is based on children's writings and reaches approximately twenty thousand school-children in a tri-county area. From the viewpoint of the university students, the company experience involves classroom preparation in the form of a *Handbook for Teachers in Creative Drama and Writing Ideas* [24] and in the participatory production with children in elementary schools. Creative drama follow-up workshops in the classrooms for children and teachers, inservice teacher programs, and the services of a professional drama specialist are successful adjuncts to the program. Actors are university students enrolled in the children's theatre course. Money for materials and transportation is provided by the Arts in Education Project.

Drama/Theatre Framework for California Public Schools   This process-concept framework for a program in theatre arts for all students K–12 was published in 1974.[25] It was developed and prepared over a five-year period by the California Office of the State Superintendent of Public Instruction in cooperation with a Fine Arts and Humanities Framework Committee. It was designed to function "as a statement of policy by the State Board of Education; as a guide to district superintendents, consultants, and school administrators; as a guide for curriculum planners; and a guide for the classroom teacher until more comprehensive courses of study have been initiated."

Following its publication, drama specialists offered extensive workshops throughout the state to implement the guidelines, but because of sudden drastic tax-cutting initiatives in the state, educational programs in the arts were severely curtailed and efforts to advance theatre arts in public school education came to a standstill. In 1980 the state's department of Education launched a new direction for the arts in education. A committee of thirty-two, eight each from art, dance, drama/theatre, and music, was formed to prepare a new Fine and Performing Arts Curricular Framework. Each discipline is represented by educators from all levels as well as community groups responsible for bringing arts experiences to the schools. Each discipline will have its own section in addition to an interdisciplinary section. The new document will supplant all related frameworks; the long-range plan also includes implementation activities.[26]

Drama in Education in Institutions of Higher Learning.

A 1978 survey conducted by the ATA through the University College Theatre Association (UCTA) indicated some substantial programs, undergraduate and graduate, involved in training students in drama in education.[27] The survey, which elicited responses from all fifty states, showed that degree programs in children's drama at the undergraduate level are offered at ninety-eight institutions; forty-three institutions offer a master of arts or master of fine arts degree; and six universities offer programs in which students may pursue a doctoral degree with an emphasis in children's drama.[28]

Eight of the institutions of higher learning that offer a master of arts or master of fine arts degree with an emphasis in children's drama are described here briefly. The programs reflect a broad range of geographical locations and emphases. The institutions are listed alphabetically.

Arizona State University, Tempe   The Department of Theatre, College of Fine Arts, offers a master of arts degree in the area of children's drama and has applied for a master of fine arts degree as well. Major objectives are (1) to help develop leaders in the area of drama with and for children and (2) to encourage quality drama/theatre experiences for *all* children in Arizona. In addition to course work, practical experience is gained through the Imagination Corporation on campus and in internships in local schools, recreational programs, and community theatre programs. Concurrent with the outreach program, the children's drama faculty, which is actively involved in the state's AAE program and in workshops for area teachers, involves graduate students in these experiences.[29]

California State University, Northridge   The Department of Theatre offers a master of arts degree in theatre with an emphasis on children's drama. The program emphasizes courses and fieldwork in creative drama, theatre for children, and speech and dramatic activities in school and community programs. Seminars in children's drama and a thesis or thesis project are required. Two children's theatre productions are included in the major university theatre season with one production touring the Los Angeles metropolitan area for Junior Programs of California. Laboratory theatre emphasizes experimental productions by graduate students with opportunities to produce theatre for child audiences. Four children's theatre productions, presented each summer in a Teen-Age Drama Workshop, provide opportunities for graduate students to direct, teach, and become actively involved in the practical aspect of the program.[30]

University of Kansas, Lawrence   The Children's Theatre and Creative Drama Program is an integral part of the University Theatre Program that functions within the Department of Speech and Drama, College of Liberal Arts. A student may pursue a children's theatre "speciality" within a theatre major on the master's or doctoral level. In addition to comprehensive course work, the program includes two major productions each year for child audiences. The fall production, which is usually on a fairly "large scale," tours Kansas City theatres and plays a total of ten to fifteen performances to some twelve thousand children. The spring production with a small paid company plays at the university and tours throughout the region, performing from twenty to fifty times to an overall audience of approximately thirty thousand. Academic credit may be earned for these performances.[31]

New York University, New York City   The Program in Educational Theatre of New York University is offered through the School of Education, Health, Nursing, and Arts Professions. The program "consciously brings the fields of education and theatre together in classroom, workshop, stage, and street; in lecture; in new plays and forms of entertainment; and in research and experimentation in order to study and to develop their fundamental relationships and to expand their aesthetic and academic dimensions."[32] The program offers training in all phases of "educational theatre." It gives attention to the various advantages of drama in the special education of exceptional children and adults. The program offers bachelor of science, master of arts, doctor of philosophy, and doctor of education degrees.[33]

University of North Carolina, Greensboro   The master of fine arts program with emphasis in child drama is offered through the Department of Communication and Theatre. The program includes course work in creative drama, children's theatre, puppetry, mime, theatre management; a practicum in creative drama in the schools with children; opportunities for directing, acting, and touring with theatre for audiences of young people; and practical experience in creating, performing, and touring puppet shows and audience participation plays.

Northwestern University, Evanston   The master's program in theatre and the doctoral study in theatre are offered through the Department of Theatre of the School of Speech. Students admitted to the master's program in theatre or interdepartmental studies in drama/theatre education usually take no more than five of nine courses (theatre) or six of eleven courses (interdepartmental) in drama/theatre in education. The total number of child drama courses depends on the background and experience of the student in various areas of the theatre and the needs of the student to qualify for a particular career. Course work focuses on creative drama, children's theatre, children's literature, puppetry, theory and practices of drama in education, and studies and workshops in theatre practice. Doctoral students delve more deeply into their areas of specialization to lay the groundwork for the dissertation and qualifying exam.[34]

The University of Texas at Austin   The Department of Drama offers programs at both master's and doctoral levels. Five areas of concentration in the master of fine arts program include theatre for youth, creative dramatics, and teacher training. The degree demands advanced knowledge of educational drama, crafts of the theatre, and dramatic production for children and youth. Its aim is to prepare students to use drama with and for young people in schools, recreational programs, and regional theatres. Students develop their skills in actual situations with children and youth in demonstration classes on campus and through teaching assignments in local schools. Research for the thesis and work on the departmental children's theatre productions provide further experience.[35]

University of Washington, Seattle   The School of Drama offers a master of fine arts degree in child drama with three areas of specialization. The program consists of course work and opportunities for involvement in projects and practical experiences in creative dramatics, children's theatre, and puppetry. Although a minimum level of competence is required in all three areas, the student is expected to develop a professional specialization in at least one area. During the program, off-campus involvement with schools, community organizations, and professional children's theatres is encouraged and supported.[36]

Summarizing and Looking Ahead

The drama in education movement, introduced by Winifred Ward early in this century, moved slowly but steadily over a forty-year period. It advanced largely through her efforts and those of her colleagues and former students. A new surge of activity in the mid-1960s was the result primarily of federal legislation and support for the arts in education. This led to research, the development of instructional materials and models aimed at fostering aesthetic education for children in the nation's schools, and the establishment of a grass-roots movement for the arts in education at state and local levels. Action by the National Council of Teachers of English advanced drama centrally in language arts curricula and introduced drama theory and practices from England.

Currently, even within a strong national 3 Rs educational trend, drama in education continues its forward movement. This reflects the comprehensive and varied efforts of the ATA and CTAA; state Departments of Public Instruction, state arts agencies, and the AAE; research in drama/theatre in education; publications; and the cooperative efforts of individuals in schools, institutions of higher learning, and communities.

Out of the flow of past and current events, four major thrusts emerge as promising for the future of drama/theatre in education. First is the inclusion of creative drama in children's education by increasing numbers of classroom teachers. These teachers continue to request more inservice training courses, texts, handbooks, and instructional learning materials that focus on drama processes and concepts. Second is the continuing improvement in degree programs that emphasize drama/theatre in education and in teacher training at colleges and universities. Third is research and its potential for influencing the entire field of drama/theatre education. Instruction needs to be informed by research into the nature of the drama/theatre creative processes, the nature of child development, "mind/brain learning" and aesthetic growth, and the nature of effective teaching processes. Fourth is the significance of interested people in turning the tide in this cause. Teachers, artists, administrators, community leaders, children, youth, preschoolers, and the elderly are needed as catalysts and advocates. Although "people power" at national, state, community, and local levels is increasing, it needs to be coordinated.

A clearly defined course for the future of drama and theatre arts education cannot be foreseen. Even with the emergence of several strong thrusts, it is too early to judge if a forceful channel will be cut or whether several current forces will merge to form a new direction. A prominent national educator stated recently that drama and theatre arts could be programmed into the basic education of all children immediately *if* the public demanded it. To convince the public to demand it becomes the concerted goal of everyone determined to help change the current and course of this "dramatic river."

NOTES

1. *Creative Dramatics: The First Steps* (Evanston: Northwestern University Film Library, 1960).
2. *Coming to Our Senses—The Significance of the Arts for American Education*, a panel report, David Rockefeller, Jr., chairman (New York: McGraw-Hill, 1977) p. 47.
3. Ibid.
4. Ibid.
5. Charles B. Fowler, ed., *Summit Conference on the Arts and Education—A Report* (Washington, D.C.: Alliance for Arts Education, John F. Kennedy Center for the Performing Arts, 1980).
6. *Coming to Our Senses*, pp. 219–22.
7. Ibid.
8. Stanley S. Madeja and Sheila Onuska, *Through the Arts to the Aesthetic* (St. Louis: CEMREL, 1977) pp. xiii–xiv.
9. Gerard L. Knieter and Jane Stallings, eds., *The Teaching Process* and *Arts and Aesthetics* (St. Louis: CEMREL, 1979).

10. James Moffett, *A Student-Centered Language Arts Curriculum, Grades K-13: A Handbook for Teachers* (Boston: Houghton Mifflin, 1968).
11. Albert R. Kitzhaber, ed., with Annabel Kitzhaber, Edna P. DeHaven, Barbara T. Salisbury, and Daisy M. Jones, *Spectrum of English, K-6* (Encino, Calif.: Glencoe, 1978).
12. Brian Way, *Development Through Drama*, Education Today (New York: Humanities, 1972).
13. Jed H. Davis and Tom Behm, "Terminology of Drama/Theatre with and for Children: A Redefinition," *Children's Theatre Review* 27, no. 1 (1978): 10–11.
14. Ibid.
15. Lin Wright, "CTAA at Wingspread," *Children's Theatre Review* 27, no. 2 (1978): 1–4.
16. Ann M. Shaw and C. J. Stevens, *Drama, Theatre, and the Handicapped* (Washington, D.C.: American Theatre Association, 1979).
17. Jack Morrison, "ATA Program Notes," *Theatre News* 11, no. 9 (Summer 1979): 24.
18. *Principles, Standards, and Procedures for the Accreditation of School Districts; Description of Balanced Elementary Curriculum*, Texas Education Agency Publication AD7 825 01 (Austin: Texas Education Agency, Fine Arts Section, 1975).
19. *The Educational Theatre Continuum* (Austin: Texas Education Agency, Fine Arts Section, 1975).
20. *Theatre Arts Framework for Grades 7–12* (Austin: Texas Education Agency, Fine Arts Section, 1975).
21. "Drama Program Guidelines," Department of Public Instruction, Raleigh, N.C., n.d.
22. In correspondence with Melvin L. Good, acting director, Division of Cultural Arts, Department of Public Instruction, Raleigh, North Carolina.
23. In correspondence with Joseph McCarthy, senior program adviser, Arts in Education, Department of Education, Commonwealth of Pennsylvania, Harrisburg.
24. Helen Manfull and Frances Fairchild, *Creative Drama and Writing Ideas: A Handbook for Teachers to Accompany the Penn State University Children's Theatre Ensemble* Arts in Education Project, Central Intermediate Unit 10 (University Park: Pennsylvania State University, Department of Theatre and Film, 1979).
25. *Drama Theatre Framework for California Public Schools* (Sacramento: California State Department of Education, 1974).
26. In correspondence with Mary Jane Evans, member of the Fine Arts Committee, California State University, Northridge.
27. John Sharpham and Diane Ackermann, "Drama in Education Courses at U.S. Colleges: A Survey," *Theatre News* no. 3 (December 1978): 4–7.
28. Ibid.
29. In correspondence with Lin Wright, faculty member, Arizona State University, Tempe.
30. In correspondence with Mary Jane Evans, faculty member, California State University, Northridge.
31. In correspondence with Jed Davis, faculty member, University of Kansas, Lawrence.
32. *Program in Educational Theatre Bulletin* (New York: Department of Communication Arts and Sciences, School of Education, Health, Nursing, and Arts Professions, New York University, n.d.).
33. Ibid.
34. In correspondence with Anne Thurman, faculty member, School of Speech, Northwestern University, Evanston.
35. "Graduate Program Bulletin," University of Texas at Austin, n.d.
36. "Master of Fine Arts Program Bulletin," School of Drama, University of Washington, Seattle, n.d.

Creative Drama—
Improvisation—Theatre

Margaret Faulkes Jendyk

Margaret Faulkes Jendyk, associate professor of drama at the University of Alberta, Canada, was educated in England where she attended the Royal Academy of Dramatic Art and London University Goldsmiths' College. She has taught in the City of Leicester Education Department, at Loughborough College, and in the Hinckley and West Ham secondary schools, as well as acted in the West Country professional children's theatre. She was co-founder and co-director with Brian Way of the well-known Theatre Centre in London in 1954, where she remained until 1965, when she became visiting lecturer at the University of Washington. She assumed her present position in 1967; in addition, she has lectured and conducted numerous drama workshops throughout Canada and the United States.

Drama: *a set of events having the unity and progress of a play and leading to catastrophe or consummation.* The Oxford dictionary's definition provides an apt choice of prognoses for twentieth-century drama in education, brought sharply into focus through controversy among protagonists in the field preventing unity and impeding progress. Dichotomy and polarization in objectives and techniques of educational drama have been aggravated during the past twenty-five years by developments in educational philosophy and psychology, by the influence of pioneers in "creative" approaches to drama in schools, and by the evolution of theatre itself with its emphasis on experimentation. At first glance, the controversy seems well founded, for drama teachers have widely differing objectives embodying confusing and sometimes contradictory techniques.

15

Four major objectives for drama in education may be identified, each involving variations in teacher orientation:

1. Artistic: *Exposure to (and sometimes training in) traditional theatre arts and crafts.* While this approach may be found at any grade level, it is most commonly associated with the secondary school where the drama specialist, fully trained (most often in traditional approaches to formal theatre), will philosophize that the experience of theatre as an art "for art's sake" nonetheless integrates educational and cultural principles.

2. Expressive: *The development of personal resources, especially creativity.* The drama teacher may have some orientation to and knowledge of theatre arts, but also has a commitment to education in the broadest sense. It is likely that training, if any, has included creative drama* and, if this teacher incorporates theatre experience into the school program, formal techniques may be deemphasized in favor of process rather than product. Being less concerned with the preservation of theatre tradition, the drama specialist may well focus on improvisation as a core, while the teacher of other disciplines (such as language arts) may use creative drama techniques and disregard theatre altogether.

3. Social: *The development of social awareness, political conscience, "group trust," and interpersonal relationships.* Comparatively recent, this utilization of drama takes advantage of the trend toward "social conscience" by limiting classroom drama and theatre experience to the dramatization of contemporary events or topics and documentary material and themes of social or political import. A more dangerous manifestation of social drama embodies the use of drama techniques by amateur psychologists and some drama teachers who have been diverted by the specter of drama as a panacea for all human problems, for sensitivity training, for problem solving, and for "confrontations" in the classroom. Regrettably, teachers in this category seem unconcerned about the art of theatre, although they label their activities "drama"; there is an unfortunate trend for administrative encouragement of these activities including government grants given to drama teachers and actors with limited experience in creative drama and participation children's theatre—but none in psychology or psychiatry—to introduce creative drama programs in mental hospitals. Such identification of *creative drama* with therapy and its related fields of sensitivity training and the like, or with questionable propaganda, brings the whole field of drama into disrepute.

4. Pedagogical: *The teaching of curricular subjects including universal educational concepts such as insight, empathy, and personal enrichment (sometimes defined as "having fun").* The drama teacher, the specialist in other disciplines, and the general teacher recognize that dramatic method involving improvisation is useful as an educational tool. In this classification we find elementary and secondary teachers of English, lan-

---

* *Creative Drama* is here used as a generic term embracing *child drama, children's drama, educational drama, creative drama, creative dramatics, developmental drama,* and so forth. Later in this essay it will be used to denote a specific approach to drama.

guage arts, and social studies. In the hands of a creative and intuitive teacher, drama can be an effective learning instrument; however, many teachers who attempt to use it are unfamiliar with the basic elements of any kind of drama, let alone the techniques involved in creative drama. As a consequence, the classroom becomes a setting for chaos in the name of creativity. Recent developments have seen creative drama techniques applied to the learning of curricular material with some success as far as the mental and intellectual processes of education are concerned; but the knowledge acquired or concepts understood and *articulated* is usually at the expense of intuition, spontaneity, originality, and genuine affective involvement (which sometimes cannot be articulated except through a non-verbal form of expression), as well as the many and varied creative elements embodied in drama/theatre experience. "Activity methods" is a more accurate label than "drama" for such learning/teaching strategies.

To a great extent, those of us who have pioneered in creative drama are to blame for the increased use of our techniques in other fields. Zealous in our well-meaning efforts to convince the traditional theatre arts teachers that a nonperformance-oriented "creative" approach to dramatic art is not only desirable but essential for young children, we have so negated theatre itself that we have antagonized our colleagues and have provided strong arguments for equating creative drama with everything *but* theatre. Indeed, some leaders in the field have spent long hours trying to find alternative titles and descriptive terms in order to emphasize the dichotomy between "drama" and "theatre."

More damaging is the manifestation of confused thinking among the exponents of creative drama: some view it as an art form, suggesting that it is the child's style of theatre; others call it art, but discourage any connection with the art of theatre; some insist that it is a subject in its own right but is concerned with personal rather than drama development; still others argue that it is a basis for eventual drama experience; some deny its existence as a subject at all, designating it as an educational tool —a core for all subjects.

Further perplexity arises because the pioneers at first focused their attention on the young child, and so creative drama became associated with elementary education; but later developments applied the techniques to work with teen-agers, and it is not uncommon today to hear people talking about "the creative drama approach to theatre." With utter disregard for rationale, creative drama is described as a nontheatre-oriented activity and defined as improvisation which, historically, has always been a part of theatre art and, in this century, has become integral to actor-training—while avant garde, highly publicized, professional theatre groups have declared that improvisation is a viable theatre art form. Meanwhile, developments in theatre for young audiences (long associated with creative dramatics in teacher-training) have included the interpretation (or misinterpretation) of audience participation as creative drama; trouping companies have promoted improvisation in lieu of script, "poor theatre" in any shape and in any place, and actor-audience interaction with the proclaimed educational objectives of promoting creative drama as a classroom activity. Recent theatre-in-education developments (originating from professional theatre companies looking for grants) have seen the emergence of improvisational programs involving any number of students—from about 30 to 200—in what is termed a "creative drama experience"; linked with curricular material (to please the school board) and often incorporating specific social objectives, such programs generally include only token performance and presentation by the teacher/actors and afford minimal action and affective involvement for the students. In other words, the experience is in *thinking* without feeling or doing. Such projects generate doubts about their relationship to either theatre or creative drama.

The layman, bombarded by such inconsistencies, selects whichever words or phrases make the most sense and often ends up with the all-too-familiar prejudice against any kind of drama in education; and it is not surprising that the traditional theatre arts teacher suspects the creative drama teacher of being anti-"real theatre." At the same time, "traditionalists" who have been known to dismiss both creative drama and participation children's theatre as "pixie drama" are reluctant to acknowledge that contemporary playwrights, directors, designers, and actors have effected comparable—in some cases identical—innovations. Instead of applying such unconventional, adventurous explorations to theatre arts programs, the quasi-conservatory system in many high schools perpetuates an outdated mode of theatre that evidences an abysmal disregard for progress in either theatre *or* education. Similarly, some elementary school teachers, while fully endorsing creativity in a general educational sense, resort to conventional styles of production and performance in the name of drama expression for children. Such anomaly arises from ignorance or obstinacy.

One reason for the continuing dichotomy between the "traditionalists" and the "progressives" is that neither group envisions the total spectrum. If the whole field of drama in education is viewed in terms of the definition of drama itself—"a set of events having the unity and progress of a play"—then any course or program of drama must include a beginning, a middle, and an end. To begin at the beginning, where drama in education is concerned, seems to be an exercise in futility. The "traditionalists," focusing on formal theatre techniques, invariably begin at the end, equating process with product. The "progressives," emphasizing development of personal resources, seem with increasing regularity to end at the beginning, equating product with process. It is important, therefore, to recognize that, in drama, the "spectrum" fits the definition of "the image of something seen continuing when the eyes are closed or turned away." The "something seen" is the process whereby individual resources and creative potential are developed into dramatic art awareness which leads to a rich, dynamic experience of the product.

The beginning, middle, and end of drama in education are here considered as three interrelated phases of activity, which incorporate the educational objectives of personal development and the artistic objectives of drama development.

PHASE 1   Laying The Foundations

Since the stress in phase 1 is on personal development, while art form is deemphasized, it will be entitled *creative drama*.

It is not difficult to persuade teachers of grades K–6 that a vital function of drama in elementary education is the development of the child's resources. Educational philosophy and psychology consistently emphasize the needs of the growing child. Sometimes, because of inherent prejudice against drama, its general educational objectives have to be disguised under the pretext of fostering creativity, which is considered acceptable, even desirable, in the education of the young. But when it comes to the teen-ager in the junior high grades, or the young adult in the senior high school, vision becomes blurred. Overnight the Grade 7 student has become adult enough to learn adult ways, and any classroom activity that implies growth or "creativity for its own sake" is suspect. As for the Grade 10 student, the appointed drama specialist usually has one thought uppermost in mind: to produce the annual school play as soon as possible. Instant theatre becomes the maxim. It matters little if the students have had drama before; it matters less if they are physically inhibited, imaginatively deprived, or incapable of communicating thoughts and ideas with freedom, confidence, and vigor. The suggestion that individual resources that have long been dormant or atrophied should be rediscovered and quickened before attempting to introduce them to the art of drama is received with amazement, scorn, and even ridicule.

Any beginning group, regardless of age or drama background, needs an initial period of exploration and orientation to provide a basis for further creative experience. Creative drama therefore, is the beginning point for *all* drama.

PHASE 2   Awareness of Dramatic Art Form

This phase will be termed *improvisation*, on the grounds that improvisation embodies numerous elements of dramatic art and is a natural evolvement from creative drama.

This period of drama experience is the most misunderstood. Dramatic art and theatre are equated with *performance*; but from the preparatory stage of resource development, the student needs to go through a level of exploration into elements of drama without the pressures of public performance that preclude (or should preclude) failure. More than this, drama teachers should acknowledge the different aptitudes of children and teen-agers, and make a distinction between the drama-oriented/nondrama-oriented young adult. In elementary grades, all children can participate in creative drama; in junior and senior high schools, where drama is an option, it is illusory to assume that participating students must be capable of the kind of dramatic art that incorporates public performance. It is well known that junior high and Grade 10 students often elect drama because they are counseled to do so, or because it seems the lesser of evil choices.

Many children, young people, and adults can enjoy the experience of dramatic art within the confines of the workshop environment without the need or desire to extend that experience into public performance. Improvisation, therefore, is a middle level of drama viewed as an essential transitory exploration for some, and a terminal experience for many.

PHASE 3   Experience of Theatre Art

While phases 1 and 2 may be described as process, phase 3 is concerned with the experience and exploration of theatre involving performance; therefore, this phase earns the simple title of *theatre*.

Experience of theatre art involving performance is ideally limited to a minority, for while all can participate in phase 1, and many in phase 2, only a small percentage of senior students are sufficiently drama-oriented to pursue the art through to its ultimate conclusion; such students may well continue with theatre arts as a vocation or as a leisure activity in adulthood. Nevertheless, it can be argued that there are different interpretations and degrees of performance so that, while chronologically the concept of "three phases of drama" may imply elementary, junior high, and senior high, in fact the same three phases with appropriate modifications may easily be applied to any age group of students in the school system. Implicit in the apparent paradox is the acceptance of a style of theatre that is unconventional and therefore, for many teachers, unacceptable.

Phases 1 and 2 may certainly prepare students for traditional theatre arts programs with the emphasis on the formal (proscenium) production of a scripted play, but it must be admitted that the stress on improvisation and flexibility of dramatic form inherent in the process tends to produce nontraditional styles of theatre art emanating from student-centered originality as distinct from director-centered imposition of an established theatre form. *The combination of flexible (often center) staging, the utilization of dance and improvisation as well as script, and projected images reinforcing dramatic statements or themes relevant to youth today exemplifies experimental theatre, which has certainly earned its place in the unfoldment of twentieth-century drama.* By chance (or, some may suggest, by reversion to simplistic styles indigenous to the origins of drama and dance), the demands on the young student are less technical, enabling even the least sophisticated to participate in the product.

The Three Phases of Drama: Objectives And Techniques

PHASE 1   Creative Drama

Objective   *To lay the foundations for further creative activity through the discovery and development of personal resources.*

Creative drama is an exercise or activity involving extemporaneous speech; spontaneous action and movement; imagination; simple characterization; story-making; and uses the whole self interacting with others to create a dynamic, immediate experience. It occurs in any kind of space, uses neither written script nor conscious structured theatre art form, and involves no presentation; it concerns personal experience rather than communication to an audience. Creative drama is totally nontheatre-oriented.

Creative activity has two main thrusts: originality (involving innovation) and interpretation. In theatre terms, originality is recognizable through the play-wright, while innovation today seems to be mainly the province of the director who, with the designer and actor, is an interpreter of the playwright. In educational drama, the production or study of plays is interpretative creativity, with the teacher/director as the prime interpreter; in this category belongs also the dramatization of a story or poem with the teacher/leader as the main interpreter. In the argument put forward herein, *dramatization is to be found in later phases of drama when the stimulus and discipline of dramatic literature provide extended experience of material and awareness of form.*

In phase 1, emphasis is placed on original ideas emanating from individual students, or collectively from groups; imagination is an important ingredient of creativity that is considered not merely in relation to the arts but as an integral part of the vital, flexible, initiative drive indispensable to personal and societal responsibilities. Other interacting physical, emotional, and intellectual resources involve sense awareness; bodily freedom and control; oral communication, self-awareness and sensitivity toward others; cognitive, deductive, and divergent thinking; together with self-actualization or the realization of full potential in the development of abilities, with dynamic response to every experience.

The above may be termed overall objectives. In creative drama, immediate goals are centered on the development of concentration, absorption, and sincerity arising out of genuine affective involvement; confidence in all activities involving movement, speaking, imagination, and interaction with others; alertness, dynamism, and maximum effort in all circumstances and conditions; the preservation and growth of individuality; and the evolvement of self-discipline with personal responsibility for endeavor.

The characteristics of creative drama are recognizable in that extemporaneous speech and spontaneous action (movement) are utilized extensively, with all students working simultaneously most of the time, using the total space available. (It should be noted that, even during pair or small-group exercises, no section of the class is excluded or asked to become "audience.") There is often high noise emission from the creative drama classroom, particularly during speech activities. To the casual observer, there is an apparent lack of unity in that each student may be doing something quite different from the next; but the governing factor that ensures freedom rather than license is the structure of the creative drama session: the techniques

Any group beginning a new activity (or being introduced to a new approach) needs a clear framework within which members can operate without fear of failure or ridicule. When children or young adults feel insecure in an environment or occupation, they react in a variety of ways—none of them particularly conducive to creativity, effort, or concentration. For each exercise in creative drama there is an immediate objective, and underlying the majority is that of building confidence so that potentials may be discovered and developed.

Thus, in early sessions, students are given clear instructions on *what* to do or *who* to be and then are left with the responsibility of deciding *how* to do it (this is a challenge to some who may have grown to rely on a demonstration from teacher or parent). As soon as possible, however, the instructor begins to relinquish responsibility for ideas on what to do or who to be, providing stimuli rather than detail. An important by-product of the approach whereby all work simultaneously in a noncritical atmosphere avoiding censure or praise of individuals is a leveling of extreme personality traits: the very shy individual will begin to take a few risks, and the exhibitionist will soon realize that nobody is watching his or her antics except for the instructor, who is busy observing everyone. The accent on private and personal discovery of potential for any given exercise endorses the valued property of individuality while precluding any suggestion of conformity through uniformity. Inherent in the structured session is discipline imposed and control taken by the instructor; the simple rule of "maximum effort" plus the logic of aiming for a simple objective such as concentration demands of each participant a specific behavioral response. For example, students who chat to each other while doing an individual movement exercise are obviously not concentrating on the activity and thus cannot fully achieve the desired aim; both concentration and movement will suffer. The underlying principle asserts that maximum effort will produce development that will lead to achievement.

In the early stages of phase 1, the instructor is looking for achievement in the immediate objectives and, as these are realized, progresses to more complicated exercises; thus, having attained a certain degree of concentration and confidence while working individually, students must now discover how to apply such properties when working with others. In practice, therefore, exercises move from being person-centered to group-centered, although the total session is still firmly structured and all pairs or groups will continue to work simultaneously in activities that lack any noticeable art form.

Exercises range from discovery of space and sense awareness to movement response to stimuli: imaginative "journeys" described by the instructor and physically undertaken by the class; large crowd scenes involving speech and action; story making from original ideas provided by the class (as an end in itself without any attempt at full dramatization, although characters and incidents arising from such stories may be used as stimuli for further activities). As the format extends to include pairs and small groups, so music may become the stimulus for simple movement situations which allow for maximum phsyical, imaginative and affective involvement without intellectualization; pair and group incidents are devised with the emphasis on action, as are situations involving mainly speech. Discussion is consistently encouraged—both as a method of obtaining ideas and planning activities and as a means of direct communication between instructor and class. In early sessions, the topic for discussion is irrelevant, since the immediate objective is to create a climate for positive oral communication and to establish an environment where all ideas are valid even if they are not commonly acceptable or cannot always be used.

It has been stated that the nontheatre-oriented approach of creative drama is applicable, even necessary, for any beginning group, regardless of age and background. For young children in elementary grades, organic growth implies that creative drama with its accentuation on personal development can—and perhaps should—be an end in itself. The natural development of the child proceeds slowly from the "singleton" stage of early infancy into the social discovery of one friend at a time through to the "gang" or group stage; this process parallels the development of drama as outlined above. By definition, therefore, it would appear that as far as elementary grades are concerned, phase 1 can be the limit of their drama experience. On the other hand, it is unrealistic to deny experience of simple art forms to the elementary child merely because he is trapped in the unnatural division of an educational system that in June labels him a Grade 6 child and in September a Grade 7 teen-ager. Therefore, the teacher of top elementary grades should be looking ahead, just as the teacher of Grade 7 students must, for a while, look back.

For teen-age groups, phase 1 is an essential starting point. With young children, creative drama assists in the natural development of resources; for the older student, it is a means of rediscovering personal resources and developing those which have lain dormant. Even for the drama-oriented teen-ager or adult, the exercises and activities of creative drama are necessary for creative endeavor embodying originality and innovation beyond the requirements of traditional theatre techniques. By ignoring or denying this, theatre arts teachers prevent the full exploration of creative potential in their young students.

Noteworthy, however, is the increasing trend for some secondary school teachers to disregard *the need of young adults for artistic exploration*; through lack of knowledge and expertise in dramatic art, or because of a deviation in objectives, such teachers maintain a level of creative drama that produces in their students lethargic disinterest or indulgence in emotional, self-centered "freak-outs."

Artistic maturation is an important stage of development. As the young person moves toward adolescence, it is with varying degrees of anticipation, resignation, and frustration that the adult accepts the manifestation of emotional and physical maturity alongside the more manageable growth of intellectual powers. Less attention is paid to the young adult's artistic maturation, although art educators have long maintained that an interest in techniques and skills coincides with puberty.

The application of artistic maturation to drama discloses that, as the youngster approaches adolescence, he manifests an emerging interest in the elements of dramatic art form. Thus, for top elementary grades, phase 1 merges naturally into phase 2; for beginning groups in junior and senior high school, where artistic maturation is revealed and realized, phase 2 becomes an essential progression, as the discipline inherent in any art form provides at once a vital challenge to personal resources and a focus for heightened physical, emotional, and mental energies.

PHASE 2   Improvisation

Objective   Introduction to dramatic art form

Improvisation is an exercise, an activity, a scene or a play involving extemporaneous speech and spontaneous movement or action, *embodying elements of dramatic art*; it may evolve from original ideas or from stimuli including dramatic literature; it can lead to a detailed scenario and script writing.

This definition develops from that for creative drama. The confusion among practitioners in the field of educational drama has been compounded by a failure to differentiate between a beginning activity (creative drama), which is nontheatre-oriented, and an advanced activity (improvisation), which, historically, has always had a place in the art of theatre. The instant we view improvisation in its rightful context, it is apparent that it is neither synonymous with creative drama nor a substitute for theatre, although it may develop into theatre art.

Phase 2 is characterized by group improvisation projects; it is important to distinguish between spontaneous "ad-libbing," which is sometimes interpreted as improvisation, and the utilization of extemporaneous speech with a planned dramatic framework; also, it should be explained that phase 2 improvisation does not include the highly skilled "instant theatre" approach favored by some professional theatre groups, nor is it limited to acting exercises utilized in actor-training. Rather, movement and/or speech improvisations are devised, planned, and rehearsed from session to session and sometimes from week to week. Major responsibility is given to the groups for ideas and organization; during such projects, pairs or small groups of students can be found scattered throughout the building (assuming that such freedom is permitted by the administration), and if a deadline is given for the completion of a project, groups may well meet to rehearse out of class time.

Occasionally, the instructor may organize a project involving the whole class: a crowd scene (e.g., the assassination of the governor of a small country, or a band of robbers looting an empty castle); a movement drama (e.g., a *West Side Story* incident to a rhythmic record); after the dramatization of a story from original or literary sources, for a collage program centered on a theme and utilizing movement, improvisation, poetry, prose, song, scenes from plays, and so forth. Written assignments are also introduced, progressing from an outline of the scene to a full scenario. Even, with older students, a simple production script.

The latter is indicative of accumulative experience in phase 2 aimed at increasing the students' awareness of elements of dramatic art. For teen-age groups, each project introduces some new component beginning with the simplest involving *structure* (objective: to work out an ending for the scene) and gradually adding *climax* (build to a strong moment); *the event* (drama involves particular occasions or incidents); *characters* (individual differences, relationships, and how people behave in usual/unusual situations); *organization* (selection and definition, the difference between a story and a play); *dramatic statement* (what is the story line or what statement is being made?).

As awareness of dramatic art form is developed, production elements are introduced and artistic judgments stressed. With originality and innovation strongly in mind, however, little attempt is made to impose rigidity of form and techniques. Instead, groups are encouraged to experiment in *style* (shape of acting area, or utilization of whole room); *lighting* (for effect rather than illumination); and *sound* (for reinforcement, stimulus, or accompaniment). Properties and costumes are limited to extension of character instead of becoming a decorative essential so that objects and items of clothing or pieces of fabric are representational or symbolic. A special project utilizing *projected images* (overhead and slide projectors each with polarizing equipment enabling them to be used for realistic or abstract images, and opaque projectors for graphics and collages) adds a further extension that contributes to the concept of creating an environment rather than "designing a set." All the above experiences are an introduction to theatre production and design.

Personal development continues, with special emphasis on expansion of experience and on acquiring a high tolerance level when working in a group. The instructor becomes in part the initiator—providing continual opportunities for further unfoldment—and in part a resource person who solves problems and organizes time. Responsibility for creativity is shared by the instructor and the groups and collectively within the groups. Discipline is achieved in three ways: from the instructor, from the group, and from the art form itself. The peculiar distinction of the group project is that it enforces maximum effort from each member; peer pressure demands this, but a simple rule is made that, in the event of absence (excused or unexcused) during the preparation of a group project, the defaulter must withdraw, although he or she is given the option of preparing a "solo" as a makeup opportunity.

Discussion continues to be a fundamental part of the process and is based on an evaluation of achievement in the particular objectives given for each project. Also, group projects are now presented to the rest of the class in a workshop situation: it is made clear that the presentation is for the purpose of seeing what others have been doing, and applause is disallowed to reinforce the nonperformance, noncompetitive principles. Through positive discussion, standards, criteria, and aesthetic values are absorbed and, as the work progresses, are applied by the students in practical work and in discussions.

Since phase 2 takes its place in the spectrum of drama as the natural unfoldment of artistic awareness for the young adult, achievement is now measured in artistic terms—not limited, however, to "acting" only. Drama has included movement, imagination, production concepts, organization and planning, and writing; toward the end of this phase, individual strengths and weaknesses become evident. It is possible to identify the potential writer, director, designer, or actor among those who may be particularly drama-oriented; it is also possible to recognize the enthusiastic "nondrama" person who enjoys the artistic experience but has neither special talent nor the desire to take that further step, which is involvement in theatre art.

The elementary teacher, studying the exercises and projects incorporated into phase 2 of drama experience, will readily declare that many such could not only be undertaken by these grade levels but also would be of benefit to them. This is true in the sense that, with any group, ideas can be adapted and techniques modified. Thus, a dramatized story, a "group play," or a movement drama can provide stimuli for creative writing and for arts and crafts and can become a positive exercise in simple forms of organization; the use of media as an art extension linked with drama or literature has been successfully introduced to elementary students. If the premise of a correlation between artistic maturation and adolescence is accepted, however, then the goals of such projects differ according to the age group. The readiness factor for the extension of experience is probably the most important assessment that every teacher has to make at any given time; of all experiences, the readiness level for any kind of performance is of high significance.

PHASE 3   Theatre

Objective   *Experience of improvisational theatre art*

Much has been written on the pros and cons of performance by children and teen-agers, and these arguments need not be restated. But it is worth noting that most of the dialogue has been based on the concept of theatre performance that embodies adult techniques of acting and staging with performance to the general public. If the word "performance" with all those connotations is removed and replaced by "presentation" involving originality, dynamic natural action, and speech in an intimate environment as a workshop event for peers, friends, family, and selected guests, most of the reasons for objection are removed. An informal, "open-day" type of presentation can involve any age group, provided there is a valid reason for it, the students are at the right readiness level, the content and style of activity is within their natural capabilities, and the "audience" is private.

Unfortunately, even if such ideal conditions are observed, the decision to give a presentation transforms process into product and creates a pressure on instructor and students. One useful way of solving this problem is to call the presentation a "demonstration" or an "incomplete production." This allows the instructor to explain to invited guests what the objectives of the project have been and, in the interests of the total concept of personal and drama development, that the presentation is an example of work that has reached a particular level of attainment.

The stress on originality and flexibility of production styles encouraged during phases 1 and 2 results in an approach to theatre that is close to contemporary experimentation. More often than not, center-staging will arise, incorporating the use of levels with flexible representational or symbolic "sets." The action will include movement/dance and improvised dialogue, although script writing will occur; and dramatic literature, scenes from plays, poetry, and contemporary songs may be interwoven to reinforce a topical theme relevant for the young student. Lighting, sound, and projected images for effective enhancement of the dramatic statement produce a theatrical event that defies classification because the intention and formation has been a "collective creation" by a group of original thinkers.

Alternatively, a play per se may be devised, embodying more conventional structure while still incorporating many of the above dramatic elements; or a story may be taken as a framework for development into an imaginative theatre event. For instance, one legend about a priest and the devil actually has only five characters: the Priest, his Cat, a Fisherman, his Wife, and the Devil. A play may be developed as follows: The characters: the Priest and his Cat, the Fisherman, and the Islanders; the Mainlanders—pleasure-seeking and easily tempted by Satan and his Devils who are constantly among them and from time to time become supernatural beings or the elements of a storm that continually destroys any bridge the Islanders try to build.

The Mainlanders and Devils represent a *Vanity Fair* image through movement; the Islanders discuss their problems through improvised dialogue; the Priest and the Devil work on (and partially script) the bargain they make. The bridge is "built" in two ways: (1) through realistic mime including the climbing of ladders to represent cliffs, with lighting effects and the apparition of devils for the storms that destroy it; (2) through a symbolic dance drama as it is eventually completed. At various moments throughout the presentation, projected images depict religious pictures and artifacts, devil faces and forms, the village and the river, together with abstracts during the dance dramas. Costumes are limited to pieces of cloth and masks for the Devils. *The total production involves all members of the class in both action and technical production:* dialogue and movement are worked out by groups and/or individuals; lighting is planned, projections are created, and when students are not involved in a scene, they are working a spotlight or the tape recorder or a projector.

One of the greatest misconceptions of this style of theatre is that anarchy prevails and artistry is absent. This can indeed happen if the instructor abdicates accountability for organization, supervision, and the maintenance of artistic integrity. The instructor/director in phase 3 takes responsibility for artistic decisions and aesthetic judgments, and for continuing to expand the students' awareness of the art of theatre. Student responsibility has progressed from self (phase 1) to the group (phases 1–2) to the art form (phases 2–3) and ultimately to the audience which deserves something better than "deadly theatre" inexpertly performed and produced.

By encouraging student-originated theatre exploration, the theatre arts teacher contributes to the dynamic unfoldment of theatre in the twentieth century, for some of these young adults may become the playwrights, directors, designers, and actors of the future. At the same time, this style of theatre exemplifies the demands of educators, administrators, parents, and politicians for the encouragement of initiative, flexibility, leadership, cooperation, tolerance, and various other qualities considered desirable for adults in the "person-centered society" advocated by the Worth Commission on Educational Planning.

The evolvement of theatre and drama in education throughout history has bequeathed to each generation a heritage of prejudice from without and controversy within. It should come as no surprise, therefore, to realize that many school boards and hundreds of schools deny to thousands of children and young people the right to experience drama as an integral part of their education. Only drama educators care enough to rectify and improve a situation that may well deteriorate within a decade. Surely, through progress with unity, we may avoid catastrophe and realize the consummation of our education and artistic aspirations.

REFERENCES

Peter Brook. *The Empty Space.* Harmondsworth: Penguin Books, 1968.
Philip Coggin. *The Uses of Drama.* New York: George Braziller, 1956.
Peter Slade. *Child Drama.* London: University of London Press, 1954.
Brian Way. *Development Through Drama.* London: Longmans Green, 1967.
W. Worth. *A Choice of Futures.* Edmonton, Canada: Commission on Educational Planning, 1972.

Thoughts on the Creative Process

Virginia Tanner

The late Virginia Tanner was for many years director of creative dance at the University of Utah. She was as well known to leaders of creative dramatics in this country as she was to teachers and students of dance. She gave demonstrations for the Children's Theatre Association and presented her young dancers at Jacob's Pillow, the Connecticut College School of Dance, the Seattle World's Fair, and the 1970 White House Conference for Children. Miss Tanner's influence on dance education has been widely felt through her guest teaching assignments, which took her from New England to Hawaii. She was selected as "Master Teacher" by the National Endowment for the Arts and the U.S. Office of Education, for whom she taught in its Artist in the Schools Program. In 1963 Wilson College in Pennsylvania recognized her with an honorary doctorate. In this essay Miss Tanner described the creative process as she saw it. Having her students become professional performers was never her major interest; helping them to become more sensitive to the world around them and guiding them to discover their potential in movement were her goals.

For many years it has been my privilege to be surrounded by the beauty, the joy, the excitement, as well as the hesitancies of childhood. What a challenge this has been!

Teaching creatively starts with imagination and ideas. Most children are filled with both—ideas they are eager to express and ideas they must express if they are to live fully as children and later as adults. To a child anything seems possible. His world is filled with fantasy, which is frequently dimmed when parents, teachers, and friends turn down the lights in his treasure house of imagination. A child quickly realizes whether or not you offer sincere warmth, understanding, and interest. Only when rapport is established will he unlock the many facets of his heart and allow you to share your treasures with him and his with you. The key to guiding the child to self-fulfillment lies in sharing those moments that involve thinking, feeling, and exploring experiences. As these experiences take place the child spreads his roots in fertile soil.

When one has an honest respect for children, there is a constant search to open new channels that will increase the child's awareness of the world around him and give a deeper meaning to his daily life. In this setting most of my activities over the years have taken place.

Early in my professional studies, I realized that, in the name of dance, much damage was being done to the young. False values were being fostered in immature minds as parents were encouraged to buy "sophisticated" kiddie costumes for the local dance review. The child was being denied the real beauty of expression through dance. By approaching dance as an art form I gradually learned to recognize many basic truths; and in doing so I developed a teaching philosophy that has inspired many persons to work creatively with children. The creative approach to movement not only provides a means to enhance coordination and poise, but it also makes a marked difference in the lives of children.

During the past few years, a great deal of time, investigation, and study have been expended throughout the world to discover ways to learn more about this elusive quality called creativity. I wonder what would have been the result if, during the initial measuring of an individual's potential intelligence, equal time had been allotted to measuring his potential creative ability, and then a search had been made for ways to stimulate the growth of both these inherent qualities.

There is a great deal of truth to the statement "All God's chillun got wings," but far too often those wings have been clipped before they have known the joy of soaring. The seeds of curiosity present in man at birth can lead him to become a dedicated person with tremendous drive for his chosen work. Yet only a few, with so insistent a creative gift that it flourishes in spite of everything, realize their potential and make a unique contribution to science, art, and the teaching profession.

But what of the hundreds of thousands of children who, at the age of four, seem to possess this cherished capacity, and then, by the age of nine, no longer utilize it as a source of rich fulfillment? Could it be that unimaginative teaching methods, lack of perception, hours of unguided television, and stereotyped toys destroy the very thing that will help bring to each one his greatest moments of happiness? Are we ignoring the need for personal growth and fulfillment that allow a young person to formulate genuine friendships and know the joy of using leisure time with purpose and study hours with eagerness?

The educated, creative man knows who he is, where he wants to go, and what he wants to achieve. Certain environmental agents can make this level of self-realization possible: sensitive parents, access to good libraries, stimulating teachers, religious belief and understanding, and the steady encouragement to utilize personal resources constructively in every phase of life. Wherever creative work flourishes, someone has established communication with his inner self. The creative force must not be permitted to waste itself. It must be encouraged, stimulated and given time to develop. During its growth, there must be guidance from a creative person.

This brings to mind an experiment conducted at a midwestern college. Two groups of highly sensitive students were selected for the control groups. Both units were given ideal situations as far as atmosphere and resource material were concerned. One group was left to itself and the other was guided by a highly creative teacher who could direct or encourage as the need arose. After a given time limit, the works of both groups were compared. As anticipated, the explorations of the directed group were far greater than those of the unit that had no supervision.

To be free to use one's imagination fully requires great discipline. Within each new freedom achieved lies the routine achievement of techniques and discipline—factors frequently misunderstood by people when the word "creativity" is mentioned. Readiness never comes by chance or by luck, but only when opportunity and disciplined technique, plus freedom of exploration, are joined. Working imaginatively with people does not simply mean "today we will listen to this music and follow whatever it suggests" or "take these paints and paper to draw whatever you feel" or "take this set of blocks and build whatever comes to mind." This approach represents only a minute part of creative guidance. The whole complex process should reflect the constant urging of the mind and body to reach out in new directions, to find more than one way to solve a problem so that within the structure of each new venture, the individual may gain more knowledge, understanding, and truth. These are the rudiments of working creatively with people. Nothing can take the place of persistence and discipline. Talent will not. Genius will not.

There is creative energy in all human beings. Louis Horst once said, "Each of us is born with genius, but some keep it only a few seconds." Our particular purpose is to open ways that will encourage the child to question, to investigate, to solve problems in more than one way, and to attack the problem at hand with a zest. In effect, to go beyond that which is easy. This is our responsibility, and I believe we can teach most facts creatively.

Knowledge and technique in skills cannot be overlooked or slighted. If we have no tools, our investigation reaches a blind wall. To be encouraged to search, to think deeply, takes time. And children as well as adults need time—time to try again, time to share, and time to have sensitive questions answered judiciously.

One day a little boy brought a book about rockets to class. "Teacher, may we dance about my book?" Until an idea was used from his book, this youngster could not participate wholeheartedly in any other activity. To solve the problem, we had small groups of children stand in four corners of the room that we designated as New York, Florida, Washington, and California. A rocket was launched from New York. It had to go very fast across the floor (our pretended sky) and land in Florida. Rockets were launched until each child had a turn. Finally, rockets were sent aloft simultaneously from California and New York. Each one had to travel rapidly through space, avoid collisions, and land in a different state. Before the class was over, rockets could be sent from each corner simultaneously. There were no collisions and yet each child moved quickly in space and landed in a new state. This experience allowed David to use the idea of his rocket book; and it taught the other children space patterns, to move with speed, and a valuable lesson in organization. And, needless to say, we had fun too.

When confronted with David's request, I could have said, "Oh, David, there are so many other fun things for us to do today. Let's save your idea." But I realized that his idea was so important to him that a way had to be found to use his book, not just as a pillow to rest on, something to jump over, something to hold high as he went skipping, for these ideas had no real relationship to the context of his wonderful book. He wanted to dance about rockets.

Keeping a child excited about investigating ideas is very important. One day a five-year-old greeted me with a special sparkle in her eyes. Excitedly, she burst forth: "Miss Virginia, I discovered the 'backward going' skip, and I'll teach it to you." What a joyous moment when we went skipping backward together! Now you may think this a very ordinary thing. But pause for a moment and ponder its true worth. For this child the discovery that she had the coordination to skip backward was a new moment; nothing like it had ever happened before in her life. I was extremely happy to have had the privilege of sharing that moment with her! I might have said: "Oh, someday everybody can skip backward," and that spark, which could ignite further discovery, might have been smothered. Part of the richness of adult-child relationships is developed by the adult's ability to see through the eyes of the child. If the adult does not make room for the unexpected and can direct only his own set of plans, some of the most vital moments of teaching and learning are lost.

My son's first-grade class was given an opportunity for a delightful creative experience. Each was to select a leaf that had a particularly pleasing shape. Our little boy was curious about the many shapes he found in leaves and encouraged his family to go with him on a walk to help him find exactly the leaf he was looking for. He was delighted to find a large oak leaf that had an unusual coloring and special perfection in his eyes. He proudly took his leaf to school and entered into the project enthusiastically. The children were to use the leaf as the body of an imaginary child and add a head, two arms, and two legs. Steve took a longer time to finish his child than was allotted, and when the teacher came to investigate why he was taking so long, she discovered that he had added a cap in one hand and an umbrella in the other hand. "Just in case it rained, Mom," he told me. The teacher quickly picked up his paper and with a pair of scissors, she snipped off the added cap and umbrella. It took weeks before he again dared to investigate beyond the limits of the assignment. He was embarrassed in front of his classmates, and his teacher had disapproved of his creative exploration, thus killing his enthusiasm for a long time.

I shall never forget the day a seven-year-old came to class with a troubled look on her face. I didn't pry or even inquire what her problem was, but sent her off to do her special trick at the barre. Later in the class she stopped me right in the middle of something we were doing and said, "Miss Virginia, it hurts." "What hurts?" I inquired. "My tooth. It keeps pushing and pushing and pushing and it hurts all the time." The question flashed in my mind, "Could I help this child understand, through dance, this very puzzling incident?"

We gathered near the piano, our favorite talking place, to learn more about the tooth and why it hurt as it pushed its way through the gum. What an informative discussion we had. We discussed the reason why she was in pain and then we discovered similarities in seeds as they burst through their jackets, chickens as they hatch, and a pupa as it emerges from the cocoon. Before we were through, one little girl said, "My mommy told me that my baby sister pushed her way out." With this idea of energy and growth as the focal point, we curled up as small as we could to discover many ways to push with our shoulders, our feet, our backs, our heads, until finally we broke through a make-believe barrier. Then our bodies began to stretch—opening up as fully as possible. When the class was over, each student, especially the child with the aching tooth, had a deeper understanding of this tremendous principle of growth.

Once while teaching a class of five-year-olds, I took a piece of plastic and enclosed it in my hands. "What's too big to be in my hands?" The children's answers were delightful. "My house," "the piano," "our baby," "your shoes." "Oh, yes," I said, "they are all too big. Now watch. It's something special, so special that I believe you will want to dance about it." As I opened my hands, the plastic piece slowly and beautifully unfolded. The children were enchanted and wanted to see it again. As they watched, they began unconsciously lifting their backs. The starting point in the movement pattern was similar to the previous story, but this time, the energy used was gentle because the motivation was different. The idea is the hinge upon which all art swings; and in dance as an art form, it is the idea that determines the movement patterns chosen. Fast rockets are different from erupting teeth. The *reason*, the *idea*, directs the shape—the form of all worthwhile learning, of all great art!

In my classes we share a capacity to see with what we call our "magic eye." This eye is located near the sternum, and we learn to use it to see the beauty around and above us. It helps us to "think tall." Try lifting up your back and opening the area across your shoulders. It will work for you, too. The children watched and discovered motion in the plastic piece. They knew how to use their magic eye—and they were learning to move with purpose, as they danced with their entire bodies. I had given them a piece of plastic, and each child was deep in thought as he watched the beauty of his plastic unfold.

As they began to dance, expressing what they had seen, several children tucked the plastic close in the curves of their small bodies, and when they opened up, so did their bit of magic material. Then, holding their pieces of plastic by the corner, they began dancing in a joyous, lyrical style, watching it lift, glide, swing, turn, and float as they released it or held it in their fingers. This was a delightful and meaningful experience, for the children were being encouraged to look, to feel, and to explore.

One vivid teaching experience that I recall was triggered quite by accident. My husband often calls me "Pollyanna," for I have a habit of tucking unpleasant things way in the back of my mind and then forgetting them. Because of this habit, I don't remember what made me angry one particular Thursday, only that I was. I remember that the anger seemed to fill every fiber of my body. By 4:15 P.M., near the time for my seven- to eight-year-old class, no one had come to my rescue to teach for me and I had to go to them—anger and all. It was impossible to forget my own feelings, yet to do so is one of my cardinal rules both for myself and for my teachers. The class must come first.

The children were quick to sense something wrong, so I called them over to the piano and began class by asking them, "Have you ever been really angry, so angry that you could explode?" "Oh, yes," they said. Immediately I threw out another question: "If I could see only your feet, could you show me with them how you felt?" Within seconds, fireworks were exploding. Such a variety of "feet things" in anger I'd never seen! They jumped and went down on their backs, kicked the wall, used fast and jerky patterns, and long, slow ones that seemed to build up and explode.

We then talked about other strong feelings that we had had; and for children so young, they had experienced many things that had caused them to feel deeply. One child said that she'd had something happen that very day in school, but she wasn't quite sure what her feeling was, maybe just disappointment. "Could you share it with us?" "Oh, yes," she replied, "it was during arithmetic."

They had been asked to choose a number lower than ten and then to write any two numbers that could add up to their chosen number. Her choice was eight. After doing several combinations, she suddenly thought $3 + 2 + 3 = 8$. Excitedly, she went to the teacher with her new discovery. At the moment, the teacher was not ready to accept more than the given problem and she was sent back to her seat.

Suddenly a light turned on in me and I asked the children to go from the piano to the record player and back, using three different foot patterns.

Among the group, all eight patterns were used—walking, running, leaping, skipping, galloping, sliding, jumping, and hopping. We were now going to use these patterns to solve Jenna's arithmetic problem. "You are in school—doing arithmetic," I told them. "But I am your teacher. This time I will give you the answer, and you must discover how to solve it. The answer is eight. You must use any foot pattern such as skips, slides, and jumps (three things) and finish by the count of eight."

Again, fireworks! But this time, such happy ones. The children worked, they questioned, buzzing about their numbers and combinations. Over in the corner, one child was busy counting on her fingers. She did three jumps and then held down three fingers. Two fingers were left on that hand, so she did two skips. Several seconds later, she figured out (again by counting) that she needed three more things to make eight. By now she'd forgotten what she'd done with the first five fingers, so she began over, repeating the process.

Before the end of the class hour, most of the children had their answers and could do them quite efficiently. I knew that they would be working at home on this newly found way to solve an arithmetic problem and that Jenna was more than pleased, not only because she recognized my approval, but also because we had taken her idea and shared it in such a fun way with the class.

Needless to say, I too felt better and had begun the process of wrapping up my "Pollyanna" package of intense anger. This experience did not end here. In fact, it kept us busy for several weeks and eventually developed into a charming dance play called *Our Day*, in which we presented the events of a typical day—from getting up in the morning as sleepyheads (because of Daylight Saving Time) to solving arithmetic problems at school.

Searching for ideas to help the children has dictated and directed most of my activities over the years, even when I have been vacationing with my family, shopping, reading, or just listening. I am constantly on the alert for new ways to assist the child in exploring the realms of movement within his understanding of his marvelous instrument—his body.

Some time ago, the thought occurred to me that I had never approached movement through the use of simple lines—bent, straight, and curved. At the time, a group of nine- to ten-year-olds was exploring ideas with me and "Miss Anne" in their Art in Relation to Dance program, and we spent four months finding new ways, each week, to approach this one idea. This gave us time to look, to imagine, to search, and to share. Pooling ideas often led to exciting results, emphasizing the group's ability to select movement patterns wisely. Eventually, the more interesting patterns were integrated into compositional studies that were exciting to the students.

Since then, I have often thought how important it is when children possess the tools of knowledge and imagination to cultivate a project in which the overall result is a source of constructive pleasure. It seems to me that if we could devote a portion of time seeking that which is significantly pleasing, sensing what would promote pleasure for others, and realizing where beauty lies, then again we would be sending the roots of genuine happiness deeper into fertile soil. All too frequently young people are technically trained in a chosen art form with no opportunity to explore on their own. I believe that if improvisation on basic principles and ideas was encouraged as the technical training is pursued, we could give new freedom and inspiration to many more people.

In trying to solve the complex social problems of today we tend to ignore a special kind of hunger. If our children could have their creative selves always fed, their destructive selves would gradually starve.

I have gone to many sections of the United States to demonstrate principles that have helped me nurture creativity. At one of these times when the Children's Dance Theatre performed in the East, Walter Terry of the former *New York Herald-Tribune* wrote after seeing the performance:

> From the first there was beauty. But more important than the loveliness of the setting was the vital innocence of the dancers themselves. They looked like children and not miniature adults. They danced themes of their own choosing and of their own creation. It is difficult to describe the most potent intangibles. But the best I can do is to say that the children danced as if they had faith in themselves, had love for those who were seeing them, actively believed in their God, and rejoiced in all these.

The *Christian Science Monitor* added: "This work is the result of an idea, a search for beauty and truth that never ceased unfolding." Children involved in such work are not likely to become "school dropouts" or juvenile delinquents.

As I recall our first visit to the East, an incident at Jacob's Pillow comes vividly to mind. While a mass "bravo" echoed throughout the theatre, one of the starry-eyed children whispered, "Miss Ginny, why are they calling for Provo?" which, as you may know, is a city in Utah.

Within this philosophy of teaching, we try to help the child have enough of a professional attitude about dance so that it can extend into his other endeavors. We guide them to discover their own potential in movement by helping them to go beyond that which is easy; by enhancing their awareness and knowledge of the tremendous power of rhythm, both breath and metric; by letting them discover the joy of clean line in movement; but always encouraging them to move with ease and agility, balance and control. They are encouraged to contribute patterns to the many dances that have been composed and then to compose their own dances. These have been our goals through which the children can find beauty—a beauty that comes from belief in self.

How do you achieve these goals? Where do ideas come from? How do you know what to teach each age level? How long do you work with each child before you give up? What do you do for the student who depends upon and is satisfied only to follow other children, to use other children's ideas rather than his own? Can you teach the child rhythmic movement without a pianist? These are all thought-provoking questions to which I have found answers through a deep respect for the child and trust in my "intuition" based on experience.

One little boy was hesitant to join in the class. In fact, he did not venture away from his mother until the third week. Finally, he became so excited by the crepe paper streamers being used as a teaching prop that he decided to share in the fun and become a real member of the class. This situation raised one question: How long do you work with a child before you give up? Briefly, the answer is that primarily we do not stop until the mother gives up. As long as the parent cooperates and does not become discouraged, a wholesome atmosphere is maintained within which we can work.

Another question arose from the hesitancy of some children to use their own initiative in searching for ideas. What do you do for the pupil who depends upon and uses other children's ideas rather than explore for himself? Teaching a child to use his own ideas is a very important part of all teaching.

In the beginning, some children must copy others to get ideas, but during each class, they are encouraged to think for themselves. Simple movement ideas that can spark teaching will come about by asking lead questions that are within their understanding; in doing so, the child is encouraged to find his own patterns. For example, How far can you stretch? Can you reach as high as the ceiling? Can you reach down to the floor without bending your knees? Could you make a tunnel and have both feet and only one hand touch the floor? These simple ideas motivate a child to do the movement for himself.

Let one group touch something prickly and sharp, such as a starfish or cockleshell. Have another group touch something smooth and round, such as a small ball or a hard-boiled egg in the shell. Ask the children to show you a pattern with their arms that reminds them of what they touched. See if each group can find words to describe what they think the object was like. "Prickly," "bumpy," "hard," "sharp," "rough," "pointed" may be words to describe the shells; while "smooth," "round," "hard," "curved" may be used for the ball or egg. With this vocabulary you can help them find contrasting movement patterns.

In one course on creative movement, a teacher who had applied these ideas to her first-grade class related that, as a result, their trip to the bakery had a great deal more meaning. The children wanted to dance about their experience. They had seen large paddles mixing the dough, the slow rising of the dough, the way the dough was cut, and the loaves of bread moving in rows. This visual experience served her class as impetus for creative movement.

Another teacher found that "moving" need not be set aside as a special project. It can be put to immediate use for many ideas that arise during the day. She related that early one day the children had been making tunnels with their bodies, and later in the afternoon they were learning to recognize the letter *m*. It was then that little boy said, "Teacher, an *m* is like two tunnels hooked together." Her students had no difficulty in remembering *m* from that day on.

Students must be given ample time to think about the things they are being asked to do. Equally important, the teacher must thoroughly understand the movement problem being presented to the children. Again, ask leading questions: Do you really know what you are going to do? How are you going to start? Will you stay in place or move about? These questions stimulate answers and ideas that will help the shy child transfer the general movement idea into patterns of his own.

Many simple objects can be used to inspire movement—a feather as it gently floats and falls to earth, a ball as it bounces and then gradually stops and rolls. Any one idea of motion can serve as the impetus for creative exploration. Take a swing, for example. What is there that has a swinging movement? Of course, most children have experienced being in a swing and realize that the path of movement is one that goes forward and back as well as up and down. But other objects move in a swinging motion. The pendulum of a clock, windshield wipers, clothes on a clothesline, a golf club as it strikes the ball, a girl's skirt as she walks are just a few additional ideas; and each would give rise to different movement patterns. These differing patterns can be investigated by using this principle: First let the arms swing, then the legs, then the torso; now change levels, each time deciding where the base of the swing is. Choose your own amount of time and tempo—sometimes slow, sometimes fast—continuing until you feel the phrase is completed.

The potential for movement stimuli in literature is tremendous. However, there are essential qualities of excellence in children's literature that teachers must learn to recognize. In searching for poems to inspire children in creative movement, I try to watch for several elements:

First, adaptability to movement—

> Want to see 'lectricity spark in kittie's fur?
> Want to see 'lectricity make her motor purr?
> Want to see 'lectricity make her headlights shine?
> Well, meet me in the alley after dark some time.

This beautifully crystallized idea and many other delightful pieces, some of them reprinted below, are all found in Vilate Raile's book *So There*.

Second, making a fanciful statement about something real—

> What if the Spring
> Should fall?
> What if the Fall
> Should spring?

I didn't say it could
did I
But it would be a funny thing.

Third, one of my favorite devices for inspiring children to explore is to trigger their sensory images—sharpen their capacity for sight, sound, touch, taste, and smell—and then to encourage their use of imaginative words—

Ice cream has such
a quiet taste
So cool, so smooth, so mild
That I don't see how
it could help
But make a better child.

Fourth, an emotional outlet that can arouse a feeling of empathy—

Inside I'm purry as a cat
When it's Spring
I wonder why I feel like that
When It's Spring?
Giggles push to be set free,
Songs sing inside of me,
Feet go tripping off in glee.
Mother says she tells by me
When it's Spring.

Most teachers, particularly those in elementary education, do not have access to accompanists, so it is only natural that the question be asked, "Can you teach the young child creative rhythmic movement without a pianist?" Yes, of course it can be done, but the teacher must first know what rhythm is and appreciate some of its mechanics.

Because of the vital part that rhythm plays in our everyday living, from birth to death, I have concentrated on finding ways in which to enhance and increase the child's awareness of rhythm and those elements of dance related to it. An extremely simple yet delightful way to help children become more aware of rhythm is to take the syllables of a word or group of words and clap the rhythmic structure that you hear as the words are spoken. Because there is rhythm in everything, this idea opens up an endless variety of patterns. For example, find the variations in cities and states. Salt Lake City, Utah, sounds different than Seattle, Washington. After the children can clap the pattern, see if they can transfer it into their feet. The sentence "I won't do it" is a valuable one to explore, not only for its rhythm pattern, but also because it allows the child to express a negative thought which becomes a relished challenge. Note value, meter, phrasing, and quality should all be a part of the child's knowledge, understanding, and ability to utilize in many ways.

One might make tapes of various sounds that give rise to movement. The many different ticking noises made by clocks, the wailing of sirens, people talking, the train as it leaves the station, the music of a merry-go-round, the surf at the ocean—these are a few sounds that might provide the stimulus for movement, for conversation, for their own stories.

Exploring the sounds of various percussion instruments can also be exciting to a class. Movement suggested by the gong, bell, or triangle is quite different from movement suggested by the drum, the wood block, or the sand block. If the students listen to these sounds, they will find that each instrumental sound inspires a different pattern.

Another means of teaching creative rhythmic movement without a piano is to investigate interesting children's records. Many very good records are readily adaptable to teaching rhythm, and new ones are being marketed all the time. All the Bowmor records, the Silver Burdett series, *Adventures in Music*, and my own record, *Come Dance with Me*, are stimulating.

Verbalizing about teaching creatively is a very difficult process, for the minute an idea is written down, it acquires a quality of rigidity and can become stilted unless it is viewed imaginatively and used as a springboard to additional ideas rather than as just a "thing" to teach. There are so many questions a teacher should be able to answer by means of imaginative, flexible ideas. How do you take the children's ideas of the day and build a section of the class around them and still accomplish some of the needed goals of the hour? Can you relieve tense situations with your own gentleness and turn these situations into rich experiences? If you do cherish the rich imagination of children, can you guide and develop it?

The answers to these questions are some of the keys to enriching each child's potential and his power of communication both as a dancer and as a human being. In other words, do you have an all-seeing eye—one that sees everything that goes on, all at once, all the time; one that recognizes whether each child is understanding, contributing, and doing anywhere near his capabilities? This all-seeing eye should be so perceptive that by your use of it each child can be encouraged, enriched, and given a feeling of security in knowing "today I discovered something new; today I did my best."

There should be moments of stillness within each class wherein a child can think, recollect, imagine, go back over the problem at hand, or listen. These moments can be extremely valuable, not as a discipline device, but as a challenge to the creative self. Discipline problems, as such, are rare where creative teaching is being done. This does not mean that there is always quiet order; much conversation goes on as children are busy solving problems. The involvement of each child with the problem at hand is what is important. True discipline never comes with threats, embarrassment, or punishment; it comes through the teacher's capacity to conduct the class with enough excitement, enough challenge, enough firmness, enough regard for each child to encourage self-awareness and thence self-discipline.

Of great importance is the teacher's willingness to change her pattern of teaching if the children are too restless. Sometimes a very quiet voice, a special piece of music, a rhythm pattern on the drum, or the sound played on a gong will attract the children who are not giving full attention and arouse their curiosity so they will want to find out what the group is doing. Of great importance is nipping a discipline problem in the bud rather than excusing the child who causes confusion with, "Oh, today he's not ready to partici-pate." I realize there are no ironclad rules on this, and that each situation is different, but the teacher who tries not to notice the confusion is only asking for more of the same.

In conclusion, I'd like to share with you responses from two teachers who were in one of many workshops that I have had the opportunity to give. These reactions express the thirst, the need, the desire on the part of most teachers to become more involved professionally with creativity.

> Creative movement has affected the way I will look at things from now on. It has reaffirmed my belief that teaching cannot be done in neat little packages to be used over and over again as each year passes. I will need to sharpen my intuition, to become more proficient in identifying the needs of my children in order that they gain the maximum. What a joy to discover that I could use my whole body and that dancing as we now understand it can be for the layman and that we can help our little people discover, through movement, so many things that will enrich their capacity for language arts, rhythm, communication, and awareness of their world. How happy I am to know that I can help my children use their creative wings this coming year. In my teaching I am sure that I have not nudged them hard enough for them to go beyond that which is easy. Next year I hope to leave imprints—ever so gentle imprints.

The second one:

> For two years I have worked with children almost totally stripped of creativity, imagination, and the power to make use of any inner self. These deprived children have had their lives crammed full of "nothing." They have learned to hate school with its pressures, frustrations, and its constant reminder of their failures in life. . . .
>
> But suddenly, an unseen door has been thrown wide open, and on the other side lies a wealth of fresh ideas and approaches to help these unfortunate youngsters. I have seen things I never knew existed. The ideas extending from them are inexhaustible. I can envision already great possibilities in their approaches to math, to art, to music, to everything we do. . . .
>
> If in this next school year I can help these children in this direction so that they no longer say "School is junk," I shall think that I have found the pot of gold at the end of the rainbow. . . . I approach September with a new energy and enthusiasm. No longer will there be deadwood subject matter for me; now I look upon it as driftwood, with its freedom, its freshness, and its quiet challenge.

It is vitally important that teachers not only be aware that there is a better—a more creative—approach to routine classwork, but that they also receive encouragement and support in their creative endeavors from administrators.

A last example of the thoughtless damage done and its invisible effects: One afternoon, months after my son's experience of having the cap and umbrella cut from his leaf-child, he came to me and asked, "Mom, what can I do now?" I answered him by asking if he had done anything in school that he really enjoyed and would like to try again. He thought for a moment and then a twinkle came into his eyes as he said, "Oh, yes!" For an hour he was very busy. When he cocks his head a certain way—and his tongue goes to the corner of his mouth—I know he is completely involved in an idea. He had taken a large piece of art paper, colored pencils, and many tiny leaves from the bridal wreath bush. The picture he made was not of one child but a whole army in action, including airplanes with pilots, parachute jumpers, men in battle, some of whom had been wounded. All his people were made of the tiny leaves; each one armed for combat. After it was finished he came to me and said, "Look at my picture, Mom. And she's not here to cut it up."

Dr. E. Paul Torrance, professor of educational psychology at the University of Georgia in Athens, is an outspoken critic of educators who fail to do justice to the creative impulse. He believes that "society is downright savage in its treatment of creative people, particularly when they are young."

The price of stifling creativity is incalculable. In America the brakes are jammed on the creative velocity of children in various ways. Many authorities on the psychology of creativity, including Dr. Torrance, put part of the blame on what they term America's "quick success" orientation. In our hurry toward "success" we are not prepared or willing to cope with the frustrations and delays that are inherent aspects of true creative work.

The unprecedented need in our society today for creative talent calls for some truly revolutionary changes in educational objectives. We need to ask more than ever before what kind of people our children are becoming. If you find some answers disheartening to accept, then may I offer these solutions to the problem in the form of a plea:

Don't turn down the lights in the child's treasure house of imagination.
Please don't cut off the "caps and umbrellas."
Develop your "magic eye" as well as your "all-seeing eye."
Inspire the child to go beyond that which is easy, to explore the difficult and the new.
Listen to his questions with sensitivity and answer them judiciously.
Above all, respect the child you teach.

Drama and Childhood:
A Personal Reaction

Gerald Tyler

Gerald Tyler is well known to drama educators in virtually all parts of the world. Educated at The College, Bishop's Stortford, The College of Saint Mark and Saint John in London, and the University of Leeds, he has devoted his entire professional life to community theatre, children's theatre, teaching, and organizations that further the work in these fields. He was founder of the Leeds Children's Theatre and the Brighouse Children's Theatre, and has initiated and organized numerous drama and folk festivals for both adults and youth in England. He was county drama advisor, West Riding, Yorkshire Education Authority, from 1948 until his retirement in 1974. Mr. Tyler was founder-chairman of ASSITEJ, and founder-representative for the National Council of Theatre for Young People. In addition, he has designed drama courses for teachers, lectured throughout the United Kingdom and America, conducted tours of Europe, and written for a variety of publications. Out of his wide experience he has evolved a point of view toward children and drama that he shares with us in this essay.

The common factor in the approaches of teachers to creative dramatic work and theatre for children and young people must surely be a concern for the all-round healthy development of their children. No two teachers will approach the subject in quite the same way, nor will the methods necessarily be identical. Every child is a unique human being, even though some emotions, thoughts, and physical characteristics may be generally peculiar to all. There are as many good ways of teaching a subject as there are good teachers; I should like to be one of them.

Personally, I believe in the importance of the folk—folk stories, songs, and dances, folklore, and folk drama. Experience confirms belief that within the folk is a storehouse of wisdom accumulated and handed down over the centuries of the growth of civilized humanity. It is the wisdom passed on by one generation to guide the next along the road to as secure and happy an existence as circumstances will allow. Indeed, I should go so far as to say that, in spite of the heavy veneer of modern progress, the farther one departs from the folk and the more one ignores their advice, the deeper and more danger-ous are the waters in which one swims. We are making so many discoveries in education that appear to be at variance with the past that it seems to me that anyone who is busy preaching the benefits of coeducation at every level, or advocating large schools, or demanding the abolition of physical punish-ment in schools, or supporting a cult of youth or the breaking down of taboos would do well to stop and ask the folk what is their wisdom in these matters.

The present world is moving fast. But is it sure of its direction? And is that direction a right one? When the folk seem to demand gods or a God to worship, how far is the government of a country ever likely to succeed in demanding of its people an acceptance of state atheism? In the store of folk knowledge from unrecorded time there lies material that touches every human being in the world. There are things in folk that evoke immediate, universal, and sometimes irrational responses: things that seem to touch human beings not in the head or the heart but near the solar plexus. Why is it that the old mumming plays and folktales never fail to capture the attention of young people and to keep their fascination with the aged if there is not something strong and necessary within them?

In the rush of modern times many mothers have omitted teaching their children the old rhymes and stories around the evening fire. It has been left to teachers to do this job at a later stage. Some new-style intellectuals, with a passion for telling children the truth, have even failed to understand the fundamental truth of the existence of Santa Claus. In the countries of the Eastern bloc the old British children's favorite, *Punch and Judy*, is frowned upon because it is thought too violent for children to see. In Britain *Punch and Judy* comes out like a hardy perennial in spite of the regular beatings Punch gives his wife, the way he bashes the baby, and then finally hangs the hangman. There has been an epidemic of real baby bashing in England recently, but I believe it is more likely the result of a lack of opportunity to see Mr. Punch than the result of his unsocial actions. Charlotte Chorpenning made an excellent play from the story of *Little Red Riding Hood*, but the end of the play differed markedly. The story's ending, more in keeping with folk tradition, has the wolf eat the grandmother and be found later by woodmen while he is sleeping at the riverside. The woodmen cut open the wolf's belly, the grand-mother pops out, and they fill up the hole with a large stone and sew him up again. The end is fantastically violent and unreal; yet the end Chorpenning gave to the play—the capture of the wolf, who wishes to live like a man but is put in a cage—is diabolical by comparison.

Cruel-hearted stepmothers are common in folktales, but however hard this may seem on some excellent stepmothers, the stories cannot do without them. The princesses must have their good and bad fairies, and the heroes must have their dragons to slay and their princesses to rescue. The themes are evergreen and come up like spring daffodils for every newborn child. We must give all children the opportunity to hear the stories, just as we should also give them the chance to live in the open air among real daffodils.

Some children nowadays appear to have outgrown fairy stories at an early age. Does this mean that the stories are wrong, or is childhood suddenly moving too fast? Are pressures put upon children by television and modern life destroying childhood? The modern child is still surrounded by dragons and wicked ogres. It may be that a good dose of fear of the smooth-tongued witches and evil wizards of folklore is a better antidote to the sly work of drug pushers than the books to be seen in some American schools on the classification of hard and soft drugs. Are we losing out on the opportunity for children to learn through fantasy rather than meet all the dangers through the hard, immediate, and specific facts of modern life? This early period of learning and adjustment is vital and should not be made to pass too quickly. Our present attitudes may lead to more jobs for psychologists, bigger and better mental hospitals, and free contraceptives for all at the age of ten—but surely these are not compensations to be desired.

For a long time I have been somewhat dubious about many things that are said and written about child drama, creative dramatics, and theatre in education generally; and this article is my attempt to explain the whole business to myself in my own way. It owes nothing to Jung or Freud, and if Robert Ardrey and Konrad Lorenz seem to support me from time to time, then it is good fortune indeed.

It began nearly half a century ago, when in the middle of a general science lesson my teacher and friend rolled out the phrase "ontongeny recapitulates philogeny." Sonorous, catchy, and mysterious in itself, it opened up a great world of interest. We learned that the human individual grows from a single cell, soon to divide and multiply and then to follow the evolutionary journey of development. On it goes through the cell-dividing stage, the amphibian stage, on through the stage of the higher animals where the human fetus much resembles that of a dog, and on to become distinguishable as a human being, to be guarded and protected until the end of the nine-month gestation period. Then follows the next mystery, for the helpless mite arrives in a strange world with little or nothing to help it survive; yet somehow it must adjust to the world around it and come to terms with a complicated pattern of existence. Within the short space of three or four years, the child will have accumulated as much knowledge and have become as adapted to his environment as he will do in any similar period of his future development. It is truly remarkable how all the host of sensations, impressions, and illogical human regulations of behavior are absorbed , accepted, and made his own.

It is doubtful whether the child could cope with the mass of new experiences were it not for the important contribution made by his private play. Play is his principal learning time, his rehearsal time, his preparation for the future. It is strange that his learning about his place within the environment seems best when passed between reality on the one side and rhythm, verse, ballad, and song on the other.

The role and function of drama in child education is a subject of considerable controversy. Personally I find that many people are so inclined to have and defend their own definitions that it seems best to rely on the *Oxford Dictionary* for clarity and it is by the *Oxford* definitions that I abide. Theatre is there defined as a building where plays are performed, but it can also mean the theatre arts and dramatic literature. Drama is defined as plays, literature, and situations having excitement. Education is defined as the bringing up (of the young), systematic instruction, development of character and mental powers. To educate is to provide intellectual and moral training.

From these definitions it seems to me that the purpose (i.e., role and function) of education through drama and theatre may be stated as follows:

1. To bring children into contact with dramatic literature, play making, play writing, and the presentation of plays
2. To introduce them to the pleasure of theatregoing and plays of the past and present both at home and abroad
3. To inculcate a critical approach to the theatre and to other dramatic products of the mass media
4. To encourage them to devise their own plays and to explore the possibilities offered by a variety of dramatic situations
5. To encourage study of all the related arts, particularly those involved in theatre
6. To respect moral ends in all work undertaken since, as by definition, education is directed to the moral aspect

This last point is emphasized because there is an observable tendency on the part of some young teachers to regard the taking of moral attitudes as wrong in educational theatre, with the result that children are sometimes subjected to ideas beyond their experience or critical powers and to language that society would not wish to encourage. An amoral attitude is in danger of becoming an immoral one. It would seem that our educational obligation toward the child and its parents is to eschew attitudes of personal indulgence and to remain, for the child's safety, in a conservative position.

Directly one begins to make such statements as "drama develops imagination," "drama is self-expression," or "drama has curative effects," one comes up against the fact that the same claims are made for every other art with equal justification. Drama is seen to be only one means of expressing personality or feelings or ideas and of developing imagination and creativity. This level is where drama is at one with all the arts as a force in education and, indeed, as one of its most important contributors. It is to be seen not in isolation but related to music, poetry, dance, sculpture, and to any other medium through which people can express their thoughts on the world around them. Little will be communicated, however, unless the techniques of the chosen medium are acquired, nor will there be truth in what is communicated if truth is lacking in what is expressed.

Because the nuances of speech provide a multitude of shades of meaning by which a person can express himself with exactness in great detail, drama has become a means whereby thoughts and feelings can be communicated with a greater immediacy than through any of the other arts, particularly so since the instruments used are the human body, the voice, and the personality. It is at this level that one can talk of expressing personality, exploring personality, or of exploring and portraying human behavior. By studying the effects of one's teaching, one may come to draw some tentative and general conclusions regarding development of confidence or personal adjustment or release of tension.

Now I am postulating a deeper level, one below the one just considered. On this deeper level one can look at life and at humanity and try to see what one can of the human spirit at different times: as it is today, as it was far back in recorded history, and indeed as it was as far back as we can probe into the history of the race. At this point I wish to go back to the human child last seen arriving in this strange world, each one unique but each one showing some general characteristics. What impressions are collected and what powers are being developed during the period before birth we do not know. How the computer of the brain begins to take in impressions, relate them, produce and reject answers during early childhood is a mystery. One thing we can do is to watch children, try to see what interests them, how they react toward and learn from other children, and observe the patterns of childhood as they emerge.

Here I have set down from general observation of my own children and others around me, a number of actions that children make and things that they do, which seem to come naturally to them and give them satisfaction. They have been arranged in a rough chronological order—rough because they vary to some extent from child to child according to his readiness and to the environmental opportunities offered to him to develop. Rightly or wrongly, I have, as a matter of convenience, omitted the early stages of foot-and-hand exploration and gone straight to the time when the child is on his feet and able to move around on his own.

Some Observed Tendencies and Characteristics of Childhood

1. (up to 4 years) Need for security, the presence of mother, home and family; to be talked to and played with. The environment gradually extends and the child needs to be taken out. He needs to make noises, run about, climb, swing, to experience rhythmic motion and sound. He attaches importance to things of his own—cup, toy, etc. He develops socially—sometimes has a secret, invisible friend.

2. (4 to 5) Need for apparatus and pieces of costume for being postmen, soldiers, etc. He mimics parents and tradespeople. He plays at being cars, engines, planes, often being the car, its parts, its noises, and its driver all at the same time. He collects things. He engages in free movement and dance; he is interested in witches, fairies, and magic.

3. (5 to 6) Tendency to want to be leader, captain, king. He rushes around violently and noisily, often aimlessly. He plays games, likes mechanical toys.

4. (6 to 7) Has fears, compulsions (must tread in the squares). He plays cops and robbers, cowboys and Indians, and capturing games begin. Girls make up dances. Both boys and girls say or make up funny rhymes, take part in processions.

5. (7 to 8) Defeats the evil chance. Makes things begin and likes organized games. He creates camps and dens. Private reading can be enjoyed.

6. (8 to 9) Shows an interest in masks and likes to play drama games, bows and arrows, join in a group. He has secret ideas.

7. (9 to 10) He plays out stories in a solitary way but also plays with others, "You be X and I'll be Y." He has codes and passwords and explores farther afield. Reading is well advanced by now.

8. (10 to 11) He likes practical things, enjoys arts and crafts, has standards. Drama now quite advanced.

This whole section is set down with humility and diffidence because children vary so much. The lonely child and the imaginative child will adopt a secret friend at a very early age. The dominant child will dash around the playground and also become a leader at an early age, while a more reserved child may never develop these tendencies. It is so hard to generalize on many points of behavior. These observations and the classification may not find favor everywhere, but it must be a fact that there is a pattern and a succession of such characteristics while the how and the why and their function remain a matter of theory and research.

In *Play, Drama and Thought*, Richard Courtney's masterly examination of the intellectual background of drama, drawing as he does upon the scholarly work of educationalists, psychologists, and philosophers, the concept of the recapitulation theory is dismissed as a speculation rather than a theory. This may be so, and my article certainly has more depth of feeling than of scientific study. This is neither the time, place, nor necessity to set up an argument between Patrick White, Joseph Lee, Carl Groos, and Stanley Hall, but I must point out that considerable changes of thought and fashion have taken place in psychology and in anthropology, in particular since 1930. Perhaps on reexamination this particular speculation may now find more respect. Can it be that if the history of the individual does recapitulate the history of the race, in the mind as it does in the body, then perhaps the order of arrival of the characteristic actions and personal play of children may say something about the history of the development of the racial mind? Personal characteristics and the order of their arrival may suggest, or help us determine, good lines for dramatic work with children. It may also tell us where to tread carefully and when not to interfere.

Richard Courtney refers to the successive culture patterns in man's history echoed in children's play, which have been set by various American writers. They are given as the animal stage, the savage stage, the nomad stage, the agricultural/patriarchal/early settlement stage, and the tribal stage. Upon these pegs the various aspects of children's play are hung to make a reasonable and understandable pattern of development. All I can say in reply is that what someone learns for himself plows a furrow in the mind and that all learning must be tested as well as absorbed. Obviously I am in general agreement with these findings, which would seem to support the recapitulation theory.

It is significant that if one turns to that famous work of the last century, Sir John Frazer's account of the beliefs and practices of primitive peoples entitled *The Golden Bough*, there is a startling relationship to be seen between many of the characteristics of childhood and what is related of the practices of primitive peoples, and indeed, for that matter, to some beliefs and suspicions of the more developed. Again, this is an observation that has been made by other people, but it may be pertinent to ask how many teachers of drama have even the abridged edition of *The Golden Bough* on their shelves or use it as a source book for drama work with young people.

There are accounts in Frazer of the practice of magic; of masks and face

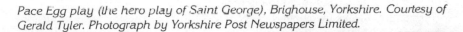

Pace Egg play (the hero play of Saint George), Brighouse, Yorkshire. Courtesy of Gerald Tyler. Photograph by Yorkshire Post Newspapers Limited.

painting; of the worship of fire, sun, moon, trees, rocks, ancestors, and animals. He deals with ceremonies attending birth, initiation into the tribe, marriage, and death. There are accounts of the festivals surrounding the seasons, hunting, and war. There are weather invocations, sacrifice, the scapegoat, virgin birth, and a host of other beliefs and customs. He covers a wealth of material that is highly dramatic, so much of it related to childhood and often finding a deep understanding in people everywhere.

Much of what is said of this link between the manifestations of childhood and the primitive practices would seem to give an authority for the use of some of it in our own dramatic teaching. Many primitive customs and ceremonies involve processions, which children enjoy, especially little girls, whose preoccupation with the wedding ceremony begins at an early age. The mammoth Prague exhibition of child art with paintings from almost every country in the world showed that the most frequent and universal subject was the wedding ceremony. The May Day processions and gala processions with their dressing up and their garlands and ceremonials never cease to attract the young. They are important, too, in the teaching of drama, for within the simple ceremony lies, apart from all the color and excitement, the never to be mentioned elements of technique and control. To keep one's place in a procession, to carry one's pose safely and one's person with dignity, is a great step on the road to self-confidence and acting. To let one's dolls talk to one another and to hold conversations with them holds the beginnings of characterization. "Come and watch me, Mum," is a command that carries the early signs of wanting an audience. And when the child says to a friend, "I'll be May and you be Joanna," then drama is really moving.

Masks are always fascinating and carry a touch of mystery and repulsion. They can be frightening and give the power to frighten, an aspect that boys in particular respond to. Makeup appeals more to girls, but daubing the face is something that becomes a Brave. Here lies a subject with wide scope in both drama and general education. From painting a horrible face to devising a tribal face lies a wealth of learning. Caste masks and the married status, the painted faces of the Orient, masks of Gods and demons, animal masks, and the formalized masks of the Egyptian gods carry one's learning across the world and up and down the centuries. It is of such universal interest and human importance that it would be possible to build a whole program of dramatic activity based on disguise and the human problem of the mask and the face.

Among the many intensely satisfying lessons I have known was one developed from a simple piece of information that a friend had seen in a kangaroo dance done by Australian aborigines. In it one man pretended to be the kangaroo and in the dance was killed and borne back to the village in triumph. A class of slow learners (eleven-year-olds) made up a circle dance from which the kangaroo detached itself, moving in and out of the ring. Then one of the spear-carrying dancers began to follow him in and out and around the circle. The circle became a line and still the stalking went on, until the kangaroo moved forward in front of the hunters who, in formalized rhythmic movement, came down and speared him in one strong symbolic action. All the dancers then mimed picking up a kangaroo and carrying it dancing back to their village for a general celebration. The absorption and concentration throughout the performance proved its satisfying nature both for the participants and for those who watched.

Man has always been preoccupied with his fragile security here on earth. He early developed a respect for the sun, which gave him warmth and ripened his harvests. If the sun failed to rise in the morning, there would be perpetual night and everything would die. The sun's blasting heat at noon also demonstrated his power for no one could look at his brightness. In the Bible we read of the people who were wailing for Tamuz, the Sun god, as he was leaving them in autumn. We can be sure that this would be followed by a spring rejoicing on his return. The celebration was often a dance and later a play enactment where the god was killed and rose to life again. This death-and-resurrection cycle is the foundation for the folk plays from ancient Greece to Hungary, from the Basque country to Britain, where the mumming plays become known as Guisers in Cornwall, Soul Cakers in Cheshire, Galations in Scotland, White Headed Boys in Ireland, and Pace Eggers in Yorkshire.

As I write this on Easter Saturday morning our Brighouse Pace Eggers have just set off on a visit to neighboring towns and villages. They went off in their white smocks decorated with rosettes, the Black Prince of Paradine being distinguished by wearing a black one. All the Pace Eggers except the doctor, dressed in a formal black suit and top hat, wore mortorboardlike hats with hoops of garlands high above them and paper streamers beneath; the streamers are the vestigial remains of the masks that at some early time covered the face. In some places today the Fool will sweep out a ring among the crowds and Saint George will slay Bold Slasher a dozen times in mortal combat, only to be revived in a comedy passage by the doctor. The words are doggerel and often without sense, and the entire play is but fifteen minutes of knockabout in the crowded streets on a cold day. The collection of money or pace eggs is the reward, but even that small compensation will go to the theatre workshop to help pay the rates! The play is like the sun; it only sinks to rise again next spring.

Nor are the myths and legends to be regarded merely as possible sources of child interest, for both these areas of recorded stories run close to the folk. Many appear to have a strong element of history. King Arthur and his knights, the wilder and more imaginative Welsh stories, and the legends that surround Robin Hood are all part of a background where fantasy, history, and folklore meet.

From where I sit at this moment I am looking across the valley to the hillside on the Kirklees estate, where Robin Hood lies buried. His history is shrouded in legend, but his name and exploits live on. He has all the necessary attributes for both play and study, and like other legendary figures, he has lived on because within him are the universal characteristics of a folk hero. He was a warrior in the grand manner, one whose prowess in battle and whose quickness of wit made him admired. He took from the rich and gave to the poor; he was a man in distress of the law, who nevertheless stood for fundamental human justice. And all this is based on historical fact. As one of those men who followed his lord, the Earl of Lancaster, to defeat in a battle at Boroughbridge, Yorkshire, in the early fourteenth century, he was as a contrariant against King Edward II and was obliged to take to the woods to escape capture and death. He was an outlaw. His name has been a household word and Robin Hood plays have been a feature of the English May Day festivities for centuries. Many writers have embroidered on the historical facts, but it does not require much from any child's imagination to look through the trees into the valley and see Robin Hood and his band cautiously picking their way to Wakefield, where a secret welcome would be awaiting.

On quite a different approach to Robin Hood, consider the dilemma of the people of Wakefield caught up in a quarrel between their liege lord and the king! For whom should they fight? Should they join the armed men on their doorstep to whom they owe immediate loyalty of the king, a man they do not know but to whom they owe loyalty through their lord? The battle having been lost, retribution will follow; what action can the men take and what is likely to happen to those left behind? How can the men who take to the woods and become outlaws meet their wives and families? Who will be their enemies and who will be spies?

Here are a dozen problems to be discussed and solved, incidents to be played out in improvisation, stories to be made up and plays to be created. The problems are real and personal, the problems of any civil war. The great advantage, as I see it, is that the problems in this situation are similar to those in the Middle East and Northern Ireland, but they can be played out without the pressure of the politics of today. The problems of the present day are never good material for school drama because these questions are too near and too complex. No teacher is in the situation to express any more than an opinion about them nor the child to understand them. What can any child know about the rights and wrongs of the situation in the Middle East, and what can he know about the causes of the troubles in Northern Ireland? The use of modern controversial happenings and other such internal and external political struggles is an open invitation to children to be pushed politically at an early age, when the purpose of the teacher should be to develop in them a critical intelligence so that they can meet with reason the hysteria, rumor, shallow argument, newspaper reports, and manipulation by persons with ulterior motives in the years ahead.

Another confirming experience regarding the use of folk drama and primitive culture entered some forty years ago when I was reporting the Maddermarket Theatre Festival at Norwich and interviewed the director, Nugent Monk, in his fine-galleried Elizabethan music room. He said, "The Maddermarket Company began here in this room with a performance of the Norwich mystery plays." I expressed surprise that he should start with a mystery play with a company of amateurs and he said, "On the contrary, the mystery plays are right because they are easily understood; the stories are known, the dialogue is simple and straight lined, the emotions come naturally to the actors and the technique of acting has become more sophisticated as the years have gone by."

This lesson had a great effect on me, and I went away and devised a syllabus for drama with secondary school boys from eleven to fourteen years. It started with tribal dances, weather invocations, ceremonial processions, mumming and other folk plays and led on through the tropes, mystery plays, moralities, and interludes to scenes from *Ralph Roister Doister* to exciting, well-known extracts from Shakespeare. I was teaching in a tough school for boys in the hungry 1930s, and the program worked.

It also told me that material from the classics, chosen with care and presented with imagination, had great appeal. Good language and universal truths are not wasted on young people. The last thing that one should do is to play down to them; just find ways of capturing their interest and do not bore them. Nobody should have Shakespeare all the time, but that is not to say that Shakespeare should be ignored at any age. Improvisations about two warring families who create such a nuisance that they are warned to keep the peace and after another brawl breaks out are stopped by the law and brought up for punishment can be played out without reference to *Romeo and Juliet*. The story can as easily be read in the newspaper.

The careful selection of material for dramatic work, whether it be original or taken from the ready-made, is most important. Drama is a form of art and the art process can be said, at its simplest, to consist of the selection of ideas, words, things, or actions put together to make a statement. On this definition much that is created daily in a drama lesson might be considered to be art, except that work must not stop at the basic process. The artistic value of the product will depend upon the quality of the selection and the quality of the statement to be made. The care in the selection and the choice of subject need our careful guidance.

Creation is never easy; to most people it comes very hard indeed, and there are no easy ways for the drama teacher to do his job. He can follow somebody's book or walk in the wake of some drama prophet. He may, by so doing, obtain some reasonable results, but in the end he must be an artist himself and work out his own salvation. To do this he must have the knowledge, the feeling, and the experience to test the materials and have the skills to produce the artistic result. All art would seem to rest on a bedrock of technique and this is true for both teacher and pupil. Both must build up their resources, their critical intelligence, and their techniques and hope for the final miracle. In teaching there is always a balance to be found in encouraging the child's creative work and in building up his resources for better work, for allowing free expression and for subjecting results to critical examination. There have to be disciplines somewhere and finally they must come from within.

Violence is one disturbing feature of drama in schools and theatres today. It reflects what is happening in the world outside. Young people have a compulsion toward scuffling and fighting; it is within them and cannot be ignored. It is no new problem. The folk would say that violence is within man and will recur time and again. The message of the Bacchae says the same thing and concludes that man must therefore learn to live with violence and control it. Discipline and control are the key words in drama teaching with youth. Children need a circle of security within which to live, explore, and experiment. As they grow older, the circles of environment and of security must extend also, but freedom of expression must always be kept within those bounds of security by which the young person does little harm to himself or to others.

The bounds of society are its taboos encased within the laws. It is one of the glories of life that youth is romantic and idealistic and it could be said that there is something wrong with the young person of eighteen or nineteen who does not know all the answers and wish to set the world to rights. Society must listen with sympathy and answer with reason, but it would be a society of idiots that let youth rule the world. Rebellion in a controlled situation is acceptable, but he who seeks to turn society into a jungle must expect a jungle answer.

Another concern in the field of drama with young people is the undercurrent in the theatre of a preoccupation with experimenting and wandering into the areas of the mind where the influence of the supernatural abounds. It may be an exploration of self or group cognition, but it does imply a journey into the uncharted twilight area of the mind. Few would deny the value of the work of Artaud, Grotowski, or Peter Brook; but they are danger signals rather than signposts in one's dealing with young people. A six weeks' course in psychodrama with young drama teachers would also seem to be a dangerous procedure, unless it is a course on what to avoid. Straightforward drama teaching of the free-form kind has problems enough, without seeking others; and while the work is based on the best of art, helpful curative effects will come as a by-product. There is a vast difference between letting art do its own work and structuring work to meet imagined needs of disturbed pupils. That is the job of the psychologist whose training is long and deep and who, even then, knows that he knows little.

Tassos Lignadis, of the Moraitis School in Athens, in writing about school drama, refers to mimicry as an attempt to escape from the limitations placed upon one by objective time scales. "To play," he says, "is to take oneself out of time and to finish the game is to submit once more to the limitation placed on one by society." In fact, he believes that growing up can be defined as learning to limit or even stifle one's imagination. The above consideration should be borne in mind in any attempt to describe the theatrical possibilities of an age group whose very existence is an absurd, raw, erotic, immediate, and dangerous drama.

If there is an underlayer to the level of unconscious knowledge seen in children's play and exemplified by what can be seen in the behavior of primitive peoples, then I speculate that it is a matrix or flux of early memories and instincts that cannot as yet be separated or defined. Yet there does seem to be an even deeper level or thread that runs vertically through them all. The question is, Where do inspiration, revelation, and ultimate truth lie? One can see man's struggling, emerging thoughts and reactions in Frazer's *Golden Bough*, but one can find more inspired thought in the Bible or in the Egyptian stories of Isis and Osiris.

Human beings are thinking animals, not governed by instinct alone, and are therefore capable of the best and the worst. A friend once remarked that every vile thing that the human mind can conceive has probably been perpetrated at some time or another. It does seem, however, that within us lies a universal tendency toward law and order, and in the struggle between order and chaos, good and evil, it is order and goodness that prevail. It is in the passion play of Osiris, in the festivals of Marduk, and in the passion of Christ that these truths are revealed. Through our drama work we have the power to make them known. Above all else we must observe the child and keep him in mind, for it is surely in inspiration or revelation that Wordsworth wrote in *Intimations of Immortality from Recollections of Early Childhood:*

> Not in entire forgetfulness,
> And not in utter nakedness,
> But trailing clouds of glory do we come,
> From God, who is our home.

Reflections on a Spring Day

Agnes Haaga

Agnes Haaga is professor emeritus of drama at the University of Washington where for thirty years she was chairman of children's drama (1947–77). She is a fellow of the American Theatre Association and a past president of the Children's Theatre Association. She headed the American delegation to the first International Congress on Theatre for Children and Youth in London, 1964, and was a member of the ad hoc committee to draw up the resolutions for the creation of ASSITEJ. A Northwestern graduate, Professor Haaga has received numerous honors and awards as a leader in the field of children's drama, the latest being CTAA's Special Recognition Citation for her services as fundraising and finance chairman for the Association's Winifred Ward Scholarship program.

It is the first Saturday in May, the opening day of the boating season in Seattle. And *what* a day! On such a day as this with spring "moving in the air above and in the earth below and around him, penetrating even his dark and lowly little house with its spirit of divine discontent and longing," Mole cried out " 'Bother!' and 'O blow!' and also 'Hang spring-cleaning!' and bolted out of the house."[1]

I say "Hang writing" and with Sean and Deirdre, my two dachshunds, bolt down the hill to Lake Washington. The whole world seems to have declared a holiday. The lake is filled with sailboats. Those who aren't sailing are messing around the boats in the public boat basin or bicycling or walking or playing or just *being*, rejoicing in the day.

We stroll along our usual path near the edge of the lake. We stop. There's something *new* in the familiar landscape—a rope is hanging from the limb of a willow tree at the water's edge—a thick rope with a big knot at its end. As I pause to consider enjoying a swing, a fair-haired boy of eleven discovers the rope. In one long sustained flowing movement he throws himself down the bank onto the rope and out over the water. After a few swings back and forth he explores other aerial patterns. A wide circular swing takes him around the tree and back again. Then he swings out with a *S*-shaped movement. At the height of his flight he twists his body to the right and swings back to the bank, creating a figure 8 in the air. With a whoop of delight he re-creates the figure 8, chanting, "Around the moon and back again."

"Around the moon and back again"—shades of Aristotle—"the imitation of an action in action"—the movement of the *S*, spontaneously turned into an 8, an impressive physical movement—something stirs within; there's a quick shift and the movement becomes an action—a space flight. The space above the water is quickly transformed. It becomes space, outer space. The "actor" involved in an action gives himself a name . . . several names, Space Ship, and finally Space Man. His movement was that of an object, Space Ship; but in chanting "Around the moon and back again" his dialogue names him Space Man. Simple though it be, "Around the moon and back again" is dialogue—the action spoken. And as for the theme of all this, the signficance of the complete action; well, I could meditate the rest of this lovely day on possible levels of meaning.

How naturally *movement* evolved into *dramatic* movement and then into dramatic *action*. How simply the moving child becomes something or somebody moving; something or somebody *doing* some thing. *Imagining* is at the heart of it—imagining oneself a character in action—imagining characters in action . . . in an action, a deed done—*drama*. The sixth-grade classes at Renton Park Elementary School near Seattle call their drama hour "mind's eye." "Because," say the youngsters, "you see something in your mind's eye, and you *do* it."

And often in your mind's eye you have transformed what you have seen—given it a new name depending upon your use of it. Children, like poets, seem to be engaged much of the time in "giving to any object, or thought, or event, or feeling, the name that makes its nature shine forth."[2] Pier Morgan, a university student, captured in a series of line drawings the action of a pre-school boy as he—

starts out alone
discovers a *rope* lying on the sidewalk
encircles the rope like a *bridle* around a telephone pole and gallops in place
rides free of the pole twirling the rope in the air like a *lasso*
centers the rope at the seat of his pants like a *tail*, still galloping
the gallop slows to a walk; the *tail* becomes a rope once more and is trailed
   behind the boy as he strolls down the street "doing nothin'"—so he says

Too bad someone in the Federal Energy Administration did not wonder and ask, "What can you *do* with a gas-ration coupon bearing the image of George Washington as do dollar bills?" It wouldn't take an imaginative youngster long to come up with an answer. "Put it in any standard bill-changing machine in any laundromat and collect a dollar's worth of change in return." No one did ask, so 4.8 billion gas-ration coupons (printing cost: $12.5 million) will probably have to be destroyed.

My musing is interrupted. A young man on a bicycle has stopped; a baby is strapped in the seat behind him. The baby points his finger in the direction of the two dachshunds and says, "Pup-pees." "Pup-pees," repeats the father with the same rising inflection of the voice. "These 'pup-pees,'" I inform them, "are six years old." The man apologizes, saying, " 'Pup-pees' is the only name we have for all four-legged creatures of the canine variety."

I think of all the names *I* have for these two creatures—My Joy and My Burden; Consciousness Achieving the Form of Sean and of course, Consciousness Achieving the Form of Deirdre. The latter names are newly acquired ones motivated by a recent visit to the Seattle Art Museum and gazing upon Morris Graves' soft, haunting, lovely painting *Consciousness Achieving the Form of a Crane*. Birds are a recurring subject in Graves' paintings and yet, "the objects he draws are not birds, but the bird after it nests in the mind, and his minnow is the stuff of the soul . . . he thinks with images: If the skull is a shell, the bird is the thought."[3]

A wind rises from the south end of the lake setting everything in motion. Headsails billow out in front of those boats running with the wind. Boats caught running oblique to the sudden, strong current of air bend sideways, their sails horizontal to the water. The riggings of the boats tied to the docks become wind chimes. Pennants snap. The rope hanging from the willow branch swings in unison with the branches. Frisbees, picnic napkins, human tresses, lake water, Sean's and Deirdre's ears, all respond to and are caught up in the rhythm of the wind. Then just as suddenly the wind subsides; headsails droop, horizontal masts become vertical, the music of the "wind chimes" fade; all things move gently, and Sean and Deirdre turn their ears right side out with hearty shakes of their heads.

My sister, Rita, at the age of five came in one day with two new names for a wind not unlike this one:

> The wind is God's hug,
> The breeze is His kiss.[4]

Then she ran across the room, caught her baby sister up in her arms, and gave her a big hug and a little kiss.

Naming motivates action; action motivates naming. How many names little children can find for an upward, rhythmic movement of the body. How they love to curl up tightly and unfold slowly, reaching and growing skyward. "*Who* are you growing up and up and up?" How they delight in an interruption in the rhythm at just the right moment. "*What* might stop you from growing?" Ah, here it comes—the Universal Adversary—Trouble—a Problem—the Villain—the Antagonist—or as one child called the disrupting agent—the big *No No*. How many times he must have reached upward for something, almost grasped it and then heard, "*No No!*" There was once a little boy who when asked his name always replied, "No-No-Johnny." He really thought that was his name, for he had never heard Johnny minus the No-No.

Children are quick to respond to key dramatic questions. I barely asked the question, "What stops you from growing?" when one little girl had thrown herself bodily across another child who was growing upward as a rose. She pressed the "rose" down to the "ground," then seeing my expression of puzzlement and concern informed me, "I'm the sidewalk she's growing up under." Well, that could stop a rose—but not quite. This "rose" began to grow sideways; squeezed out from under the "sidewalk" and continued her growth skyward. "Roses," said she, "just grow and grow and grow."

"They have Helpers," suggested a playmate.

"Who would help roses to grow?" I asked.

"The rain." "The sun." "People!"

What action does this begin to imitate? Ah—Joseph Campbell's single hero emerging from behind a thousand faces, archetype of all mythology, receiving a call to go beyond where he is—a call to adventure. He has his No No's, including his own refusal to answer the call—in which case there is apt to be a transformation to a lesser form of life. He has his Helpers, within and without. Saying yes to the call initiates a transformation to a new identity, a fuller life.[5]

A raucous barking breaks into my thoughts. Sean and Deirdre are chasing a pair of ducks. They always manage never to catch the ducks but delight in the chase. Some children are playing in the shallow water at the swimming beach. They are improvising rules for a game of water tag—"You can't leave the water"—"You're safe if you touch the posts." Then come shouts of "Not It!" "Not It!" "Not It!" "You're It!" There are screams as It chases the Not Its. A Not It is caught and becomes It. How intense is It's desire to get Not It. How equally strong is Not It's determination not to be caught. Such conflict in a simple game of tag.

This same intensity is present when we have played a game of tag in drama—working in pairs, each pair imposing a handicap on itself, e.g., hopping on one leg or walking stiff-legged to slow down the pace but not the intensity of feeling. All understand what they want—to get Not It or to escape It. Great fun! After this action comes *naming*; first *general* names for It and Not It—Chaser and Chased, Hunter and Hunted, Antagonist and Protagonist, Bad Guys and Good Guys, Villain and Victim. But drama is the art of the particular so we move on to more *specific* names, more concrete images as we imagine ourselves characters in an action—Cop and Robber, Cat and

Mouse, the Wind and the Sea, Snoopy and Red Baron, the Early Bird and the Worm, Broom and Dust, Wolf and Red Riding Hood, the Fates and Oedipus, Fear and a Child, Machine and Man. Hunter vs. Hunted—is there any earlier plot known to man?

Up on the grassy hillside above the beach four boys are engaged in what appears to be a game of hide and seek. But not quite; it has been modified and renamed Army. The players carry toy rifles, highly representative of the real thing. Three are in hiding; a fourth, the Seeker, goes forth, rifle poised for action, to search out the foe. I am far enough away to see all the characters in action. The Seeker is edging his way around the refreshment stand. A second boy is on the opposite side of the building, his back pressed to the wall, as he inches his way along to venture a look around the corner of the stand. A gentle movement in the bushes beyond indicates that one gunman is under-cover there. A fourth boy is lying on the ground. When the Seeker spies him and fills him with gunshot, he raises up and protests "I'm dead! I'm already dead!"

"O.K. O.K. O.K. You're dead."

"And so are *you*," shouts the undercover man emerging from the bushes with a "Pow Pow Pow." The Seeker drops. Now the back-to-the-wall boy dashes around the corner and after a burst of gunfire stands triumphant. But there is a surprise ending. Unseen by me and apparently forgotten by the four boys, a fifth boy has been lying prone on the roof of the low building. He lifts himself and his rifle and with a giant "POW!" brings the action to a climax and an end. The dead rise to life; there is a new initiating Seeker, and the action starts again.

As the play continues, I ponder this more complex Hunter vs. Hunted plot worked out by the players in the course of the action. The name of the game is Army. You reach for more specific names for Hunter and Hunted and you come up with but one name—soldiers—who at one and the same time are the hunter and the hunted, the killer and the killed. My immediate response to this violent action is how wonderful that there is this harmless, imaginary way to release aggressive human energy—no broken heads, no blood, nobody hurt. And the significance of this action? Ah, here I hit a snag. How simple if the name of the game were War; then the commentary is: "War = killing and being killed." But the boys have complicated the situation; the name of the game is Army and the significance of this violent action is: "Army = war = killing and being killed." True? In part, yes; but in whole? What about the situation where "Army = United Nations forces = peace keepers" or "Army = strength = national security?"

Whether this dramatic action of Army had taken place outdoors as it did or indoors (or out) in company with an artist/teacher, one would have to admire the tight mini-plot that evolved in the course of the action. There was indeed a straight dramatic line of action leading up to a surprise climax and ending; all those involved played with conviction, interacting with each other in a highly concentrated way. This was indeed an intensification of experience with an immediate replay.

Here is where the adult leader would make a difference in procedure. With an adult involved as a partner in the proceedings, there would be no immediate replay but a time of relaxation after the playing—a time for some feedback, evaluation, clarification. The focus of this clarification depends so much on the who and what and where and why of the individual group. With little children the clarification of the experience in which they have been involved might simply be individual children sharing the name they had given their upward rising movement. Sometimes involvement can be so great that it welcomes further expression in another art form and you have paint and brushes on hand so the children can now give color to what they just endowed with character and action. Living the same experience twice but in two different art forms may be a most satisfying kind of clarification.

Older and more experienced players may want to look at the experience in dramatic terms, becoming aware of the dramatic elements involved in the mini-plot. Here would be the place, it seems to me, to explore the significance of the action calmly, and with goodwill and humor recognize half-truths as in the case of the Army game.

Sometimes it is broad generalizations that pop up in the playing that need exploring with much interest and curiosity by children and adult. Once in exploring the characters in Walt Whitman's poem "I Hear America Singing," one boy puzzled and distracted the others by staggering irrationally about, bumping into people, furniture, and walls. Afterward in taking a look at our efforts, we voiced our puzzlement and asked him who he was. He looked surprised as though it should be very obvious to all who he was. "I was a sailor."

"How were we to know you were a sailor?" I asked.

"Well," said he, "I was drunk."

"Oh?"

"Well, sailors drink."

"And when they drink," said I, "they drink to great excess and they stagger all over town bumping into people and—?"

The boy woke up quickly. "O.K.," he said, "I was a sailor, one, individual, and particular sailor who was drunk—O.K.?"

The whole group said, "O.K."

The observation of the boys using the old game of hide and seek as the springboard for their Army game and watching them work out a plot in the course of the game reminds me of a plot that was generated by a square block. In the circular player area of the famous Penthouse Theatre on the University of Washington campus are some sturdy wooden blocks about eighteen inches square. There are also a few blocks shaped as though three of these squares had been welded together in an L shape. The blocks can be assembled into tables, chairs—whatever the players need. One of the boys in the sixth, seventh, and eighth grade drama group arrived early one afternoon, piled the blocks up like a pyramid, and sat himself down on the top block. To the first girl to arrive he announced, "I'm King of the Mountain."

She must have had a bad day at school for she put him down with a cold reply, "You're King of the *Squares*." He was taken aback, not by the words (he was bright enough to appreciate the play on the word) but by the tone of her voice. But he bounced back with, "If *I'm* King of the Squares, *you're* the biggest square in my kingdom."

This kind of "naming" can begin to hurt. As we are not out to hurt or to be hurt in drama, I moved in, not as leader or teacher but in a character appropriate to the dramatic situation. "*I'm* the greatest square," I boasted. "I can do the most square things in the squarest way." I began to walk square, adding robotlike music to accompany my movements. The girl laughed and joined me in a square dance—as did others arriving and tossing coats and books aside to get right into the exploration of squareness. At the suggestion of one player we embarked upon a square day—brushing our teeth, eating, etc., all in sharp horizontal and vertical movements.

Midway into the day's square chores I injected a key dramatic statement to open up possibilities for conflict, legitimate dramatic conflict. "Enter Trouble!" Before I had time to ask who or what the Trouble might be at least three players replied, "A *round* person." One of the three promptly stepped into character. "I'm King of the Rounds."

"What do you want here?" I asked.

"To be King of the Squares!" was the reply.

All looked to their Square King. "I'm going to *stay* King of the Squares!"

"On guard," cried the Round King.

A battle of swords ensued—in slow motion so no one would be hurt. All the Squares picked up the slow-motion style responding with cheers, groans, and moans as first one king and then the other seemed to be winning.

Then came a moment of stunned inaction and silence. The King of the Squares was "run through." The slow-motion camera stopped and then rolled again as slowly, oh so slowly, the Square King fell from his mountain, crag by crag—a drop and a pause, another drop and pause—until he lay at the bottom. From the top of the mountain the new King exclaimed, "Squares, bow down to your King, your new King." All bowed. Then with a twinkle in his eye (eye of the boy or eye of the King?) the King announced, "Edict Number One: All Squares must change their shapes; all Squares must become round; do you hear? *Round!*" They heard and they did become round, changing with much effort from a sharp-cornered rhythm to a circular movement as they completed the day's routine activities and retired to sleep, curled up in round balls.

We gathered in an intimate circle to exclaim over the plot created in action. We had joy in the *doing*; we have joy now in the experience of *clarifying* and *appreciating* what we have done. If we are like our Creator in our power to create, does it not follow that that likeness includes the power to appreciate our own creation; to rejoice when it is good? *And* to acknowledge when it delights us not and why? The group looked at the plot that had evolved. They were interested in the significance of the action, in the satirical style of the playing. They wanted to try another ending. What about having the "square-rounds" rebel, overthrow the King, and thus free all to be round, square, oblong, horizontal, vertical, whatever each wished to be? They exclaimed and laughed as they envisioned the climax and all the possible ways of moving as each person in the kingdom found his or her own form and rhythm and moved in that individual shape and way and yet was in harmony with all the others.

There have been times when a spontaneous experience of this nature leads into a long, continuous drama demanding research and a steady but willing commitment. "Who would dream that a simple poem like "Imaginings" wherein we are invited to create a world of our own desire behind a little red door would lead a group of teenagers into the mysteries of creation and the atom? But such was the result when one boy found behind the door a book containing the answers to all the mysteries of the world. What were those mysteries? For each his own mystery, from the awesomeness of space, the perplixity of love, the marvel of universes revolving within universes, to the moment when the Cause of all causes started things causing. The result was an exciting experience in dance and drama wherein the scientific and the biblical accounts of the Creation were found to contain no contradiction. In the process the leader as well as the youngsters had to "bone up" on atoms and elements and Genesis."[6]

The circular space of our famous theatre-in-the-round on campus was by choice the locale of my university classes and children's groups in drama. I've always been fascinated by circles—

> —The circular form of children's games.
> —"Let's all form a circle," says the teacher.
> —"I can draw you a picture of God," says the child and draws a circle. "See, no beginning and no end."
> —No beginning and no end—all are equal in the circle.
> —"Find your own place in space" and the child with outstretched arms turns himself about delineating in the air a circle.
> —The expanding circle of communication—the child first communes with himself and then with one other and, in drama, only with those within the context of the dramatic situation. The little boy playing the Soldier in the Nativity story stands nose-to-nose with Joseph and whispers, "Go back to where you were born; you got to be counted." "I can't hear you," says an adult sitting close by. "I wasn't talking to *you*," replied the Soldier. When the players reach the age and the level of experience when they delight in communicating with those within the dramatic situation *and* with those who are looking on, there is no "don't turn your back to the audience" nonsense, for in our circular playhouse the audience is all about us. Our circle of communication has expanded naturally and painlessly to include the audience in the drama.

"Oh, I like our circular playing area," I say out loud. And as I speak I become aware of a little girl standing in front of me and the two dogs—a little girl with dark curly hair and blue eyes. Her name is Kathy and she wants to play with Sean and Deirdre. As she plays, her name, her looks, and her spirit remind me of another Kathy. At age seven she arrived for the afternoon session in creative dramatics with a book in hand and in one long unpunctuated sentence not only supplied the content but suggested the procedure for the next hour. "Here is a book of Mother Goose rhymes you pick out some *good* ones and tell them to us and then we'll choose which one we want to *do* with our partners and you ask us some *questions* and we'll make a little play all of us at the same time with our partners." In that moment I felt deeply my vital role in the creative and dramatic process these children had come to engage in for their own enjoyment and benefit. Kathy, by her action and words, was acknowledging that there is an art in guidance, in the selection of dramatic content, and in the procedure that is a partnership of the children and the adult involved.

In the sharing of the rhymes I came to "Peter, Peter Pumpkin Eater," told the rhyme and posed two questions: "Why couldn't Peter keep his wife?" ("What was the problem?") *and* "Why, once inside the pumpkin shell, was she so content?" Kathy and her partner leaped up and begged for this rhyme. their wish was granted, and they immediately went into action as had all the other twosomes. Kathy picked up a cardboard box that happened to be on the edge of the playing arena. She put it on her head and blindly thrashed about. "Peter," she cried, "there's no room in this house, no room, no room for anything—I'm leaving." And off she went, oddly enough with the "house" still on her head and mumbling, "No room, no room!" "Peter" quickly assembled some chairs in a big circle; then with a digging motion removed one chair from the circle and dug vigorously all about inside the sphere of chairs. That chore completed, he chased down his "wife"—led her into the pumpkin house; took the old "house" off her head, and stood back to see her reaction to the new one. Kathy as the wife moved about the round house, entranced and finally gave voice to her ecstasy, "Ahhhhhh space, space, space at last!"

How much space has been covered in our walk today, physical and otherwise. How much time, too; for the sun has dropped behind the hill, the boats are all nestled at their moorage, and we too will soon be on our way home. We rest for a moment on the rolling green slopes of the park across from the boat basin. The azaleas, the rhododendron bushes, a few late-blooming camellias and fruit trees fill the air with their vivid colors and their scents. All week long the gardeners have been tending them—pruning, weeding, loosening the dirt around their roots, spreading pungent sawdust over the flower beds to contain the weeds and enrich the soil.

It is the nature of these plants and trees to grow and develop. Each is programmed to grow according to an individual and unique design within.

"The rose is a rose is a rose," never an azalea or a rhododendron. But there are helpers without, too—the rain, the sun, the gardeners.

Each child is blessed with an inner design of his own and endowed with innate powers to grow and to develop, to perceive, to think and to imagine, to create. In him, as "in the prophetic artist, genesis again will create the firmament and the day and night and the world of plants and animals, and into this creation he will enter and he will be its voice and its guardian

> and will give to everything its name
> > which is poetry
> and to everything its sound
> > which is music
> and to everything its color
> > which is painting
> and to everything its shape
> > which is architecture.
> and to everything its motion
> > which is dance
> and to everything its metamorphosis
> > which is sculpture."[7]

And I would add—

> and to everything its action
> > which is drama,

> becoming increasingly aware in the process of his own
> > unique self and his interrelationship with
> > all creatures and all creation.

This power is there, within all of us—to be recognized, appreciated, nurtured, turned to most joyous and meaningful account. But it too needs the helpers—the rain, the sun. The gardener's work and mine are much alike.

NOTES

1. Kenneth Grahame, *The Wind in the Willows* (New York: Scribner's, 1929), p. 3.
2. Max Eastman, *Enjoyment of Poetry* (New York: Scribner's, 1932), p. 29.
3. Frederick S. Wight, John I. H. Baur, and Duncan Phillips, *Morris Graves* (Berkeley and Los Angeles: University of California Press, 1956), p. 1.
4. Rita Haaga, *Is the Wind Still in the Willows?* (Private Printing, 1969), frontispiece.
5. Joseph Campbell, *The Hero with a Thousand Faces* (New York: Pantheon, 1949).
6. Agnes Haaga, "Recommended Training for Creative Dramatics Leader," in *Children's Theatre and Creative Dramatics*, ed. Geraldine B. Siks and Hazel B. Dunnington (Seattle: University of Washington Press, 1961), p. 205.
7. Mary Caroline Richards, *Centering in Pottery, Poetry and the Person* (Middletown, Conn.: Wesleyan University Press, 1962, 1964), p. 94.

Co-Respondents:
The Child and Drama

Ann M. Shaw

Ann M. Shaw's professional experience began when she was appointed creative dramatics specialist in the Evanston public school system. Subsequent teaching has included Western Michigan University, Hunter College, Teachers College of Columbia University, and Queens College, where she is at present a member of the faculty of the Department of Communication Arts and Sciences. Dr. Shaw has been a consultant in creative drama and communication development to National Follow Through Centers in Georgia, Michigan, and New York City, and has been a leading proponent of drama in the education of disadvantaged children. She is co-editor with Cj Stevens of the collection Drama, Theatre and the Handicapped, *published by the American Theatre Association. A contributor to many professional journals, Ann Shaw is on the board of directors of the American Theatre Association and currently chairperson for the U.S. Center for ASSITEJ. Her bachelor's and master's degrees were granted by Northwestern University and her doctorate by Teachers College. In this essay, Dr. Shaw discusses her view that the potential of improvisational drama in education derives from its relation to life and to drama as an art form.*

What has the child to do with drama or drama to do with the child? As the framer of the question, I readily admit that the implicit assumption reflects my point of view: I believe that the child and drama are inextricably linked; and I advocate the deliberate, purposeful inclusion of improvisational drama in the education of children because I believe it can contribute to the process all of us are forever involved in, that of becoming and being human.[1]

If that sounds like a "declaration of faith by a true believer," it is. My intuitive sense that drama and the child are naturally related predates the time when, as a sophomore in college, I originated the idea of improvisational drama with children. My creation of what I supposed to be a new dramatic form was stimulated by my desire to combine my passion for theatre with my pleasure in children. It was based in the process that had developed from leading neighborhood children in "Let's pretend that . . .," a kind of play in which we made up and developed problems in spontaneous dialogue and action—our only audience the family cats and the town dogs who were sometimes drafted to be part of the drama.

My image of myself as a creative genius was shattered when my theatre professor told me Winifred Ward had been working with children in creative dramatics for twenty-five years before I "discovered" it, that she was not the only proponent of this form of drama, and that several universities offered courses or programs of study related to drama and the child. So ended my brief career as a pathfinder! Still, it was something of a relief to find that I was not alone in my interests and that there were those from whom I could learn.

Always a believer, I have become increasingly concerned with the need for the formulation of an intellectual basis for that belief. The following discussion certainly does not establish that base nor does it constitute a philosophy. It is intended to indicate my search and my current views. At best, it is only a partial answer to the opening question.

The kind of drama experience I shall be talking about is called by a variety of names: creative drama, improvisational drama, child drama, developmental drama, education drama, informal drama. I shall use the terms *creative drama* and *improvisational drama* interchangeably simply because these terms seem to be in most frequent use in the United States and are usually familiar elsewhere. Variously defined by exponents, it seems safe to say that an explication of any of these terms would include reference to a process in which a leader guides participants in exploring and expressing ideas through spontaneous enactment. Improvisational drama is appropriate to any age group; it is particularly suited to the interests, needs, and learning styles of children.

My view of creative drama and its potential in education is grounded in what I take to be its relation to life and to drama as an art form. I shall begin with a brief description of the capacities and processes that distinguish humans and are the base of the improvisational drama process and then suggest several aspects of drama which ought to be kept in mind as we advocate and practice improvisational drama with children. With this as background, I shall offer a definition of improvisational drama and discuss my views of several issues which are central to an attempt to examine the particular contribution improvisational drama might make to the growth and development of the child.

Symbolic Process and Drama

To begin at the beginning, then, we humans are the animals who perceive and create the world symbolically. Susanne Langer contends that "symbolization is not the essential act of thought . . . but an act essential to thought, and prior to it."[2] She views the brain as not simply a great transmitter, but better likened to a great transformer:

> The fact that the human brain is constantly carrying on a process of symbolic transformation of the experiential data that comes to it causes it to be a veritable fountain of more or less spontaneous ideas. As all registered experience tends to terminate in action, it is only natural that a typically human function should require a typically human form of overt activity; and that is just what we find in the sheer expression of ideas.[3]

The symbol behavior of the young child often takes the form of overt imitation of experiences and behaving as if the child were the person, thing, or in the circumstance imagined. Thus the young child acts the mother feeding the baby, acts the jet plane streaking across the sky, acts the birthday party. Hans Furth, discussing Piaget's distinction between sensorimotor knowing and symbol behavior points out:

> When a three-year-old child plays "mother" or "going to bed," the child's gestures could not take place if the child's knowing of mother or sleeping were tied to physical actions. Sensorimotor knowing of sleeping, you will recall, is *actual* sleeping. When the child plays sleeping we can conclude that his knowing is beyond the senorimotor stage, that it is no longer entirely tied to the external action, and that therefore the child is capable of representing his knowing in *symbolic* sleeping.[4]

In the symbolic behaviors of children we find the earliest manifestation of the processes and form that characterize the art we call drama. Because drama was developed we have come to call this kind of play "dramatic play." It is important to remember that this form of symbolic behavior gave rise to drama and avoid the tendency to speak of improvisational drama as if it were antecedent to life.

The child's interest in dramatic play is obvious. I once walked behind a little boy in Harlem thinking, for a few minutes, that he was either crippled or had a nervous disorder for he moved with a strange little hop and a jerking motion of his head. As I came closer to him I realized that he was intent on a pigeon that was going down the street in front of him and was imitating its walk. After a minute or so, the child turned into a horseback rider and a neighing, bucking horse, which, after being brought under control by the cowboy, galloped down the street. Suddenly, the horse was pulled up short opposite two men who were tearing up the street with a jackhammer. The child's hands which held the imaginary reins grasped the handle of an imagined jackhammer, and with feet spread in imitation of the construction worker, the child impersonated the sound of the jackhammer and the actions of the man operating it.

In the first and last instances, the child was involved in imitating what he was actually seeing and hearing. As horse and rider he was involved in what Piaget would term "symbolic imitation," the figurative gestures making the remembered/imagined event present and expressing his knowing of it. Watching a child involved in dramatic play is a little like watching a one-man band. The child often acts several aspects of an event simultaneously as in horse and rider where he "Whoas!" for the cowboy, whinnies for the horse, pulls on the reins, slaps his own thigh for the flank of the horse. Still, this form of child's play is no more an exact copy of what has been or is being observed than theatre is an exact copy of life. Literal as the imitative play may seem, examination makes it clear that the child had transformed reality into selected, heightened gestures. As the child develops, these figurative gestures become increasingly selected, condensed, and sustained, as though the child somehow understood the principle of aesthetic economy expressed in the phrase "less is more." In a single well-chosen gesture as in a well-honed phrase, a host of meanings are projected.

It seems clear that conceptualizing the world outside one's skin requires the overt enactment of aspects of the "not me" world. This symbolic play is instrumental in developing the ability to discriminate self and other, breaking the bonds of intellectual egocentrism, becoming socialized. Cameron states:

> Social communication depends upon the development of an ability to take the role of other persons, to be able to reproduce their attitudes in one's own response, and so learn to react to one's own behavior as others are reacting to it.[5]

As the child's intelligence develops, the enactment process becomes internalized. However, the covert process of imagining—or imaging—self as other or in places and circumstances not physically present to one's senses continues throughout life and characterizes much of our thinking when we hypothesize our future, reconstruct the past, and plan for the present.

It may well be that the imaginative projection of self that requires overt enactment in the early years is the foundation of divergent thought and underlies all hypothetical thinking. Theodore Sarbin, a leading exponent of role theory, says:

> It is by now a truism that the learning of social roles—in fact the learning of any concept—is associated with the ability to treat an object or event *as if* it is something else. One has to adopt the *as if* set in order to group apparently diverse objects or events into a common concept.[6]

Behaving "as if" is the bedrock of symbolic behavior and fundamental to learning in any intellectual discipline. Drama is the field that is most specifically and literally derived from this human capacity. Enactment of our remembered and imagined experiences gives form to subjective feeling and celebrates our individual knowings. In this sense one might regard drama as the earliest or most fundamental manifestation of man's capacity to create aesthetic forms.

Perspectives on Drama

Drama is an art. "All art," Susanne Langer states, "is the creation of perceptible forms expressive of human feeling."[7] Irwin Edman sees the function of art to be the intensification, clarification, and interpretation of experience. He says the arts "suggest the goal toward which all experience is moving; the outer world of things, the inner world of impulse mastered thoroughly by intelligence, so that whatever is done is itself delightful in the doing, delightful in result."[8] Drama concerns itself with expressing selected perceptions of the human situation in the form of characters in conflict where the image of human action is presented in the form of human action.

One cannot be long involved in a community of persons concerned with drama without realizing that there are a number of views of what drama is. This has made it particularly difficult for advocates of creative drama to articulate our relation to the traditional positions and programs of departments of theatre in colleges and universities. Development of the area of improvisational drama has been further impeded by the fact that those of us who are primarily concerned with drama in relation to the child define drama differently. While agreement may not be reached, communication may be served by a brief examination of interpretations of the term.

Many employ the term drama in the sense of the first dictionary definition: "a composition in prose or verse portraying life or character by means of dialogue and action and designed for theatrical performance; a play."[9] For these people, drama is the literature of the theatre and may exist as drama solely on the printed page.

Others use drama and theatre as interchangeable terms referring to the purposeful presentation of selected aspects of human life or human skill, whether these aspects are real or illusionary. For example, people who hold this view would apply the terms drama or theatre to the circus act in which Gunter Gable-Williams actually rides a tiger who is actually riding on the back of an elephant, as well as to the portrayal in dialogue and action of the murder of Desdemona in Shakespeare's play *Othello*. The key here is the performance of actions designed to arrest attention and involve the spectator with little or no formal distinction made between those performances which constitute actual danger and those which present the illusion of danger. Circus performers whose lives and livelihood rest on an appreciation of these differences are dismayed by the increasing tendency of audiences to respond to their skill and feats of physical daring as though the danger were pretense. Bernard Beckerman distinguishes between theatre and drama, advocating a view of theatre as an art of presentation and drama a special form of that art in which "one or more human beings isolated in time and space present themselves in imagined acts to another or others."[10] The distinguishing element in this definition being "imagined acts," that is, the presentation of illusions of reality.

In each of these preceding views of drama a staged presentation to others is implicit or explicit. A divergence of opinion is expressed by those who hold that drama need not necessarily involve either the presentation of plays to an audience nor a literary composition, that its essence lies in the purposeful selection of aspects of human experience which are heightened and expressed in dialogue and action by persons who behave as if they are the person living the experience which has been imagined. While many of us in improvisational drama do not totally reject the more traditional views, surely all of us, if we connect our work with drama at all, must agree that drama is not dependent upon a literary composition nor on the formal presentation of plays to an audience.

The broadest interpretation of drama is advanced by those who consider it to include any action that arrests attention and intensifies an experience, (e.g., seeing or being involved in a car accident), and by those who insist that drama and life are synonymous as may be gathered from such statements as "Everything we do is really drama" or "Actually, all life is drama."

As you can see, interpretations of drama range from the literary work that may be considered the most objective form in that it has permanence and may be repeatedly examined, to an experience which is indistinguishable from life itself. Personally, I find the first view sterile in that it omits the dynamic of human presence; I find the last view puerile because it misses distinctions of function and form.

Here are two statements on drama that reflect my thoughts on the subject and indicate the predilections I bring to the following discussion of improvisational drama. The first is a definition developed by the Attleboro Conference group.[11] It has provided us with a useful base for our discussions of issues related to drama, theatre, and the child.

> Drama is the metaphoric representation of concepts and persons in conflict in which each participant is required either to imaginatively project himself into an identity other than his own through enactment, or to empathize with others doing so. This action is structured, occurs in real time and space, and typically demands intellectual, physical, and emotional engagement and yields fresh insight into the human condition.[12]

The second is a statement by Kenneth Tynan that has been eloquently employed by Dorothy Heathcote in her discussions of drama and the child. It captures the emotive power of drama. In *Declaration*, Tynan avers: "Good drama for me is made up of the thoughts, the words and the gestures that are wrung from human beings, on their way to, or in, or emerging from, a state of desperation."[13]

Improvisational Drama: A Point of View

The remainder of this essay is made up of personal assertions and thoughts on selected issues and topics pertaining to improvisational drama and the child. Each issue and topic deserves fuller treatment than I have been able to give it here but may be sufficient to indicate my present point of view.

Subject or Method?

The power of improvisational drama to inform the lives of children is generated by

1. The fact that the process of improvisational drama is grounded in a form of symbolic transformation of experiential data (overt enactment of the "as if"), which is essential to the development of human intelligence and is a fundamental way by which the child makes meanings.

It is this that leads many to regard creative drama as a potent methodology rather than a subject and to advocate creative drama as a teaching approach to all aspects of the curriculum.

2. The nature and function of drama—the art that involves us in the creation and apprehension of metaphors expressive of the individual's response as he confronts life pressures, makes decisions, and deals with the consequences of chance and choice.

It is this that leads some to insist that creative drama is a subject that has legitimate claim to its own time and place in the school day.

Frankly, I consider improvisational drama to be richest in import for the child when it is defined and practical in such a way that it includes both the process of making metaphors and the metaphor made. In conjunction with my colleagues Frank Harland and Anne Thurman, I have described creative drama as the improvisational, nonexhibitional form of drama in which persons are led to imagine, enact, and reflect upon human experiences.

The potential of improvisational drama in the development of persons is best realized when we emphasize the process and the particular understandings with which drama is involved and is able to illuminate; when we purposefully involve children in the enactment of their individuated imaginings of the development and outcomes of those significant moments of personal and universal experience which *grip* our minds and hearts. To the extent that we do this we may fairly propose creative drama be considered the central humanistic study in the education of children. To the extent that we devote our energies and expertise to promoting improvisational drama as a panacea for personal development and the problems of educational institutions, we are profligate.

This assertion does not mean that I think improvisational drama is an ineffective method or ought never to be used as an approach to other curricular contents. I suspect that in the hands of a reasonably skilled leader, improvisational drama would nearly always be an effective way to capture attention and motivate interest, whatever the subject might be, because children associate it with the pleasure of play, it allows them to be actively doing something, it personalizes subject matter, and it can make abstract concepts concrete. While I question the advisability of a dramatistic approach to conceptual development in science and mathematics, except on a philosophical level, I think creative drama might well be incorporated in social studies, history, and literature. Even here, however, it is easy to founder on facts and forget the essential nature of dramatic experience. It is important to realize that while improvisational drama is developed in spontaneous dialogue and action, improvised speech and action, in itself, does not a drama make.

The point I wish to establish is this: Improvisational drama may well be an effective teaching method. But relegating improvisational drama to the role of "hired hand" to teach spelling, personal hygiene, how to answer the telephone or conduct yourself on a bus trip, and so forth, is an appalling waste of the power of drama to relate children to themselves and to others, to make vivid the actualities and potentialities of human existence.

Process and Potential Contribution

The goal of improvisational drama with children is not the development of a play for an audience, to train actors for the stage, to make required subjects palatable, nor to "keep kids off the street." As has so often been stated, the goal is the development of persons. Such a purpose places us on the side of the angels but leaves us in a similarly disembodied state unless we can be more specific about what and how creative drama might contribute to personal development. I have attempted to illustrate how the process central to improvisational drama involves the child in symbolic transformations that are instrumental to intellectual, emotional, and social development. I have argued that the understandings drama seeks to develop—that is, the meaning of personal plight and possibility, and the creation of aesthetic representations of life that making drama involves—are humanizing experiences.

To be more specific, it is necessary to look at what participation in the creative drama process requires the child to do. Throughout a creative drama session, children as individuals in a group situation are involved in (1) recalling and using their knowledge and experience to enhance their understanding and communication of the known—and to make inferences about what is unknown and has not been experienced; (2) imagining themselves, someone else, or something else confronting problems; (3) relating to and interacting with others; (4) analyzing alternatives and making decisions; (5) exploring, developing, and expressing ideas and feelings through enactment; (6) evaluating the outcomes of their actions.

The interplay of these behaviors and the dynamics of group process may be clearer by example. Recently two of my students led a group of mentally handicapped eleven- and twelve-year-olds in improvisational drama. The children had said they wanted to make a play about "a really bad accident." Somehow a plane crash on a deserted island became the focus; the leaders and group worked for two sessions playing into being their images of danger, isolation, privation, survival, group dependency. By the third session they had managed to heal the injured, secure enough food to sustain life, agree to risk trying to reach civilization, and make a raft from parts of the plane.

The third session began with getting the raft stocked and into the water. A table replaced the previously imaginary raft, and the children and both leaders climbed aboard. "Are we ready? Is everyone here?" "Everyone's here." "Shove off!" were the replies. But Linda was not on the raft; one of the children discovered this fact and told Linda to get on the raft. She shook her head "No." They asked her to get on the raft. She refused. One leader said, "I wonder why Linda won't get on the raft?" The children posed the question to Linda. She declined to answer. One child reviewed the situation for her and reminded her of the reasons they had decided to leave the island. Linda remained silent. Persuasive appeals became highly personalized. "You can't stay here alone. You might get sick and couldn't get any food." "What if a snake bites you?" "You won't have anyone to talk to." You won't have nobody to play with." Linda was not moved. One leader asked, "Well, what are *we* going to do?" and the children began to realize and respond to other dimensions of the dilemma—group responsibility to the majority and to Linda, individual's responsibility to the group and to Linda, one's responsibility to one's self. "I want to get back home." "So do I, but we can't go without her." "If Linda doesn't want to come with us, that's her problem." "But she'll die." "I guess we better stay." "Then we'll all die." "Everybody gotta die sometime." "Let's tie her up and make her come with us." "That's not fair." They turned back to Linda and faced her with their problem. A decision had to be reached. The tension was palpable. Reluctantly, Linda said, "I'm afraid. I might fall off and drowned!" This was a problem they could solve. "Here—you can sit right in the middle." "Man! I swim good. Don't worry!" "We'll hold on to you, Linda!" Cheers broke out as Linda climbed slowly onto the raft and, true to their word, they made space in the center of the raft and held her safe. Sighs of relief and sounds of celebration were audible as they "shoved off." The group was again united and could turn their attention to the voyage home.

Improvisational drama is no mindless or spiritless matter. Of course the profit for the child is dependent on the ways the leader employs the process and contents in relation to the particular group of children. With this reservation in mind, it is reasonable to state that improvisational drama promotes the development and integration of the child's cognitive abilities (his ability to think) with his subjective life (what he feels and intuits) with his affective growth (his internalization of attitudes and values) with his capacity to create.

On Leaders and Leading

It is generally acknowledged that the leader is indispensable to improvisational drama. Agreeing with this contention and in light of my concern that the potential of improvisational drama be realized in practice, I cannot ignore the subject of the leader. On the other hand, the subject is so important and complex as to deserve and require an essay in itself, a treatment it has received in a number of publications in the field. Here are a few of my thoughts on the subject of the leader and leading.

It is the leader's responsibility and function to take the children further in developing and expressing their ideas in dramatic form than they could have gone on their own. The principles of leading require perceiving and treating children not as objects to be acted upon but as persons who can and do think, feel, and create. One must subscribe to the view that the child's future is built on the present and that the child must be fully engaged in viewing, valuing, questioning, and questing now.

Of course the leader must know, respect, and like children. Equally important, the leader should know, respect, and like himself. One must know what makes drama and be able to use this knowledge in guiding the dramatic process. One must, also, understand the nature of the creative process; appreciating the importance of spontaneity and the consequent necessity to put ideas into action before the judge inside each of us says "It won't work. It's a worthless idea" and prevents one from exploring the potential of the unknown. Similarly, the leader must respect the function of reflection, evaluation, and revision in creative effort for refinement affirms our creative potential and is a main source of aesthetic pleasure.

In order for creative work to emerge, the leader must establish an environment, an atmosphere that fosters mutual respect and cooperative effort, where ideas are listened to and valued, where imagination is fired and fun is shared. If the dramatic process is to function fully, the leader must emphasize enactment for enactment is the method of inquiry and mode of expression that distinguishes improvisational drama. Basically, the leader helps the children get at and develop their ideas by selecting stimuli that focus attention, arouse imagination, and evoke a response; guiding the children in making decisions about dramatic content and in expressing their ideas in dramatic action; encouraging the group to analyze and evaluate their work.

So far as I know there is no one best way to begin work with children in creative drama. Successful beginnings seem to depend upon the leader's preferences, the abilities and needs of the children, and factors related to the situation in which one is working, such as space, time available, general atmosphere, and so on. I do try to make certain that I begin with something which will grip the children's imaginations, will involve all of them simultaneously in enactment, and will result in their feeling success and pleasure.

People often ask me to evaluate the kinds of improvisational drama experiences that are recommended for children and to suggest how the experiences should be sequenced. There was a time I thought I knew what should be included and in what order, but experience has caused me to question my assumptions. Sense-awareness exercises, movement experiences, and theatre games are all valuable in developing concentration and self-confidence, stimulating creative responses, and establishing group rapport.

On the other hand, beginning with story dramatization or creating dramas from a topic or problem can produce similar results. Whether these activities provide a necessary skills foundation for story dramatization or creating dramatic scenes as was once generally assumed is, I think, open to question. For the reasons presented earlier in this essay, I do think one's main emphasis should be on creating dramas rather than on exercises and theatre games.

For me, leading children in creative drama is always a demanding and fascinating experience. Sometimes it is a frustrating experience as well! As a leader one is constantly challenged to find a balance between subjective and objective involvement. Unless the leader can become honestly intrigued with what is happening, is excited by the play with possibilities, and cares about the outcome of the experience, the whole effort is dulled for the leader's concentration and vitality shape the child's response. Besides which, I am a firm believer in the leader's right to have fun too. However, unless one can simultaneously maintain one's objectivity, it is difficult to assess and deal with the needs and strengths of individual children, to guide the process sensitively and intelligently, and to resist the temptation to take over the drama. In this moment-to-moment process, knowing/sensing which decisions must be made by the children in order to give them ownership of the creative process and event, and which decisions the leader must make in order to involve all and deepen the experience is one of the great challenges of leading groups in improvisational drama.

In beginning this essay, I said that I regard the potential contribution improvisational drama might make to the life of the child to reside in its relation to life and to drama as an art form. I have suggested that the child's symbolic development is acquired through and manifested in processes which are the life source of drama. I contend that one of the basic ways we humans come to enlarge our knowledge of the world, understand ourselves, and relate to others is by purposefully imagining ourselves acting and interacting in relation to circumstances which are not actually present. Improvisational drama has the great advantage of employing this discovery process, a process that is primary for the child; not alien but familiar, not painful but preferred. The instinct to play, the mimetic impulse, the necessity to symbolize, and the pleasure we derive from expressing our knowings in symbolic enactment are the life source of drama, the art form that creates dynamic metaphors of the human situation illuminated through human action.

As I see it, improvisational drama should be viewed and practiced as a form of drama in which children play their images of life into being; as an experience that requires children to seriously engage in thinking, feeling, relating to others; in imaging, creating, and communicating credible representations of human actuality; in valuing life and appreciating the singularity and universality of human experience.

There is much to be studied and known before we can lay claim to the potential outcomes I have posited or fully answer my opening question, What has the child to do with drama or drama to do with the child? As I continue in my efforts to contribute to the development of a conceptual base for improvisational drama with children, I am concerned with involving children at the deepest level their intellectual and emotional capabilities allow in exploring and expressing their "knowings" of life and in envisioning and creating alternative life situations.

NOTES

1. Philip Phenix uses the phrase "being and becoming human" in his book *Man and His Becoming* (New Brunswick, N.J.: Rutgers University Press, 1964). I have reordered the phrase to emphasize the idea of growth.
2. Susanne K. Langer, *Philosophy in a New Key* (New York: Mentor, 1951), p. 45.
3. Ibid., p. 47.
4. Hans G. Furth, *Piaget for Teachers* (Englewood Cliffs, N.J.: Prentice-Hall, 1970), p. 28.
5. N. Cameron, "Experimental Analysis of Schizophrenic Thinking," in *Language and Thought in Schizophrenia*, ed. J. S. Kasanin (Berkeley, Calif.: University of California Press, 1954), p. 60.
6. Theodore R. Sarbin, "Role Enactment," in *Role Theory: Concepts and Processes*, ed. Bruce J. Biddle and Edwin J. Thomas (New York: Wiley, 1966), p. 199.
7. Susanne K. Langer, *Problems of Art* (New York: Scribner's, 1957), p. 80.
8. Irwin Edman, *Arts and the Man* (New York: Norton, 1939), pp. 34–35
9. *Webster's New International Dictionary* (2nd ed.; Springfield, Mass.: G. & C. Merriam, 1934).
10. Bernard Beckerman, *Dynamics of Drama* (New York: Knopf, 1970), p. 20.
11. The Attleboro Conferences were organized by Ann Haggerty, Bart O'Connor, Barbara Sandberg, and Ann Shaw to provide specialists in creative drama and/or theatre for children a forum for an exchange of views on issues central to the field.
12. Attleboro Conference, III, 26 October 1973.
13. Dorothy Heathcote, "Improvisation," *English in Education*, 1, no. 3 (1969–70): 27.

Drama as Education

Dorothy Heathcote

Considered one of England's outstanding educators, Dorothy Heathcote is currently professor of drama at the University of Newcastle upon Tyne. Her course in drama in education was the first of its kind to be introduced into the curriculum for British teachers. Students come from all over the world to study with her, and her teaching assignments have taken her to the United States and Canada. Mrs. Heathcote left school at the age of fourteen to work as a weaver in a wool mill. At nineteen she won a scholarship to Northern Theatre School and was tutored by Rudolph Laban, J. B. Priestly, and London stage designer Mollie McArthur. She has presented work in action over the BBC and her recent films, Three Looms Waiting *and* Dorothy Heathcote Talks to Teachers, I *and* II, *have been shown throughout the United States. Her successful use of drama with the disadvantaged has attracted much attention. In this essay Mrs. Heathcote explains her philosophy of education that accords drama a core place in the school curriculum. She sees drama as practice for living, in which the areas of feeling and social relationships are of major concern.*

It seems sensible to me that, if there is a way of making the world simpler and more understandable to children, why not use it? Dramatizing makes it possible to isolate an event or to compare one event with another, to look at events that have happened to other people in other places and times perhaps, or to look at one's own experience after the event, within the safety of knowing that just at this moment it is not really happening. We can, however, *feel* that it is happening because drama uses the same rules we find in life. People exist in their environment, living a moment at a time and taking those decisions which seem reasonable in the light of their present knowledge about the current state of affairs. The difference is that in life we have many other things to consider at the same time and often cannot revise a decision taken, except in the long term. So drama can be a kind of playing at or practice of living, tuning up those areas of feeling-capacity and expression-capacity as well as social-capacity.

Poets do this in their poetry, painters in their painting, writers in their books, and filmmakers in their films. All these art forms, however, require technical understanding and often elaborate equipment; drama requires only a body, breathing, thinking, and feeling. We begin this practice of playing at an early age because we realize that identifying with others is a human act of which we are capable. It is in the nature of drama that we start exactly where we ourselves are, with our own "prejudiced" views. The diagnostic potential in drama is, for teachers, therefore, very valuable. I believe that classes have the same privilege as other artists in ordering and reordering their worlds, as they gain new information and experiences.

So for drama with our classes we must select an incident for review (not an easy thing, this isolating of key incidents), and this incident has then to be clothed with such elements as place, period, persons present at the relevant time, season of the year, or any other "fixing" device. This fixing is really the work of the class and reflects their prejudiced view. Some fixes need little assistance; others require much more elaborate preparation; but it must feel real to the players, not to some future audience. Broadly speaking, I use a very simple guide if I am in any doubt. There seem to be three ways of structuring the situation (there are probably a hundred but I have managed to isolate these three): simulation, analogy, and role.

If you choose simulation as a device, you often need to bolster reality by facts, being, and feeling. Much drama in school works on the simulation level, but it is hard for teachers to keep it believable when working with an uncommitted class. If you choose to begin with analogy, emotion can usually be the fixing device. This is the easiest approach, as it is in the true theatre tradition, which is about the spaces between people being filled with meaningful relationships. All too often children never get to that kind of experience in their drama. The third way of starting is with a person who is already fixed, for example, a derelict or a policeman or a rent man, who demands (because of his own strongly fixed role) an immediate emotional response. I often work in role at first because it fixes emotional reaction. I find much prejudice against this way of working, though I maintain it is the equivalent of good paint or clay and proper tools. The proper tools of drama are emotional reaction and the state of being trapped, a state from which one can escape only by working through the situation.

Now we have a starting point. Next we need to know what this starting point is likely to teach our classes because of what it will demand of them. This is the difference between the theatre and classroom teaching. The theatre makes us think, wonder, and identify through our watching position (I know that some theatre also allows us, or pressures us, to participate more actively); the drama of classrooms allows us to employ our own views while experiencing the nature of the tensions so that, in the act of making things happen, we think, wonder, communicate, and face up to the results of our decisions and actions. The most important part seems to me to be the chance to build up the power to reflect on our actions. Without this reflection process, the full use of the work is never exploited. This process demands the buildings of a storehouse of images and the language with which to reflect.

Some work started in classes serves the short term as, for example, when I recently introduced a class of infant children to the Goddess Pele (the guardian of volcanos in Hawaiian literature). I wanted to make a double thrust into the area of these manifestations because I considered it more efficient to learn, on the one hand, that modern man has a scientific explanation for events, but that in ancient times man had other explanations for the eruptions. I introduced the two kinds of truth. Both kinds seem of equal importance to me, depending on which point of view stretches a class the most at the time. Both certainly deserve recognition. A much longer project, which altered radically the behavior of a class of eleven-year-olds, was the founding of a city-state in which only eleven-year-olds could live. The city-state made laws, developed a system of education (school every other year!), dealt with sickness, negotiated with adults, arranged for food, and handled finance. In the Goddess Pele experience the class stayed as it was and entertained her presence. She could come and go as required. In the city-state, however, though the children were themselves, they began to live according to other rules and to take on different burdens of responsibility.

All drama, regardless of the material, brings to the teacher an opportunity to draw on past relevant experience and put it into use; language, both verbal and nonverbal, is then needed for communication. The qualities of sympathy and feeling are demanded as well as aggression and its results. This is not always comfortable for the teacher, for the expression of the class sometimes threatens her. But if we grant that it is the artist's right to begin from where he is with his view of an idea, then we must also grant that right to our classes when they create. A second opportunity, of course, is *our* right to insist on the other side of the coin—that of reflecting on the results of our view of the event. In such arts as pottery and painting this is easy; it requires only the hands to stop and the eye to view. It is more difficult in drama because the means of expression is the same as the means of looking, namely, the person himself. Art cannot exist outside the person and take on its own life. It becomes a memory of the event.

I am much criticized for "stopping to consider," especially when "it's going nicely, thank you," but it is for this very reason that I *can* stop. I know that the

Dorothy Heathcote at Northwestern University. Courtesy of Betty Jane Wagner.
Photograph by Gordon Wagner.

event can be rediscovered. Reflection about work is one of the best ways I
know to elicit trust, for I can stop work in order to show enthusiasm, to
challenge, to demand more, and to show my own involvement as well as my
noninterest in value judgments. The outsides of the work matter to me only
when they begin to matter to the class; of course, some classes like to feel
that they are doing a "proper play" from the start. I want them to feel this, too,
in that case, until they find themselves more interested in the ideas than in the
shape. The shape is just as interesting; but not everything can be done at
once, and I prefer to leave that aspect until later. I am primarily in the teaching
business, not the play-making business, even when I am involved in making
plays. I am engaged first of all in helping children to think, talk, relate to one
another, to communicate. I am interested primarily in helping classes widen
their areas of reference and modify their ability to relate to people, though
good theatre can come out of this process, too. But first I want good people
to come out of it. One difficulty of drama is that often the behavior of a class
threatens us because it seems inapplicable to the circumstances we are
interested in exploring. Purple trees in paintings do not threaten us as much,
for they stay on the paper and are obviously the personal viewpoint of the
artist; drama, on the other hand, threatens the very spaces we occupy, and
the attitudes of others threaten the very air we breathe.

The procedures are as follows:

1. We make the world smaller by the isolation of an area of concern.
2. We involve groups of people who, in turn, are involved in group decision taking. Groups can work in fantasy or life situations (truth). These are the same; only the rules are different. But whichever they choose, they must realize that in drama there must always be the acceptance of the "one big lie." This is an agreement to pretend that we are in the situation we have chosen. The truths are the truths of how we see the situation, our own behavior, our own language and expression, our own significant actions and the truths we find to be important to us in the situation. I have discovered that all people understand the idea of the one big lie. It is like giving well-mixed paints or good wedged clay to classes, and it eliminates the silliness that often characterizes children's work at first. One reason for self-consciousness is, of course, that the person of the child is used as the material; another, that the rules are hard to perceive. This is unlike the rules of paint and clay, where the clay falls apart and the paint runs off the paper if the mix is not right. The mix in drama is just as fundamental to the success of the work as it is for the visual arts.
3. We establish certain ground rules:
   a. First the situation must be defined. There must be a beginning that each person can recognize as true to the situation. In games the rules stand at all times when the game is played, and the players learn them once and for all. Drama rules may appear to change because the actual start must use the present capacity of the class to relate to each other. In drama the space relationship is the social health of the class, plus the nature of the game it is about on each occasion. This demands very special skills to be mastered by the teacher; books alone cannot teach them, though as we learn how to isolate factors, it will become possible to teach teachers more rapidly than we do at present.
   b. Group views must be put to use so that the drama starts where the groups are (simply because you cannot start from where you aren't). This means that the leader/instigator must find a common starting point. If the common starting point is negative, then the negative must be used—positively, of course. This is why, when I am asked what I teach, I can only give the answer, "I teach children." What else is there to teach at first, whatever the subject area? It seems to me that we all teach children until such time as the classes are committed to an interest in the particular discipline and a desire to learn the skills of that discipline. To commit classes, however, requires strategies. Far too little time is spent in training for strategies or for holding staff conferences regarding those usable strategies that successful teachers stumble upon. Indeed, there should be no need to stumble upon strategies. The study of these should be a constant inservice part of running a school.
   c. There must be some instigation to review progress. Progress can easily be seen in the visual arts, but drama often disguises progress or shows it falsely; for example, if the action moves quickly, the result can be mistaken for quality. A slower approach can suggest lack of progress. I usually take on this responsibility at first because it is difficult for a member of a group to get the ear of the class. Once the social health of a

class has improved, it is easy for others to assume responsibility, and they should be encouraged to take it.

The first leaders are often those who have language confidence, though not necessarily the most ability. Later the demand shifts from talk to action, from the repetition of facts to the understanding of feelings, by the demand for skills of different kinds (often not socially acceptable, such as picking locks or brazening out a stand against authority).

I am much criticized for instigating early review. I do it because one thing that must happen in learning is the development of a sense of commitment to work. I will not guarantee that classes work; what I will guarantee is that I will always keep the work interesting. Another advantage in early review is that it prevents rot from setting in, without its looking as if one had stopped for that reason. So review can be a "failure saver" as well as a "slower down into experience." Reviewing, to me, is a strategy.

d. Strategies must change according to the class and the drama. Because I often work in role at first, there is an assumption that that is the way I shall continue to work. In an organically changing situation such as teaching, one is constantly seeking to make the first strategies redundant, while seeking to serve the class in other ways. I am weary of explaining to my profession that I do not do the same things every time; I start where the class can start and from then on, as we become more understanding of each other, I try to build a working relationship, in which we can take more liberties with feelings, make more demands upon each other and move more as a team.

A class with poor social health requires a more delicate strategy than one in better health, where there can be some self-help. So strategies are of two kinds: those that stimulate the class to working and those that further the action in the drama. Progression lies in the growing ability of the class to accept the discipline of the drama form and to put the work before personal interest. Concern for each member of the group, ability to take more thoughtful decisions, the courage to risk making and rejecting suggestions—all these are progressions.

There are also the art-form progressions. These are closely related to the above, of course, but there are the extra dimensions of awareness of the overview: the avoidance of anachronisms, the checking of facts, the groping with unfamiliar skills and pursuing them past weariness, the never giving up until it feels right. In other words, it is conceding that sometimes the work matters more than the individual.

There is also the confidence of making the form work for you, revealing how those rules, which seem so limiting to the inept player, help to release the brilliant player. When a class can take liberties out of knowledge rather than out of ignorance, we can rejoice. This is rarely achieved in drama because much of the time students never really understand the rules.

e. The work must go slowly enough to give a class an experience. This is very difficult with classes of poor social health because they do not want to go slowly. Another reason for strategy! I never object to any ideas the class wishes to work on, but I do interfere with the pace. I cannot say that this is right, but I believe pace an important aspect of work and I do much to ensure that it contributes to the best experience. This is an area that a class cannot manage for itself.

f. Tension of some kind must be present in the drama. Teachers rarely understand how to provide it. The simple factor in making tension work is that something must be left to chance but not more than one thing at a time. So long as there is that one factor and no one in the room knows precisely when that thing will occur (though everything has been set up so that it *must* occur), we have tension.

Subtle tensions are useless in a class that will only respond to cruder ones. An example of such a tension might be waiting in the dark for an intruder to enter a room. Or a less crude one, demanding more patience while awaiting one's turn to be interrogated, knowing that one of the group will be found guilty. The pressure must come from within the situation, not from the teacher/role insisting that it be done right.

Every conceivable situation can provide the tension to suit any type of class. I remember a group of delinquent children (fourteen-year-olds) who moved very quickly through a series of such tensions, each one making the group work harder than the preceding because each one demanded more of them while allowing them satisfaction. The first was a mugging; the second a verbal threat to a lady of wealth to blackmail her son; the third a painful forging of a document that would fool the guards; the fourth a telephone call made under the nose of the police, warning a friend of a police raid. Finally, the wait outside a temple to find out whose baby—yes, baby (and they themselves were the mothers)—would be chosen to be sacrificed in a prayer for rain. They also did the ritual mourning.

One feature of using tension in teaching is the opportunity it offers for using the same situation while it apparently changes for the class. An example of this was seen with a group of retarded children working on the theme of *Macbeth* (not, of course, the text, for they could not read):

Tension 1   Aiding the King safely through a forest in which dwelt a wild, often hunted, but never captured boar of great strength and size.

Tension 2   Finding that the lair of the boar was occupied and needing to be sufficiently silent while in that area.

Tension 3   Finding that the boar was loose and might attack at any moment.

Tension 4   Finding that the old guide, who would have been able to predict the boar's reaction, had fallen sick and could not help them.

Tension 5   Realizing that darkness was falling and they were lost in the forest.

This class explored fear and responsibility each time, while apparently changing their play. Each time they carried over more of the factors involved in looking after kings. They also "grew" a vocabulary in order to discuss the subject of fear. This came about because of "teacher interference." Before the teacher can interfere, however, the class must understand or make a decision as to which factor it will reinforce and why, while apparently changing the tension. I chose the problem of having to keep the King safe because I believed it helped the class to avoid using their own instinctive aggressive behavior, which would have been to kill the boar and thus rid themselves of the situation quickly. If a solution comes too easily, there is no opportunity for a class to be stretched.

g. Feelings and thoughts that exist inside persons have to be made explicit to the group so that it can see and respond to the expression in the group. In drama this expression takes place through what can be seen to happen, what can be heard to happen, and what can be felt to happen.

The elements of darkness and light, stillness and movement, sound and silence are held in a constantly changing expression of life. In drama these must be in use from the very start, and I personally try from the beginning to introduce classes to the use of them so that they begin to be selective about the way they will make their statements, though I do not necessarily discuss them in any technical way. I might say, "How will we first know that a monster has been here while we were away?" From the answers I receive I move the class to active decisions, which can be seen to employ these elements.

It is the use in common of these elements that make classroom drama and theatre kin. In theatre they are used for their effect on other people whereas in teaching they are used to make the impact on the very persons who create the work. Drama is about filling the spaces between people with meaningful experiences. This means that emotion is at the heart of drama experience but it is tempered with thought and planning. The first is experienced through the tension and the elements; the second, through the reviewing process. Out of these we build reflective processes, which in the end are what we are trying to develop in all our teaching. Without the development of the power of reflection, what have we? It is reflection that permits the storing of knowledge, the recalling of power of feeling, and memory of past feelings.

All too often we phase out emotion in our classroom work as if it were unimportant. (Certainly emotion is harder to deal with than thinking because children do not expect to use their emotions in school.) If we take the emotion out of drama, there is only the burden left. I recently heard of a group of "Roman soldier juniors," who were expected to attack a British fort in a "noisy way but without making a noise." I do not blame the teacher, who was trying to avoid disturbing the class next door. I do not blame the children, who mouthed all the words they would have spoken, had they been permitted. They were neither fish, flesh, nor fowl as they tried to do a noisy thing quietly, while trying to be the efficient fighting machine they understood the Roman soldiers to have been. They had to do all the external things while being denied the internal experience they needed in order to find their truth. If they could have made a silent attack, out of the necessity of a silent approach, they might have managed it.

I blame only the training of the young teacher, which led him to think that what he was doing was drama.

Please note that I am not quarreling with the fact that the children could make no noise—only that they were expected to do and believe in noisy things while keeping silence. If they had decided to try to attack in silence, then their movements could have been a real experience of battle. Likewise, if they had been allowed to assume a bargaining position, which would have demanded a careful choice of words, they might have experienced the significance of the spoken language while facing an enemy who misunderstood the words and the promises.

I believe that the child and the actor have to follow the same rules. It is not possible to simplify these rules; it is only possible to simplify the demands we make. Some potters make clay work harder for themselves than others do; some painters do the same with paint; some actors say more with fewer gestures; and some musicians get more out of fewer notes. The processes are the same for the great and the mediocre, but the expressive use that is made of these processes is the varying factor. Surely we owe our classes the real material that our artists have to use. Drama is possibly more liable to criticism than other art forms because the rules exist in use, by people in action, and they never exist outside that reference except in the memory.

The elements of darkness/light, stillness/movement, and silence/sound offer an incredible range of expression. They embrace all clothing worn, all places in which persons find themselves, all words said, all groups formed, all sounds made, all gestures employed; and the teacher must master the flexibility of the elements so as to make them available at will to their classes.

The method of teaching classes is usually via the theatre exercise. But exercises have a built-in, self-destroying force, particularly when used with uncommitted classes. They have a drive toward ending themselves. True drama for discovery is not about ends; it is about journeys and not knowing how the journeys may end. Once there is real commitment to this way of learning, there is a reason for studying the factors we employ in order to isolate and practice techniques.

But let us give a few examples before we start on the means by which ideas are communicated. We have crippled our children beyond the breaking point by insisting on rewardless labor before they are given the opportunity to experience any reality. Learning about being a person comes from trying out, not by practicing for it. I am not saying there is no value in exercise skills. I am saying that we must have some motivation for doing a thing before we start imposing our theories. When drama is exercise-driven, the natural discoveries that come from emotional involvement cannot arise. Pace, pitch, tempo are discovered in the heat of the moment. Exercises exist to take emotion out, so that coolness and repetition can exist. I know you can devise exercises for emotion, but why should you with children who have the real thing so readily available just waiting to be tapped?

Recently I was working with a class of nine-year-olds who were just becoming interested in the Luddite rebellion, which took place when the first spinning frames were destroyed by the incensed weavers in 1812. The children set up a frame in "heat." That is, they knew nothing about such frames but in confrontation with an owner of a mill, who was impatient to see the frame working, they not only built it slowly from hints given in role but they also developed a sense of responsibility as skilled workers, brave men who dared build such things in troubled times. They developed at the same time a distinct feeling of the rhythm of building together. Exercises do not work so efficiently. Their value lies in the way they help to isolate a factor and let special attention be paid to it. I say that exercises are for those who have already tasted the riches of a tough and real experience. Far too many classes never get to the reality of their art because of time spent on exercises.

Drama, then, teaches in the following way. Taking a moment in time, it uses the experiences of the participants, forcing them to confront their own actions and decisions and to go forward to a believable outcome in which they can gain satisfaction. This approach brings classes into those areas that in the main are avoided in school: emotional control, understanding of the place and importance of emotion, and language with which to express emotion. We expect good fathers, husbands, honest citizens, fine sensitive friends, and tolerant and understanding neighbors to emerge from the classes we teach; but we have done very little to prepare them for these roles.

I should not criticize our educational system so much if we did not profess to be doing more than making children literate. We talk of career classes, for example, and then we proceed to ignore the relevant areas of responsibility that are emotionally based, except for a little advice in the form of cool discussion. We talk about religious education in our English schools and behave with arrogance toward our children. These and many other subject areas demand a steady reaction of emotional input for thorough exploration, but we often present our material in such a way that emotional material has to be treated without emotional response.

Though drama is probably discussed more today in terms of teaching and learning than it has been in the past, it is far from being fully exploited in our schools. It continues to limp along, never quite able to show its potential because the system, as it stands, preserves jealously the "one class, one teacher" syndrome, the "everybody has to be the same age in the group" syndrome, the "teacher has the secrets" syndrome, the "we can't have more than one person making decisions" syndrome, the "let's keep everything in short periods" syndrome, and above all, the "let's not have too many children surprising the teacher" syndrome. I know, of course, that pockets of super-human experiment do exist, and I do not want to denigrate these in any way. But the basic problems remain and give rise to the apathy and the social ill health in our classes.

Procedures and Practice

First, let us examine a simple table. I think that the best learning takes place when there is a balance between the two extremes, but I present them here as opposite sides of the same coin. When I am actually teaching, I am happiest in an area that lies midway between the two methods as, for example, in the Goddess Pele work mentioned earlier, where the truths of scientific explanation and myth were taught simultaneously.

> **Informal Approach** (often referred to as left handed):
>> emphasis on applying experience in the act of learning
>> using the emotions to aid understanding
>> being involved in the teaching
>> being able to challenge the teaching
>> taking decisions to modify the pattern of the plan

> **Formal Approach** (often referred to as right handed):
>> emphasis on learning from others' information
>> learning through the mind
>> convergent learning
>> objective learning
>> strong reliance on the proven

It will be readily seen that these two methods need not be in conflict; some kind of happy medium can be found in order to give the teacher security. Indeed, it is not factual information and emotion that oppose one another; it is the approach to the class and the strategies employed. The left hand relies heavily upon mutual appreciation and mutual decision-making between teacher and class. Drama is not an efficient means for straight factual teaching, but it provides a rich ground for making facts understood in action. When building a spinning frame, for example, if you are not certain of the details and are asked if all the cogs run smoothly, you either ask questions about its construction or someone tells you (there is always more information in the group than emerges at first), or you do the thing that feels right. It may elicit the question, "What about those under the shafting?"

And so it goes on until looking at a plan seems a good idea; then you may either gather around the board and draw what you think you have been building or look at a picture of a real frame. The main thing, of course, is that when you do look at a spinning frame, the illustrations must not only be of good quality but may be more complex than they might otherwise have been. The class studying the Goddess Pele worked simultaneously in the areas of correct vocabulary, technical detail, ancient beliefs, the power of Pele as seen in her person, peril to people, and the formation of new lands. In a formal approach the class would have dealt with these elements one at a time, gradually building up a factual picture. With Pele to challenge and be challenged by them, to offer her explanation in reply to theirs, the students absorbed many layers of feeling and information at once. Also, it was possible to test the understanding straight away, for many diagnostic techniques can be used during the action to test the grasp of concept and factual understanding.

The basis of all my class contacts seems to depend more and more upon a few relatively simple techniques. I plan the areas where the class will make the decisions. I also plan strategies that I shall use to get the class committed to work. This planning is always done from an inside experience approach rather than from an external tasks approach. I try to know the impact of every verbal statement I make as I make it. I select all signals with extreme care and sensitivity, even when working with my back to the wall with what I call "dragon's teeth" classes. I spend much time examining the uses of questions and the types of questions asked. I recognize a dud question and set about recovering from it immediately. One dud may take ten or more other good questions to make a recovery. I decide when and why I shall leave role and become interrogator-leader. People assume that because I use role early, I mean to go on with it. I use role in order to teach the class that emotion is the heart of drama. Talking about emotion is no substitute for feeling it. This is the advantage of being in role but, of course, it is a complicated tool and takes some patience to learn how to use it. I have not yet met a teacher who cannot use it and who does not learn more about the use of drama in her teaching as a result of its use.

I seek rather than plant information. And I never mix plans. In other words, I decide very clearly what the lesson should achieve. It may be an unplanned session when I deliberately decide to test the class in order to find out where it is; all subsequent sessions can be based on what I learn in the beginning. Or it may be a session especially designed to introduce some aspect of learning, such as the Pele work discussed earlier. It may be very specific, such as the work done to readjust opinion or to bolster confidence in order to answer questions in examination. Or it may be to help study how the text comes alive on the stage.

Drama is so very flexible because it places decisions in the hands of the classes; the teacher acts as midwife. I select all the best artifacts, literature, and reference books I can find (adult materials for the most part, as I find them superior). I do not withhold information if I can find a way to impart it. I believe far too much information is withheld from classes, or children feel that it is being withheld, which has the same effect.

I work slowly in the beginning. I do not move forward until the class is committed to the work. This does not mean that I stand still; it means that I use many strategies to keep in the same place while apparently moving forward. The social health of the class dictates this commitment, and it is my belief that all the real difficulties of drama come from social ill health. Therefore, if we want to train teachers to make use of drama, we must begin by training in strategies that develop social health as the teaching progresses. This strategy is also geared to success and approval. I work to stretch classes. I expect students to work very hard, and I show that I work hard too. I never withdraw help nor do I ever praise falsely. I give positive comment at all times, and when I want to urge further effort, I often quote my own experiences (always true but often edited to make the strongest impact and timed so as to shock the class into new awareness).

I do not expect classes to like drama automatically. I guarantee that I will do nothing to make them feel foolish, but neither will I allow them to get off the hook. I use the rules from the beginning and especially make the point that all signals, whether positive or negative, affect the work. Finally, I stress that at the present time with the emphasis upon the children's expectations, the teacher will have to initiate, guide, ask for proof of work, time the work, and be the guide and mentor throughout. With some initiative developing in the fifth and sixth forms, we are bound to find this way of working difficult and slow. Children have not been trained to trust their own ideas or their own ways of approaching work. Therefore, for the time being, we not only have to carry the burden of working against the stream but that of creating classes who will revel in taking decisions, in using emotion productively, and in exercising their skills. Finally, we must stand up against the criticism of our colleagues.

Curriculum Drama

Elizabeth Flory Kelly

Elizabeth Flory Kelly's academic degrees were granted by Smith College and Western Reserve University; additional postgraduate work was done at New York and Northwestern Universities. Her professional theatre training included two years at the Maria Ouspenskaya Studio. Mrs. Kelly's lifelong interest in theatre began in childhood at the Cleveland Play House, of which her parents were among the founders. For the past twenty-five years she has been developing techniques in what she calls "curriculum drama" while teaching in several independent schools in Cleveland. She has studied innovative and current theatre/drama practices in England and on the continent of Europe. Mrs. Kelly is presently chairperson of the Outreach Committee of the Cleveland Play House Board of Trustees and the children's theatre consultant. Her outstanding contribution has been the organization and administration of dozens of drama workshops involving thousands of educators from over sixty-two school districts and art institutions in the area.

Recipient of grants from the Martha Holden Jennings, George Gund, and Schubert foundations, Mrs. Kelly has introduced teachers to the methods of Dorothy Heathcote and Gavin Bolton and to Dr. Jean Houston's pioneering work in the importance of the arts in right-brain affective learning. Mrs. Kelly has been given Special Recognition Citations by the Children's Theatre Association of America and the Ohio Theatre Alliance, on whose Inservice Education Consultant Team she serves for the state's board of education.

Curriculum drama cannot be understood properly until we rethink the key objectives of education. Should the *basic* emphasis be placed on learning

91

skills or on learning to cope with the myriad human relationships of life? How many teacher-training courses clearly indicate the multiple, simultaneous levels of instruction with the proper priority given to each? Could a major problem in American education be found in the lack of importance given *affective* learning with an overemphasis on the use of cognitive skills? As Harold Taylor has aptly written, thinking is an activity of the whole organism "which begins in the senses . . . and involves the emotions."[1] More recently, Dr. Jean Houston and others skilled in the thinking process, have indicated that actual learning damage may occur when overemphasis is placed on left-brain cognitive, linear thinking to the exclusion of right-brain affective imaging.[2]

A junior high school English teacher is told that her curriculum will consist of teaching "clauses, verbals, and styles of writing." When she asks if that is all, she hears, "Isn't that enough? Teaching those things *well* should certainly be sufficient." The key word is "well." What do we mean by teaching well? In the recurring theme of going back to teaching "basics," we sometimes forget that little can be taught without motivation. Yet how do we motivate students without making basic subjects relevant to students' lives? Where is this relevant area of common experience in which a teacher and her "unskilled" students can communicate? Doesn't this lie in common human-ness? This universal human thread integrates all skills and helps avoid the fragmented learning that occurs so frequently when subjects are taught in isolated compartments.

We are neglecting to notice that the "point of entrance," the "magic button" that motivates learning, lies in the human level with its interplay of people relationships.

Curriculum drama is a continually evolving, unabashedly eclectic method of teaching. The fact that theatre/drama techniques involve many aspects of the other arts works both with and against its full recognition as an art form. Used as a process for learning, it naturally coordinates the other arts, but as a result of this complexity, it is frequently shunned as an impure art, and its true potential for learning is left unrecognized.

Any means that not only motivates and accelerates but even *deepens* the quality of learning should be utilized. Drama as a process does all this. As an example, long-term retention of learning occurs when flashes of recognition are interwoven with linear thinking. When recognition of *relationships* occur, memory ceases to be rote. "Drama deals with relationships" states Dorothy Heathcote.[3] With these insights into so-called new relationships, the student's feeling of drudgery, often sensed with linear learning, is swept away, and a more profound "knowing" occurs.

Frequently two or three objectives can be accomplished simultaneously through drama techniques; for example, the class can experience an integrating "group dynamics" session and simultaneously "role play" historical characters of the French Revolution. Thus drama techniques, frequently used for socializing objectives, can be effective simultaneously because of their superb *empathic* qualities in deeper understandings of subject-oriented material.

Group socialization frequently proceeds more effectively if it is approached obliquely through another learning area. It allows students to test simulated alternative life choices. The teacher guides the students in their identification with an examination of selected pressure points of human conflict. Dorothy Heathcote's techniques for imparting moments of reflection and insight into these human situations has moved dramatic improvisation into uncontestable depths of quality learning.

Similar to the scientific observations of the microbiologist Dr. Lewis Thomas,[4] drama can clarify a microcosm of life, thus enabling the teacher to relate the student's newly found knowledge to the complexities of our macrocosm.

As an example of curriculum drama's eclecticism, let me point out that curriculum drama avails itself of any educationally effective theatre/drama techniques, espousing the use of both formal theatre experiences as well as informal drama, while preserving criteria for quality education. This is the era of multimedia. Assess your own abilities in their use. If you can handle tape recorders, slides, movies, and projectors, incorporate them occasionally in your dramatic productions. Effective learning is frequently multisensory.

Although *theatre* and *drama* are frequently used interchangeably, the word roots indicate a basic difference. Theatre comes from the Greek word "to see, to view"; drama comes from the root meaning "to do or live through." When charting the variations of use of theatre techniques in education, the theatre end of the spectrum will indicate the viewing, performance, and aesthetic study of a formalized art; the drama end will indicate the informal "doing or living through" that occurs with more spontaneous, improvisational techniques at the other end of the scale. Although curriculum drama encompasses all theatre methods for teaching subject material, the emphasis is toward the informal end of the scale because of the profound educational implications in "living through" drama.

Anyone who is concerned with making theatre/drama central to society has an obligation to enlighten departments and schools of education on the learning potential within the arts. This is an area of education in which England is at present doing brilliant spadework. Because of the size of the United States and the diversity of its theatre and educational systems, we need a concerted effort to adapt, develop and bring forth our own expertise in this developing field. Too often teachers follow given curricula so slavishly that they have no time for "frill" dramatics. Administrators frequently ignore the fact that selective in-depth learning is usually far more effective than longitudinal, surface spread. Of course, there is little time to memorize *extraneous* material or even improvise when working in educationally meaningless areas. But if education is a process of skill training in order to better cope

Meeting with children. Courtesy of Elizabeth Flory Kelly.
Photograph by Anne B. Adamson.

with the myriad problems of life, how better can a student learn to cope than by projecting himself through the techniques of drama into simulated life interrelationships?

A danger lies in the use of extraneously planned or published curriculum drama exercises except for rather superficial educational purposes. Class-room teachers, unsophisticated in drama techniques, may unwittingly choose such exercises as an integral contribution to their curricula, only to realize later that the normal progression of learning has been arrested and no deepening insights have occurred. On the other hand, if a teacher is taught how to recognize and adapt potential learning activities effectively into a particular subject area, with the interests of a particular class in mind on a specific day, an exercise that might threaten to become a crutch can be recycled into an exhilarating slice of quality learning.

Let me illustrate by using a theatre exercise introduced in Cleveland at a recent teacher-drama workshop conducted by Victor Miller of the Connec-ticut Center of the Performing Arts. An opening exercise used to illustrate the components of drama was a little gem called Airport. An obstacle course of chairs and boxes was assembled to resemble a littered runway. One teacher volunteered to be the airplane. A scarf was tied over his eyes to help him simulate the conditions of a blind landing. A second teacher volunteered to act as the control tower. He immobilized himself in a strategic position just off the runway in order to guide the "plane" to a safe landing. It was an exercise filled with dramtic suspense; it established an objective that could be attained only by surmounting a series of obstacles. It also established an unusual relationship of trust between the two actors.

A few days later I was invited to do two half-hour curriculum drama sessions with a "problem" third grade. Consultation with the classroom teacher revealed a class profile consisting of three children in therapy, several disturbed remedial readers, an academically run-of-the-mill middle group, and a smattering of precocious pupils. Not unexpectedly, the gym teacher was having trouble. Learning was being impeded because of poor socialization. My drama objective—learning to work together—was administratively agreed upon.

I decided *not* to begin my sessions with a primary emphasis on people because human relationships were too central to the class problem. The first half-hour session was therefore spent on individual enactments of favorite animals coping with obstacles of nature such as thunderstorms. The children were then asked to return to the circle and vote on their most popular animal. (Of course, horses won!) They were asked if they would like to enact a story about horses. When they enthusiastically agreed, they were told to count off by fives. This caused momentary consternation, for they realized that the natural friendship cliques were being fragmented when those with the same number had to act together as a team. The incipient emotional upset was quickly subdued with the introduction of a preliminary story structure. The groups were to enact the purchasing of very special horses to be trained to make a trip up the Magic Mountain. The remainder of the day was spent on the selection and training.

On the second day, the Airport exercise was adapted to a specific third-grade level to be used for socializing purposes. The airport runway became the tunnel leading up the Magic Mountain. The control tower became the horse trainer who stood outside the tunnel and led his string of horses through the obstacle course. The eyes of the horse were not masked because such a request would have only been a challenge to peek! Eyes were to be closed because the tunnel was dark. Any horse that did peek was immediately disqualified by classmates who were watching tensely just outside the crooked "tunnel" of chairs. Each team consisted of a trainer and his team of horses. Each "horse," crawling on hands and knees while clutching the ankles of the "horse" preceding him, had to move with his team as a coordinated unit at the command of his student horse trainer. The dramatic tension was superb. Better still, a heterogeneous group of third graders was learning to work together with a unified focus.

To use drama as a facilitator for quality education, the main thrust should be on training teachers to recognize and develop dramatic elements within their own curricula. In these days of "turned off" students, a teacher must develop material that stems from where the students are in relation to their specific curricula. Unless they are handled with great flexibility, textbook exercises tend to stultify instruction by inserting what may be a non sequitur at the very moment a teacher is trying to relate more closely to a class. Such exercises can sometimes stimulate the creativity of a tired teacher, but they should never be substituted for teacher judgment and proper adaptation to avoid interruption of normal classroom learning.

A carefully sequenced approach for teaching dramatically unsophisticated teachers some educationally oriented drama expertise is sorely needed. A teacher is not working with preplotted stories and must learn to identify and structure a dramatic situation out of a general idea and still allow students to retain the satisfying feeling that they created it themselves. This entails the spontaneous use of playwrighting techniques.

Relatively simple playwrighting techniques consist of a few basic rules. A teacher must be able to identify a potentially dramatic moment within his or her subject area, to pinpoint the emotional conflict, or hotspot, that may be relevant to the students' interests and possible emotional involvement.

I will use as an example a fourth-grade teacher's problem with teaching a history lesson. The class had been studying the westward trek, and she had had the brilliant notion to have her students pack their Conestoga wagons. The class was swept with enthusiasm. They worked so intently that she decided to let them return to the project the following day. This second go-around was a disaster; chaos set in. In desperation, the teacher returned to her formal "safe" teaching methods and enrolled in a course of curriculum drama!

Later we showed this teacher how chaos could have been avoided if a "magic if" had been introduced on the second day. We explained the improvisational rule of introducing new elements into a redoing of a dramatic situation. In this manner, the impetus this teacher created would have been sustained and the learning deepened. For example, what if you are now packing under pressure because a windstorm is on the way? Or what if you find you must pack and leave immediately in order to escape an Indian attack? An additional suggestion was made: If the teacher had chosen the moment of *greatest* dramatic potential, she might have asked the students to decide what they must *leave behind*. Then additional dramatic scenes could have been planned by decreasing the storage space on the wagon, necessitating that more and more precious possessions be jettisoned.

Dorothy Heathcote lists the dramatic elements that enhance a scene as Sound or Silence, Movement or Stillness, Light or Darkness.[5] I would like to include two additional dramatic elements, both of which I suggested in this last exercise. *Time* is the first element. By inserting the threat of Indians or a windstorm, time was suddenly telescoped and dramatic pressure was increased. *Space* is the second element. By decreasing the amount of space in the wagon, more and more cherished possessions had to be left behind, thus heightening the drama of separation.

The learning process of *reliving* segments of life in order to better understand them was dramatized theatrically in Thornton Wilder's *Our Town*. Here Emily, having died in childbirth, asks to relive a day on earth. She is advised against this, but she insists. Whereupon she begins to relive her twelfth birthday, *knowing in advance* the future sorrows and separations. Very quickly the reliving of this preordained experience becomes excruciating to her. Emily bursts into tears. She returns to the cemetery saying that she never realized how fast life must be lived, with no time truly to appreciate it. Dorothy Heathcote's teacher-structured learning moments focus on a segment of life, slowing it down for reflection; they are a brilliant contribution to the use of drama in education. They allow students to examine microcosms of life in order to gain added awareness of what it is all about.

Because of the limitations of space, this chapter cannot include a detailed sequence of my curriculum drama course for classroom teachers. In outline, it goes like this. It begins with a careful consideration of the *art of theatre* with *basic* principles of acting, direction, and playwrighting tried on and familiarized. Then simple classroom suggestions for scenery and costumes are introduced. (The fewer physical encumbrances, the more time left for imagination and learning. Only an attempt at capturing the feel or essence of a location, mood, situation, or period should be attempted). Once this basic content of the course is understood, a preliminary formal-to-informal curriculum drama chart with accompanying educational criteria and examples often proves helpful:

Visits to quality professional theatre productions. Under the aegis of the school these can serve socializing as well as educational purposes. Frequently, such a visit is the perfect entrée to understanding an otherwise difficult script. I have seen the most unlikely junior high school students memorize pages of *Romeo and Juliet* after viewing Franco Zefferelli's movie. Understanding unfolds with the emotional impact of professional interpretation.

Formal student theatre productions. These can be part of the educational process. They should be assessed for their literary quality and their educational and aesthetic objectives. School time should be time sacred to quality exposure. We must ask if the time used in memorizing lines is commensurate with the quality of the text. On the other hand, in our devotion to quality, let's not neglect humor and the wittily turned phrase. *The Importance of Being Earnest* may be selected for its high style. *Raisin in the Sun* or *Our Town* may be chosen for equally valid goals. A fear of cutting to obtain enjoyable, optimum learning is regrettable.

Professional traveling troupes. When such troupes visit schools, there is less school rescheduling or curricula upset than occurs when the class attends an out-of-school production. Troupes often give quality plays in their entirety. The danger arises when quality literature is unmercifully cut to fit a forty-minute assembly slot.

Theatre-in-education troupes. These troupes visit schools and bring a new approach to the specific contribution the professional theatre can make to education. Such troupes have proliferated in the British Isles but are developing more slowly in the United States. They take a particular educational topic and develop it in a formal or informal manner. They are one of the bridges between formal theatre productions and more improvisational structures, often using a mixture of both by coming in with a formal production and then offering a workshop for a specific age group. For example, Everyman Players visited Cleveland with a production for lower elementary students called *Hey-Diddle-Diddle*, based on nursery rhymes. In addition they offered an excellent workshop for several thousand bused-in junior high students on *Style*, which was shown through costume, speech and movement from different eras. Style is a particularly difficult concept for a classroom teacher to convey without visual assistance.

Quality of these troupes varies greatly; they should probably be judged in three specific areas:

1. Professional quality of production and performance. This seems unusually high in England.
2. Willingness and ability to tap effective educational material. Such troupes must cultivate interested, sympathetic, and sophisticated school administrations in order to synchronize their choice of material with the latest educational expertise.
3. Ability to locate and develop dramatic moments within educational material. This is needed to construct a theatrically effective scripted framework that will elicit true student learning participation.

Formally written plays dramatizing curriculum material. Educational criteria for these productions should be not only an assessment of the quality of learning that is occurring (if the lines are memorized) but also how effectively the material has been dramatically handled. A delightful example of this kind of formal educational theatre was written recently by a geometry teacher.

I handed this teacher a copy of *Flatland*,[6] which explores an imaginary two-dimensional geometric world. The teacher took the basic idea of the story and developed an original plot: two scalene triangles, at the bottom of the geometric social ladder, which is based on the number of angles one has, find congruent bliss when married by the many-sided high-priest circle, who spends most of his time contemplating *his* center! When the two scalene triangles unite for a kiss, they discover they have become a four-sided parallelogram. They have upset the whole immobilized social structure of their world! The play is enriched with lyrics filled with geometric terminology.

By humanizing and converting abstract concepts into a fresh, two-dimensional world, the students have been challenged by many new learning experiences illuminated with the sparkle of theatre production. The memorization of this eighteen-minute playlet has sorted out and tucked away geometric terminology and concepts into the students' memory banks.

Jelled or structured improvisation. This is one of the next steps on the scale toward informal use of theatre techniques. This kind of informal theatre can be handled by the classroom teacher as a culmination of improvisational experiences in curriculum drama structured informally into a school perfor- mance. Because such a performance stems from curriculum material, the formalized presentation can be highly educational with built-in expansion and contraction controls to fit the size of the class.

To clarify this further, let me outline one of my own productions. An En- glish class had been studying Homer's *Odyssey*. They needed an end-of- the-year play, but the teacher wanted quality learning to continue. She sug- gested that the students create their own class odyssey. The students decided that their class odyssey had been a journey throughout the school year in search of the next grade!

The class had been recently introduced to *symbolism* through their study of poetry. Now they were asked to study each episode of Homer's *Odyssey*, capsule the action into a short paragraph, and decide what each adventure basically represented or symbolized. For instance, the Cyclops were de- scribed as self-centered antisocial monsters who could not cooperate suffi- ciently to form a community. The class decided that the one eye of the Cyclops symbolized an introverted, all-demanding focus.

The next assignment was to decide what in the students' own lives might have a similar, all-consuming focus. Their unanimous vote went to "the TV tube"! With this *analogy*, they began creating improvisations centered around television's ability to divert them from the studies necessary for their graduation. The lures of Scylla and Charybdis were symbolized by the popu- lar local teen-age shopping center. Each episode was thus boiled down to its *symbolic essence* and then a *present-day analogy* was chosen to trans- pose it into its modern school counterpart.

Let us next examine briefly the *process* by which improvisation is jelled. Several class groups may be creating around the same theme with discus- sion following each playing. This is where the teacher's expertise is needed. She guides and stimulates further in-depth thinking in a quality learning area. A teacher who complains that a second-grade class cannot repeat a scene or that the children have to perform a scene immediately or it "falls apart" probably needs to explore the Stanislavsky techniques mentioned earlier, the "magic if." Improvisational scenes should never be reenacted the same way twice. The teacher should call for a moment of positive assessment after each scene to help the group formulate the new focus for the repeat scene: "What if we now play this scene in pantomime?" "What if the two old ladies had to pool their food money in order to survive, but they really detested one another?"

In this way, the basic order and structure of the jelled improvisations re- main fundamentally the same while meanings and implications deepen as production time nears. Not only will the sequence of action automatically be learned but the student will feel that he retains a certain freedom of expression and exploration. By encouraging the continuation of thinking on one's feet, the terror of forgetting memorized lines is avoided.

Staging jelled improvisations must remain consistent with the least amount of technical distraction. Token costuming, lighting, and scenery usually satisfy the students, facilitate performance, and encourage the development of creativity and belief. Heavily costumed, a child may feel uncomfortable—simultaneously handling a shawl, a parasol, high heels, a southern accent, and a story line! Part of the learning process can consist of the student's selecting the one property or portion of costume that most effectively portrays the essence of the character. Is it his monocle? Is it her long skirt?

Young voices should not be artificially strained by being forced to project in unreasonably large auditoriums or gymnasium echo chambers. An oversize audience can so easily be detrimental to the proper development of a child's personality. The teacher's educational objectives for a jelled improvisation performance should include assisting student performers in learning to share effectively what they wish to convey to others. The learning in proper classroom improvisation can sometimes add this audience-communication experience if the scene is simply shared with another class section. But may Zeus' thunderbolts forever expunge from the classroom any teacher who exploits a child's personality for the sake of a polished performance! A teacher must never forget that naturally unfolding personalities can develop only if the medium is used basically as a process rather than a product.

Here is an example of jelled or structured improvisation that shows a coordination of the arts with core subject matter. An art teacher was introducing her junior high students to the symbolic surrealist art of Miro. An English teacher wished to introduce free-verse writing as well as the principles of dramatic interrelationships. The two teachers decided to coordinate their instruction. A specific picture was agreed upon that contained several elementary figures of stars of varying sizes, a quarter-moon, and a TV antenna placed against a somber sky.

The English teacher asked the class to *verbalize the overall mood* of the picture. The celestial loneliness was described with a series of adjectives. The students were then asked to pinpoint this mood individually with written phrases that were shared with the rest of the class. The teacher then guided the students into a *study of the figures* within this celestial mood. She asked them to meditate individually on a specific figure, trying to find its *inner action or drive*. This was to be expressed by an action verb beginning with "I want . . ." For example, "I want to talk to someone," "I'm lonely and I crave people," "I want warmth." Teams were formed with each student representing a specific abstract figure within the painting. The students took their visual positions within the composition and tried to feel their *relationships to one another*. They began to act out these interrelationships in pantomime.

Meanwhile, the art teacher, closely informed of developments in the English class, had begun to introduce *puppetry* to the same class with the making of stick dolls representing the Miro figures. The students began to realize that the inner actions of the figures could not be realized fully by immobilized cardboard cutouts. Coils, joints, and twinkling were introduced while preserving the proper mood and inner context.

The students were then asked to introduce the *dialogue* between the heavenly spheres. They had been studying writing complete sentences and were suddenly released to write lists of connotative words and then phrases, expressing the lonely desires of these figures. It became an exciting and freeing exercise in which all kinds of sound effects were written and tested orally. Although the word "poetry" was not mentioned until much later, *free-verse dialogue* was emerging.

The music teacher, who happened to have a flair for modern music, became intrigued with the literary and visual efforts of the class. He helped the students compose appropriate *songs* and *sound effects* to accompany the verse dialogue. Such sounds as whisks used on metal wastebaskets, Kleenex hummed through over combs, and erasers laid on piano strings were investigated and taped!

The day of the assembly performance arrived. A puppet booth was improvised on stage by drawing the curtains to the opening required to expose the electrically controlled movie screen. Three-foot-high corrugated paper was stretched between the lower portion of the opening with gym mats spread on the floor behind. The puppeteers thus could kneel comfortably on these mats while manipulating the puppets.

The program began with a slide lecture by the art teacher on the symbolist-surrealist Miro, which ended with the students' chosen picture. The movie screen was then slowly raised, revealing the puppets in identical positions to the figures in the picture. The lonely musical sounds began, and the figures moved to the haunting recitation of the verse-dialogue. An aesthetic educational experience had been successfully completed.

I hasten to add that frequently I and my students have relied solely on the artistic expertise of the class. I am not a musician, dancer, or artist, but I have encouraged students to experiment unabashedly with their own abilities in order to incorporate a freewheeling use of other arts with their drama improvisations. Remembering that dramatic moments frequently lie near the solar plexus, a teacher must sense those pressure points not only in the curriculum but in her specific class. A teacher who relates quickly to a group will keep her antenna tuned for reception rather than broadcast immediately a curriculum that does not relate to the group. The teacher enters alertly in limbo, absorbing what Stanislavsky calls the actor's "offstage beat" before she steps into her teaching role. If a high school class has had little experience in spontaneous performance, it may feel threatened if asked to go immediately into improvisations. Discussions, debates, and reasoning conducted from desks arranged in a circle, enabling everyone to be seen, are the easiest introductions to curriculum drama.

Many *trips* lend themselves to drama when one realizes that a dramatic plot is not expressed graphically as the shortest distance between two points. A plot can better be expressed by a rising zigzag line, illustrating an action drive from point *A* to point *B* that is interrupted by obstacles and conflicts, thus building suspense:

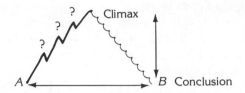

On the top of the rise sits the climax. The quick downward path to the conclusion might be visualized as a spiral that wraps up all the loose threads of the plot as it drops to the conclusion. With these drama fundamentals in mind, a teacher can find dramatic elements in much of the basic curriculum.

Curriculum drama is a method by which potentially dramatic moments within required studies are identified and developed in order to heighten emotionally the students' response to the curriculum, thus deepening the learning experience. The process of learning occurs within sound artistic principles with drama frequently acting as the coordinating art in combination with other arts.

Curriculum drama has provded an invaluable tool for value training, where alternative choices can be tried on and results and implications studied. Educating to mitigate the trauma of future shock is natural material for improvisational work, which can be sparked by questions introduced by "What if . . .?" "What if the energy crisis continues to worsen?" And an exercise in moving backward in time: "What if the French Revolution was fought with modern technology?" Change the time or place, or alter a point of view, and fresh dimensions are introduced into education.

The key to curriculum drama is for the teacher to guide creativity into quality areas of learning rather than be satisfied with prescribed exercises ill adapted to the particular moment in a particular class. The teacher must know not only subject matter; he must also remain open to suggestions by his students. Too often a creative teacher imposes his own creativity on a class, thus smothering the creative attempts of his pupils. The real trick in teaching any creative art is to be able to sense how much to give a class in order to guide and stimulate them, then to withdraw from the creative activity except for helping the class build tension and excitement. Finally, the teacher must indicate moments of reflective in-depth learning, where conclusions and deeper meanings can be formed.

The teacher's ability to tune quickly into the mood and interest of the class, his ability to find dramatic moments within the curriculum and structure those moments in order to indicate the framework within which students can feel free to create are important techniques. That true creativity is not dependent on complete freedom is one of the first concepts a class must learn. All art contains inherent structure, and the neophyte frequently needs guidance in finding the correct form.

This method of humanizing learning and relating it to where the class is has been particularly effective with inner-city children. I was asked to evaluate a student teacher's creative dramatics class with a group of deprived second graders. The teacher was desperately trying to hold their attention long enough to tell the story and cast the characters of *Cinderella*. The children did not understand kings and queens, nor were they interested in them. Pandemonium had set in, heightened by several sets of hands banging on the piano.

Suddenly the teacher grabbed up a sprig of lily of the valley she had tucked into her buttonhole that morning. "Look, children," she cried, "See what I found in my garden." Instantly she had the attention of most of the class. "What is *your* favorite flower?" she continued. She was shouted a bevy of answers. "How would you each like to be your favorite flower growing from a tiny little seed? Let's see how tiny you can make yourselves."

The focus of the class was still being shattered by an uncoordinated pair of hands pounding on the piano keys. "Softly, Sheila! Softly! Your noise is making the plants wither." Several children promptly faded to the floor! "We must have soft, growing music . . . *that's* it! See? You're making them grow." The pianist's fingers were dancing on tiptoe! "And now I shall transplant each little bud into my flower bed where it can stretch its stems and grow."

Tears silently coursed down my cheeks as I watched the young teacher gently enfold each little child and carry him or her to the "growing plot." Belief and concentration, trust and loving care, had suddenly entered that room. From there the teacher could lead her class into the study of all the miracles of the beginning of life.

How gratifying to read the following remarks by Neil Postman, one of America's outstanding educators:

> What we have to do is to make the study of one's own feelings a legitimate school activity, invested with an importance at least equal to that presently given to map-reading skills or spelling. This can be done in a variety of ways . . . from regularly scheduled rap sessions, to seminars in value clarification or role playing or adolescent psychology, to, best of all, the acceptance of the fact that no sensible distinction can be made between cognitive and affective learning, from which it follows that in every course, in every activity, a serious interest MUST be taken in the feeling of the students.[7]

Anywhere human feelings and relationships need to be studied, curriculum drama techniques are a potentially effective method of teaching.

NOTES

1. Harold Taylor, *Art and the Intellect* (New York: Museum of Modern Art, 1960), pp. 12–13.
2. Roger M. Williams, "Why Children Should Draw, the Surprising Link Between Art and Learning," *Saturday Review*, 3 September 1977, pp. 11–16.
3. Dorothy Heathcote, *Three Rooms Waiting*, 16-mm color film produced by the British Broadcasting Company.
4. Lewis Thomas, *The Lives of a Cell* and *The Medusa and the Snail* (New York: Viking, 1974, 1979).
5. Dorothy Heathcote, *Dorothy Heathcote Talks to Teachers*, 16-mm color film produced by Northwestern University Film Library.
6. A. E. Abbott, *Flatland* (New York: Dover, 1963).
7. Neil Postman, "The Ecology of Learning," English Journal, April 1974, p. 60.

Dramatizing History

Joanna Halpert Kraus

Joanna Halpert Kraus is on the faculty of the State University of New York, College at Brockport. Previously she taught at the State University of New York, College at Purchase and College at New Paltz; New York City Community College; and Columbia University, where she taught creative drama to Agnes Russell School students. Her academic background includes degrees from Sarah Lawrence, the University of California, and Teachers College, Columbia, with further study at the University of London. She is active in the Children's Theatre Association, but she is best known for her literary work, which includes stories, articles, and three full-length plays for children. The Ice Wolf, Mean to Be Free, and Vasalisa have all been widely produced. In 1971 the Children's Theatre Association awarded Joanna Kraus the Charlotte Chorpenning Cup for Achievement in Playwrighting. Her latest play, Circus Home, was written on a Creative Artists Public Service Fellowship in Playwrighting. In this essay she discusses content and ways of working in the classroom.

Confusion! Conflict! Crises! These are the critical moments of human history. This is the substance of drama.

Why dramatize history? Because history is the story of human beings caught at crucial moments in their lives, making difficult, sometimes painful, decisions.

To receive any illumination from a study of human history, one needs to conjecture on the motives propelling the performers. One needs to comprehend the indecision, the ambivalence, the vacillating opinions that existed. One needs to ponder the possible internal causes of external events.

Both the study of history and the study of drama should illustrate and illuminate human behavior and experience. One has the opportunity, via the structure of improvised drama, not only of sharing recorded factual data with students but of encouraging them to experience, kinesthetically and emotionally, the conditions under which indicents occurred.

Thus, it is in a sense inaccurate to permit only cardboard heroes and villains to parade across the textbooks of America, instilling images and ideals that often reveal sterile half-truths. Perhaps a worse sin educationally is that such a presentation is boring.

If we believe that the mind and spirit can soar in the classroom, and if we as educators concur with Dewey's premise that one learns by doing, then it is incumbent upon us to find exercises that will provide experiences for all aspects of human growth.

It is my conviction that creative dramatics, roleplaying, and participatory theatre, which involve mental, physical, and emotional participation, as well as the literate, imaginative, formal theatre script, which combines artistry with authenticity, are all viable ways of removing unnecessary dust from the tangible records of past events.

According to Charles DeCarlo, the greatest problem facing educators today is "how to encourage in an age of large organizations, individual moral sensibilities and human responsibility."[1] Or, as I see it, can we escape from the oppressing sense that events of history simply happened to us and begin to examine the consequences as a result of human action—or the lack of it?

In his eloquent essay "An Approach to Literature," Robert Penn Warren divided literary conflict among the following three areas: man against nature, man against others, man against himself. The classic divisions seem appropriate for the study of history and drama as well. But the creative artist's task springs from, rather than ends with, documentation. The artist must search below the surface. Art asks questions about the human condition.

Both the study of history and the study of drama should illustrate and illuminate human behavior and experience. One has the opportunity via the structure of improvised drama not only to share recorded factual data with students but also to encourage them to experience kinesthetically and emotionally the conditions under which, and the process through which, certain decisions were made that led to specific historic events.

In improvised drama the participant is the medium through which transpires the emotional range of human response. The substance of drama is conflict, people confronted and challenged by situations with which they must cope. Drama needs nothing more than a place for ideas to develop. Costumes, scenery, makeup, lighting, properties are the intricate trappings that provide the spectacle, the visual illusion. But this glamorous addition is secondary to the primary function: an illumination of human concerns.

Any teacher who does not use drama as a learning tool is deliberately eliminating one of the most native and natural tools at her disposal. The desire to play is part of the human condition from birth onward. The use of drama in education is simply taking advantage of a propensity natural to the human being.

If we as educators are agreed that education implies more than cerebral effort and that the mind and spirit can soar in the classroom, and if we as teachers working in classrooms concur with Dewey's premise that one learns by doing, then it is incumbent upon the teacher to find exercises that will provide experiences for all three aspects of human growth.

Most of those who teach creative dramatics agree with the official Children's Theatre Association's definition, arrived at after much deliberation:

> Creative dramatics, in which children with the guidance of imaginative teacher or leader create scenes or plays and perform them with improvised dialogue and action. Personal development of players is the goal, rather than the satisfaction of a child audience. Scenery and costumes are rarely used. If this informal drama is presented before an audience, it is usually in the nature of a demonstration.[2]

But, as one would anticipate, there are differences among the various practitioners. A pioneer in the area of creative dramatics, founder of the Children's Theatre Association of Baltimore, Maryland, and author of *Creative Play Acting*, Isabel B. Burger defines creative dramatics as the "expression of thought and feelings in the child's own terms, through action, the spoken word, or both."[3] Brian Way, director of the Theatre Centre in London and author of *Development Through Drama*, states that "a basic definition of drama might be simply 'to practice living'."[4] Drama is as concerned with exploring and mastering the emotional self as it is with discovering and mastering the physical self.[5] Though both Burger and Way have as their rationale the development and understanding of people, their structural approaches to this end differ. Burger's method, demonstrated in the creative dramatics classes that were the cornerstone of the Theatre's activity, moved from pantomime to mood to change-of-mood to dialogue.[6] Each step placed progressively greater demands on the creativity of the student. Way's circle of human development included concentration, the senses, imagination, physical self, speech, emotion, and intellect.[7] His exercises were designed to develop the individual areas, but he was not concerned with the point at which one commences, only that the circle ultimately be completed.

I believe that in creative dramatics a student experiences with his total being the imaginary circumstance. He exercises and trains his imagination while he disciplines his body to express what his mind and spirit dictate. If creative dramatics provides only an acceptable outlet for raging emotion, it is providing a therapeutic moment, which should have a therapist on hand to interpret. If, on the other hand, the experience develops the young person's imaginative powers, ability to conceptualize, argue, decide, and understand with his total being, then it is drama.

My rationale does not differ from Burger or Way, but I would add that in a country of conformity we need to develop creativity; in a nation where corruption is commonplace, we need to reintroduce individual integrity; in a period that is increasingly impersonal, we need to establish pride in identity; in a world where the generation gap seems sharply accentuated, we need to explore the causes of alienation; and in a terrifying time of tolerance for the intolerable, we need to develop a sense of commitment and responsibility, first to self, then to others.

The current bible of educators, Bloom's *Taxonomy of Educational Objectives*, lists a hierarchy of developmental skills in three separate areas of learning: the cognitive domain, the affective domain, and the psychomotor domain. In dramatizing historical material, one inevitably touches upon some of the skills or levels of each. However, the tendency when teaching any academic subject is to assume that the cognitive area is more important, that it is more important for the student to learn the dates and the names of little or unknown incidents than to explore the emotional reality of how individuals might have felt. I believe that this is shallow pedagogy. As George Shaftel recently stated, "History is not just a record of events. History deals with people thinking and feeling. Events are important, but so are feelings. Feelings impel action!"[8] Fannie Shaftel further commented that although there has been a push to increase cognitive content learning, it is a false notion to think that we can totally separate affective and cognitive areas. "Although some tasks are heavily intellectual or heavily emotive, behavior does not separate. . . . We move through feelings to factual material."[9]

One could not, and should not, avoid facts in dramatizing history. But facts by themselves are easily memorized and easily forgotten. Jenny Egan, founder of the Four Winds Theatre, which in its unique format explores past and present history, works theatrically to make the audience "feel the significance of historic facts."[10]

For too long, students have needlessly groaned their way through history. Students and tourists alike have sat and stood at historic sites, manifesting through their posture varying degrees of patient resignation, while a guide or teacher droned on. It is my conviction that creative dramatics, the participation play,[11] roleplaying[12]—all of which involve physical participation as well as emotional participation—and the literate, imaginative theatrical script that combines authenticity with artistry are all viable ways of removing unnecessary dust from the tangible records of beliefs and events which, after all, shaped the present.

> History is so much more than building and an inventory of artifacts. It is a way of living that can only be transmitted to the visitor through exciting his imagination. The dissemination of information, no matter how effective, can no longer do that. We believe that a theatrical experience, a living recreation of history can.[13]

The historian Henry S. Commager has suggested that history teachers and textbooks utilize a realistic approach to the decisions people have made in history. Many political scientists, taking their cue from the behavioral and physical scientists, have advocated the use of simulation or symbolic models of political happenings.[14]

Despite Dewey's familiar educational motto that we learn by doing, and the subsequent supporting material by Kilpatrick, Theodore Sizer recently pointed out in *Places for Learning, Places for Joy* that almost all our education is "offered vicariously and in the abstract. Children are expected to learn how others feel by reading about them. . . . We read about the Revolutionary War, and now we know how tyrannical George III was."[15]

There are two approaches to the dramatic improvising of historic material. One serves to vivify and enhance the factual content; the other serves to demonstrate the emotional content of a conjectured, though plausible scene. In either case the participant needs to confront the problem that faces the specific individual or gorup and solve it within the context of time, place, and characters. As Dorothy Heathcote has pointed out, the student in any improvised scene needs to "take up attitudes and viewpoints and for the time believe in them."[16]

The Belgrade Theatre in Coventry, England, has delved into historical material in their theatre-in-education program. Stuart Bennett wrote:

> With older children we used social history themes widely. Occupational mime was used to create an identity with a social role. The pupils were then, in their roles, given a common experience and put into a situation which they could only resolve through communication. The aim was common to good education and the main stream of theatre—to extend the participant's understanding of people and how they relate to one another. Secondary pupils explored the life of seventeenth century London through improvisation and then reconstructed the Great Fire with ourselves acting the historical roles and the pupils the people. Juniors used similar background methods to explore the Lady Godiva legend and the Middle Ages. Again all the children took part all the time.[17]

The Frozen Lands, a documentary program for junior schools, related to Shackleton's journey to the Antartic.[18]

In conjunction with the American Revolution Bicentennial Commission, graduate students enrolled in my Children's Theatre Workshop at State University College, New Paltz, helped develop an outdoor participation play based on the actual incident of the burning and destruction of Kingston by the British in 1777 (*Only One House Left*).

Previously at State University College, Purchase, my students and I developed a creative dramatics scenario on the building of the first transcontinental railroad (*All Aboard 2-6-10 Miles a Day*). The purpose was to stimulate interest in the characters, the events, the conflicts, and the

At Promontory Point, Utah, press photographers snap pictures as a dignitary pounds in the gold spike that joined the Union Pacific and the Central Pacific railroads. Courtesy of Joanna Halpert Kraus. Photograph by Leo Spies.

decisions that were part of an emerging nation. Geography, geology, politics, immigration, prejudice, treatment of the native American, economics, ecology, private enterprise, military involvement, modes of cross-country transportation, the decision-making role of Congress, use of media to communicate news—all were touched on as the children discussed, prepared, and created their version of the history that occurred a little more than a century ago.

There is a fascinating account by R. Verrier, Monks Public Schools, England, in which the instructor illustrates an approach which utilized drama, English, and history in teaching an incident that occurred during the English Civil War involving King Charles, John Pym, and Members of Parliament. The teaching was done with secondary school students placed in three groups of differing academic ability. All three groups took part in preliminary discussions, the analysis of the given situation, and refinement of the problem; but the form of the involvement and the focus differed.

> The able form of pupils showed special interest in the legalities of the situation and the "correct" ritual of events. This interest led them on to a study of documents from which historians themselves learn about events. They attempted to produce "original sources" such as correspondence between the King and the Speaker of the House of Commons as well as private correspondence between the King and his friends. The mixed ability form were interested in the reactions of ordinary people and the drama of the King's abortive attempt to arrest Pym. They produced a tape to "help" other pupils of "our age" to understand the situation. . . . The weaker form . . . centered around the plight of the wanted man, John Pym. They constructed group stories show-

ing how several families living in *any street* might react to a fugitive from Royal justice.[19]

In a recent lecture by George Shaftel discussing role playing and history, he described several role-playing situations that would permit young people to focus on ethical values and group decision making. One incident occurred in the mid-nineteenth century. Two youths playing by the river chanced to see a black man struggling in the water, a white man in close pursuit. To save a drowning man might well be an act of disinterested mercy, but to assist an escaped slave in the 1850s was a criminal offense.[20] Do they see and assist? Do they see and ignore? Whatever action taken, the young people must realize the probable consequences of their behavior. Another of Shaftel's role-playing situations dealt with the members of the Interim Committee, in the midst of World War II. They had to determine whether or not to use the atomic bomb.[21] Role-playing situations grapple with moral issues and the urgent realities of the historic period, but they also demand that young people consider the ethics and values involved, which transcend any time line.

All drama should gradually move the participant from an awareness and acceptance of self to an awareness and acceptance of others.

At Western Washington University, where I was invited to be part of the Summer Institute for Drama and the Child, students developed a participation play based on the accounts of early settlers of Puget Sound. The teacher-actors developed a scenario that illuminated the plights and predicaments of the journey west by wagon train.

One of the most poignant scenes came near the end of the play when a distraught wagonmaster called everyone together. Throughout the six-month journey the families had battled dust storms, buffalo stampedes, cholera, dysentery, consumption, floods, scorching sun, dishonest guides, and lack of supplies.

The wagonmaster gravely spoke about the weak cattle and the first signs of frost. "We won't make it unless we go faster." There was a silence. "We have to lighten the load. We're gonna have to give up some of our prize possessions and family treasures. We'll never make it unless we do."

"I've already given up my prize possession," a woman sobbed softly, thinking of her dead family.

"What are you willing to give up?" the wagonmaster urged.

The master's wife had been sewing a huge patchwork quilt that would be finished "when we get there." Now she picked it up and placed it gently on the ground. "I'll be the first," she said quietly.

Slowly, solemnly the group began to lug imaginary featherbeds, parlor organs, rocking chairs, china, dolls, and huge trunks to the center.

"Take what you can," the wagonmaster scrawled on a hastily painted sign for future wagon trains. "We couldn't."

Today, only a century and a quarter later, one can travel from coast to coast in six hours instead of six months. Each time I fly in pressurized comfort, I think of those first crossings on the Oregon Trail. In terms of our history, what a short time ago that journey occurred.

The children who came to the participation play were compassionately involved with the aspirations and suffering of the emigrants. But is that really so strange when history is presented with real people struggling with grave problems? When global neighbors less than a day's jet ride away seem to "threaten" us with ideas, values, habits, and life styles that appear totally alien, can we possibly coexist peacefully? Incidents of history trenchantly and tragically reveal our limited tolerance. But never before in our history has it been as vital as it is today that we begin to respect the varying expressions of human behavior springing from cultural differences and respond to these differences as manifestations of the infinite variety of possibility in the species.

Dr. Shaftel believes that an individual is only tested as such when he behaves within the framework of a group.[22] We do not live in isolation. We never have. And history is as much a record of group behaviorial action as it is individual aspiration. The concept of decision making or choice, action, consequence is as crucial to the structure of drama as it is to the comprehension of human history.

In using improvisational drama to vivify and enhance the teaching of historical material, there are pitfalls. If one is dealing with specific factual data and a variety of primary and secondary sources, it is often near impossible to create the well-rounded characters or a taut drama that the playwright might wish. One is bound to some extent by statements that were made or by a progression or sequence of events that may seem somewhat implausible in the latter part of the twentieth century. Improvisational dialogue may be sincere, but flat or filled with unintentional anachronisms. On the other hand, the authentic wording of a serious statement may, on occasion, be so pompous that its forced inclusion would be self-defeating. Participants may become so intrigued with external behavior that they partially neglect internal motivation and, unless assisted, ignore the emotion or the action.

In emphasizing the process of involvement, the end product may not be as devoid of anachronisms or dramatic liberties as the historian might wish. For example, in our production of *Only One House Left*, there were unintentional "O.K.s" uttered, although students knew they should avoid contemporary slang. In preparing the play we deliberately ignored the fact that the eighteenth-century Council of Safety was comprised solely of men. We encouraged both males and females to participate as villagers in order to involve all the children in the decision-making process. In the original letter sent by General Vaughn, the name Esopus was used when referring to Kingston. Since that would have only added confusion, we changed the reference to Kingston. When the president of the Council received the alarming news that the British fleet was at the landing, there is documented evidence that he sent a letter to Clinton. Rather than delay the improvisational exodus, we took a sentence of this letter and incorporated it into the news brought by the messenger who interrupted the Council meeting. We did this to build dramatic tension and to facilitate the immediate evacuation of the village.

Finally, the building of Kingston took place eight months after the fire. But during the play the action is continuous. Time passes via the one meeting in Hurley. In this instance the long passage of time, which is historically accurate, would be dramatically awkward.

The pre- and postdiscussions are a vital and integral part of the dramatization process. During the preliminary discussions, the leader should elicit what knowledge the children have and supplement that with selected specific details—pictures, photographs, maps, replicas of relevant period items, in addition to evoking the possible thoughts and feelings of the characters. During the postdiscussion, leaders, teachers, and parents can separate facts from opinions, theatrical devices from accurate details. The leader can help young people discover that all printed material is researched, written, and edited from a point of view, and that a profusion of sources may reveal a profusion of facts on the same subject.

One must also be careful to particularize general events. For example, when the townspeople of Kingston returned to their devastated homes and picked their way through the rubble and smoldering ashes, leaders softly suggested, "Find your home. See if there is anything left we can use." This gave purpose to the exploration and dramatically controlled what might otherwise have been vague wandering. Children quickly returned with apples, potatoes, wool, a family Bible, a silver jewel box—and burned British money!

One day after the fire a boy reported that he'd found a car. Puzzled, the president of the Council stated that he didn't know what the term meant. The boy frowned, thought for a moment, then grinned and said, "I mean a horse and cart!" Children often confuse historic time lines. They are apt to lump great lives together under that amorphous term, the *past*.

But dramatization of specific incidents can help intensify one's interest or stimulate one's enthusiasm in acquiring more knowledge of a place, event, or historic period. When children become intellectually, kinesthetically, and emotionally absorbed in solving a problem, whether the event is in the past or present, they are capable of passionate intensity.

From the historian's viewpoint, improvisational dramatizing of history serves as a motivating session or as a stimulus. But it is these very excursions into the thoughts and feelings of other people in the past, confronted with an urgent problem to solve, that develop the basic skills we hold so high in our current educational thinking: the ability to concentrate, to move purposefully, to develop ideas, to function effectively as an individual within a group. I have referred to the last skill as the ability to preserve the "I" within the "we," for I believe that is the ultimate test of a truly democratic society.

In an age where our children may well be ambassadors in space, should we not give some attention to that quality that puts us higher than the beasts, albeit lower than the angels—the capacity for empathy?

NOTES

1. Charles DeCarlo, "Molding Integrity Seen as Key Teaching Task," *New York Times*, 16 January 1974, sec. C, p. 79.
2. Ann Viola, "Drama With and For Children: An Interpretation of Terms," *Educational Theatre Journal* 8 (May 1956): 139.
3. Isabel B. Burger, *Creative Play Acting* (New York: Ronald, 1950), p. 2.
4. Brian Way, *Development Through Drama* (London: Longmans, Green, 1967), p. 6.
5. Ibid., p. 219.
6. Burger, *Creative Play Acting*, p. xiii.
7. Way, *Development Through Drama*, p. 13.
8. Fannie and George Shaftel, "Working with Feelings Through Role Playing," lecture-demonstration at the Association for Childhood Education International Study Conference, Washington, D.C., 17 April 1874.
9. Ibid.
10. Jenny Egan, introductory remarks at *The Raree Show*, New York, N.Y., 21 February 1974.
11. A participation play is an extension of creative dramatics in which the audience becomes part of the action and determines portions of the play.
12. Role playing is a process in which a problem is presented, generally related to value structure and human relations. Various solutions are explored, enacted, and discussed by the participants.
13. Vernon D. Dame, superintendent, Manhattan Group National Park Service. Program from *The Raree Show*, The Four Winds Theatre, February 1974.
14. Fannie and George Shaftel, *Role-Playing for Social Values* (Englewood Cliffs, N.J.: Prentice-Hall, 1967), pp. 9–13.
15. Theodore R. Sizer, *Places for Learning, Places for Joy* (Cambridge, Mass.: Harvard University Press, 1973) p. 75.
16. Dorothy Heathcote, "Drama and Education: Subject or System," in *Drama and Theatre in Education*, ed. Nigel Dodd and Winifred Hickson (London: Heinemann Educational Books, 1971), p. 57.
17. Stuart Bennett, "The Belgrade's Bones: Fifth Year of Theatre in Education," bulletin, Belgrade Theatre, Coventry, England, 1971, pp. 4–5.
18. Rosemary Birbeck, "Theatre in Education," bulletin, Belgrade Theatre, Coventry, England, 1969, p. 2.
19. R. Verrier, Appendix IV, in Dodd and Hickson, *Drama and Theatre in Education*, pp. 173–74.
20. Fannie and George Shaftel, "Working with Feelings."
21. Ibid.
22. Fannie Shaftel, discussion, Association for Childhood Education International Study Conference, Washington, D.C., 18 April 1974.

"Acting" and Children

Grace Stanistreet

Grace Stanistreet, founder of the Children's Centre for the Creative Arts at Adelphi University in Garden City, Long Island, is a pioneer in the field of the creative arts as learning. Whereas the majority of programs offer children's theatre, creative dramatics, or movement classes, the Adelphi program includes all performing and visual arts in its curriculum. This multidisciplinary approach, with its emphasis on individual development, has attracted many visitors since its inception in 1937. Grace Stanistreet has published two books, Teaching Is a Dialogue *and* Learning Is a Happening, *and has been in constant demand as a workshop leader and teacher of teachers. In 1972, Adelphi University conferred an honorary doctorate in recognition of her long record of distinguished work in the field. In this essay she explains the point of view that has guided the work of the Children's Centre from the beginning.*

Attitude

Theatre activity can help youth face and adjust to reality when it is understood by the teacher that to create the illusion of reality, the actor must be able to recognize the drama of the real. Too often, teachers of dramatic activity for children believe that fantasy, not reality, is the way to stimulate the child. They resort to magic and gimmicks as lures. They "play" at theatre. They dramatize many stories, but "acting out" is not enough; story playing does offer children opportunity for emotional release, but we have overemphasized this aspect. Growth and learning are made possible by a serious approach to the study of acting as it relates to living. Techniques for acting are techniques

115

for living, but they need to be related and applied. Children like to work seriously and to be challenged by an activity for which they have the equipment.

Theatre stripped to its essence—the presentation of life problems—is a natural means of expression and of learning for the child. An eight-year-old expressed his understanding of acting: "Acting is all about knowing who you are, what you are doing and why." Another said, "You can't do anything very well if your heart isn't in it. I think acting is all about heart and feelings." Such expressions indicate a child's response to a serious approach. Yet many teachers fortunate enough to work in this area continue to take the playful approach, which is unworthy of both adult and child. It is true that when this is the only approach a child knows, he will play along with the adult. In so indulging the adult, he may demonstrate a greater maturity than that of the teacher. The teacher who leads the child step by step to a recognition of acting as a demonstration of life and to an awareness of his equipment, and who provides the opportunity for its use, is rewarded by enthusiastic response and proof of competence.

Do I mean by the above statement that fantasy is ruled out? No. Fantasy has a place in children's acting class because it requires knowledge and deliberate capers of the imagination. But imagination, soaring without a base from which to depart and return, is like a plane that has lost contact with the control tower. Fantastic tricks of imagination, magic, and props to stimulate result in theatrical pretence unworthy of either adult or child.

Performance

Some confusion exists about the terms *creative dramatics* and *children's theatre*. Some view creative dramatics as a spontaneous activity and children's theatre as a planned, memorized, directed play. They see the activity as creative, and children's public performance as not creative. In my opinion, the activity is a long-term preparation for eventual performance. Activity concerned with any form of communication requires a receiving station, and reception by an audience can be a vital contribution to a child's development. But the audience itself must be prepared and educated to play its part. How this is done is not our concern here. And the children coming from the classroom activity to a performance must be prepared by an attitude toward performance, which views it as an enlarged classroom. The material of the performance itself should be an outgrowth of the classroom activity, not a new experience achieved through an artificial process. As we hope to extend all learning in the classroom into life, so performance can be a bridge between the classroom and the world.

A successful performance enjoyed both by actors and audience can make the activity more meaningful and delightful. But a performance by children should not be repeated. Repetition of a performance requires a special skill to achieve the freshness and newness of the first time. This requires work and study for performance sake. In children, we develop skills for the sake of their contribution to growth; for example, courage and confidence to think, feel, and act harmoniously for an immediate purpose.

In further justification of the statement recommending one performance at a time, it is my belief that the emphasis must be placed on the process by which performance is achieved. Repeated performances place the emphasis on the product rather than the process. Further, the repetition, even though dialogue may be improvised and not memorized, tends to lose the original vitality and therefore lessen the satisfactions derived.

Children and teacher must see performance as sharing rather than showing. It is an opportunity for children to learn the responsibilities of both initiator and receiver. They should see performance as a cooperative endeavor, not an exhibition of "me."

Teacher Qualifications

The teacher of acting for children must approach his work with respect and a sound knowledge of theatre as a medium of communication. He must have an understanding of the creative possibilities in conducting the formal (the play) or the informal dramatic program in the classroom. Many assume that the classroom work is creative and the play is not. Either will be as creative or uncreative as the director, or teacher, is creative or uncreative. The creative teacher-director is concerned with what happens in the course of the preparation of the play. This justifies the play as an activity for youth and determines the quality of the result.

A specialist who teaches acting to children should be able to teach acting to students of any age. The reverse need not be true. The teacher of adult actors is not necessarily a good teacher of children. But principles and concepts are shared by both. The teacher of children needs, in addition to his knowledge of theatre, to know how to apply this knowledge to serve children's needs, which means he must like children and know how children learn and grow. The teacher of children knows he teaches more effectively by indirection than by direction. That is, he must present in himself all the qualities he is dedicated to developing in children. There is in his attitude an understanding of and respect for the natural capacities of children, and an attitude of humility that admits that he can learn from his students. There is no trace of patronage, sentimentality, or superiority in his approach.

Good acting is the result of a creative process. The process may be initiated by the director or the teacher, but it takes places within the individual. This inner activity results in overt action. This is self-direction. Arriving at his ends by a creative process makes it possible for the actor to achieve the totality of being, or wholeness, that we desire for children. This goal supports those who would have all schools include acting experience for every child.

Saying good-bye at the close of the session. Courtesy of Grace Stanistreet. Photo by Hank Shulman.

But the experience can be effective only under the guidance of a creative teacher, and there are too few teachers of such understanding. Perhaps this is because not enough situations demand this quality and kind of teaching. This will continue to be true until the public recognizes the difference between a superficial and a real approach to youth through the avenue of theatre. The public must be led to understand that the superficial approach results in imitation and exhibition. The real approach produces creative thinking, feeling, and acting individuals.

One problem is overcoming the concept that acting is for the stage and only for "talented" people. Presenting the study of acting as a means of successful living and learning is not enough to change these concepts or to overcome the fear that acting lessons will make a child exhibitionistic. Indeed, it can do this if the child is studying acting for professional purposes. On the other hand, if the teacher presents acting to children in its simplest form— acting is doing—they accept and understand it. And if they are *to do* (to act), they must *be* and *think*.

Rationale

This kind of activity may be new to children, but they respond to it. It is an opportunity to use what they have and to succeed because they are not in competition. It is harder for adults to accept and understand, for they are often suspicious that acting is solely recreational, a fun thing. The following dialogue was written to help parents understand.

Parent   Why do you refer to your classes as acting classes rather than dramatic classes? You say they are classes for children and laymen, for educational and developmental reasons. I thought acting referred to classes designed to train the professional performer. Acting makes me think immediately of the so-called talented child, who is being trained for the professional stage.

Teacher   Lessons that an actor ought to learn are lessons for living life. What are the stage, drama, theatre but selected, re-created life situations and problems? Therefore, the actor needs to know first how to live his life role, how to be himself, how to be an authority of himself. This is a prerequisite to understanding and being authoritative about the roles he may assume.

Parent   But doesn't dramatics do this?

Teacher   In the dramatics club or class the lessons generally begin with an assigned role. This is what the student expects and wants. The layman, whether child or adult, loves the chance to get out of himself. It is generally thought of as a desirable "release." The truth is that the assumed role may make the student more conscious of himself, because he looks for his effect upon others. He is concerned not with *what* he is doing, but *how* he is doing. He may have changed himself externally, but internally he is unable to encompass or identify with the character. The character cannot absorb him because he is self-absorbed. He is thinking (while going through actions of his character) his own thoughts, feeling his own feelings. He is a house divided. This kind of acting for effect may seem to succeed but contributes nothing of lasting value.

   Dramatics class implies dramatic performance at some time. Often the class exists for the preparation of a performance. An acting class is concerned only with the growth of the individual.

Parent   What are some of your reasons for teaching acting to the child or to the layman?

Teacher   What are the qualities you desire to have, to make life more satisfying, to fulfill yourself? Would one of them be greater self-confidence or trust? The actor must know and trust himself. Whether or not he is aware of it, when he acts a role, he reveals himself. There is an idea that acting is good for the layman because it's a kind of defense or disguise that permits him freedom to do what he could not do in his own role—the "release" I mentioned earlier. Encouraging a child "to put on an act" does not develop his personal strength. It makes his need to hide greater. The first lessons, then, must be directed toward helping the individual trust himself, helping him not to be afraid of showing what he is—to perform rather than to put on a performance.

Parent   I do not go along with you all the way on the idea that play-acting is bad. That is what you are saying, isn't it?

Teacher   No! Play-acting has a place in the acting class but I am trying to make clear that the first concern of the serious teacher is to help the child accept himself. There is much play-acting that goes on in an acting class for learning purposes. What I am doing here in our discussion is stripping to fundamentals.

The teacher can then go on to explain her other reasons for teaching acting. A second reason may be that acting—honest, sincere acting— requires the harmonizing of all parts of the individual—the thinking, feeling, doing parts. Education is concerned with developing wholeness for health and for learning. Experience with acting is one way this can be done. What happens when you see something that offends you? Your whole being is focused in protest; you say, "Oh, no!" And when you speak there is no mistaking your meaning. You have expressed thought and feeling in words and action. This is you functioning sincerely. Good, sincere acting requires response of the whole being.

A third reason is that in our society we are judged by our public speech and behavior. I do not mean standing up to make a speech. Public speech and action is that expressive behavior called for in group situations of any kind— classroom, parties, meetings, games—wherever interaction is called for.

In the intimate familiar situation all people are capable of being individuals, expressing feeling freely without inhibitions. Very young children generally have no inhibitions. They act themselves, often to the embarrassment of adults. But they lose this freedom in time. They catch the pervading disease, "What will people think?" They become self-conscious and, to be sure, they are not different from others. They follow the crowd. They learn to hide what they think or they stop thinking. Voice and action in public becomes tentative. It is apparent that the individual's concern is with the effect of the utterance and not with the truth. Acting must be concerned with truth. Youth needs confidence to be itself in public as well as in private. I do not mean an undisciplined self and offensive behavior, for this is as unnatural as putting on an act. I mean the ability to function as freely in a group as in the intimate situation, to speak out, to move the body with ease. Notice the narrow vocal range, the limited, tentative gestures of many people in the public situation. They are dull, lifeless, and ineffective.

A fourth reason for teaching acting is that it is natural to play-act. Children learn by re-creating life situations, by being mommy, teacher, nurse, etc. And all of us enjoy in varying degrees a little limelight. Limelight is as necessary to growth as sunlight. Because it is natural, there is enjoyment in acting and thus possibility for learning also.

A fifth reason is related to wholeness. The actor's instrument is himself— his whole self. Many teachers become preoccupied with the physical instrument, forgetting there must be something behind the front, and herein lies a danger. The visible agent must be expressive of the inner agent, which is where the responsibility lies. The inner agent must be a storehouse of riches to be selected and expressed visibly and understandably. In working with children in an acting class, the teacher's concern is less with the outer means than with the inner. He feels responsibility for developing and building these inner resources. He does it by cultivating the avenues of the senses, opening them wide. He helps the child to recognize and become aware of sights, sounds, textures, temperatures, smells, tastes in the world around him. He provides opportunities to put these sensations to use so that they will remain forever in the storehouse of memory. And in widening these avenues in and out, there is the possibility of developing an ability to see that which is invisible.

A sixth reason—and though I state it last, it is by no means the least important—acting is communicating. It is strange that in a world so communications conscious, there is so little person-to-person communication. Communication is interaction. Interaction indicates that something is happening here and now. The actor must achieve not only person-to-person contact but person-to-group. He learns to assume responsibility for both initiating and responding alternately. He learns that the initiator is responsible for the response he receives. He learns that alert and active listening is essential to achieve vitality and interest. He learns the difference between talking at and talking with, the difference between recited dialogue and spontaneous dialogue. He learns to speak out and not to be afraid of the sound of his public voice.

At this point the dialogue might proceed something like this:

Parent   I see. I like "building the resources." This means developing a resourceful person. You have made a good case for acting. But how do you teach it?

Teacher   That is the most difficult question to answer, for there is no prescription. A teacher with the ideas I have given you will find his own ways to achieve these ends.

I indicated that the first lesson in acting should establish self-trust. The teacher might begin with a simple exercise, such as asking the student just to stand quietly and look at the group. Or he might ask him to look at an object, while he himself is the object of group attention. He might do any number of things to help the student achieve the ability to focus. In focusing upon a person, thing, or idea, wonderful discoveries can be made. The first and most important is that the attention is transferred from self to object. When this is achieved, personal freedom is achieved. A second thing that occurs is awareness of the relationship between self and objective. With relationship we discover identity. This illustrates the biblical phrase "he who loses himself will find himself."

These goals are not achieved one at a time or in any special order, but every exercise contributes to the progress we seek.

Parent   But doesn't the student become restless in an acting class when he is not always acting? Is he satisfied with the simple exercise you suggest?

Teacher   A good question. If the teacher is a "good actor," the members of the group are challenged constantly. Each can have a chance as soon as he is ready. Because the class is designed to have the student discover and learn for himself, there are continual surprises and delights. At no time does the teacher sit and hand out information or criticism. There is constant movement. The challenges provide opportunity for each to do what he can; and there is the expectation that what each does today will be refined and improved tomorrow. The class is a continuing investigation of capacities and means. It is not that in such classes the students never act. But they are asked to act the experience that is theirs at the level of their growth. The result is beautiful acting because it is truth, a visible expression of inner conviction.

Parent   How does this study benefit the student in his life role?

Teacher   It will benefit him according to his needs. The child who doesn't know "what to play" will discover that he can make up his play. The child who never reads will begin to take an interest in words because words are important tools for the actor. The child fearful of "wrong answers" will develop spontaneity of expression because he is unafraid. The child who insists on dominating every situation will no longer need to dominate because he's had recognition. The child failing in school because he couldn't concentrate will do better. The child who never has anybody to play with will begin to attract playmates.

Of course, this doesn't happen in ten lessons. This must be a continuing activity—part of the child's life. "Trying" an acting class, a dance class, an art class, and the like, is part of the difficulty in our society. These activities must be sustained and ongoing to have real growth value. One of the many fine things about a class in the arts, whether it be dance, music, acting, or visual art, is that as the individual grows, the work is made more challenging. The child need not be held back by a classmate who is less able. And even in the heterogeneous class, the teacher can meet individual needs because he is not bound by a syllabus nor expected to produce a group, whose members know the same things at the same time regardless of individual native equipment.

Parent   You have given me some insight, but I'm afraid I cannot visualize such a class.

Teacher   Is it important? How can I describe a class that takes its direction from needs, interests, and abilities? A class whose source of supply is the individuals within it? A class that has no text, no syllabus? It is the parents' role to investigate the philosophy, the point of view, the purpose, the principles, and the attitudes of a teacher. Then, if the investigation is satisfactory, to have faith in the teacher. Refrain from asking a child, "What did you do today?" If it is difficult for a teacher to describe such a class, how much more difficult for a child. What happens is dependent upon the conditions of the moment. What is right today may not be right tomorrow. This is true of all creative classes, whether in the arts or academic subjects.

Returning to your immediate concern about the value of the acting class, however, let me say: Acting is an art form. It is the art most closely related to life. The study of acting should mean natural transference of its values to the art of living.

Parent and reader may remain unconvinced. You may say, you speak of the lessons the actor must learn that are lessons for living. If the actor has learned these lessons, why is he not a happier, healthier person? Some actors are. Those who are not may have learned the lessons well but no one ever told them that these apply to life and living. They think they need props, stage, play, costumes in order to use the learned lessons. Techniques are turned on with the lights and turned off at the end of the play. The actor needs help to see that these lessons should be integrated with his own being and should be his to use to make life richer and more satisfying.

What are these lessons? Concentration (focus on the here and now); productive use of imagination (making it work); observation (awareness of environment, persons, self); self-projection, sensitizing the senses so they remain open; discrimination (making choices); discipline of body, voice, mind, communication (verbal and nonverbal); and elimination of inhibitions and fears. These are all lessons that can help an individual achieve the most from life. Few of them are stated goals of a public or private school curriculum; but for the teacher of acting, these are the fundamentals of his work with students.

The following dialogue suggests the concepts and some techniques needed by a teacher who is using acting for developmental purposes:

Parent   You speak of lessons in concentration. What would you do? How could you make such a lesson interesting?

Teacher   Maybe I'd put a plain card on the floor, then ask the children to focus—giving it all their attention for as long as possible, to see what would happen.

Parent   Have you any idea about what might happen? I'm sure I haven't.

Teacher   I've done it myself. One thing that happens is that everything disappears but the card. Children say, "Everything went black but the card," or "It seemed to move."

Parent   Do you think children would do this? It seems silly to me.

Teacher   It doesn't to them. They enjoy the challenge. To see how long they can stay with the card. It is a challenge to do what the teacher knows they can do, if they try.

Parent   I'm still not clear. How would you go about a lesson in imagination?

Teacher   I'd let them "Scamper."

Parent   What is "scampering?" I've never heard of it.

Teacher   It's a technique. A procedure where we take imagination on a guided tour.

Parent   I don't follow.

Teacher   Do you know the edge radio has on TV for educational purposes?

Parent   You tell me.

Teacher   Radio makes the listener work. He has to visualize in order to follow the action. TV does all the work. All the viewer does is look. Do you see?

Parent   Yes. Radio makes it necessary for the listener to use his imagination, his experience, his knowledge.

Teacher   "Scampering" is a technique devoted solely to one end—exercising and guiding imagination. It is like radio in that it supplies cues to the imagination. For example, the music bridge comes in slowly in a minor key. You are prepared for a change, a somber change. The sound man prepares a sound. You interpret it as a door closing and you are right because someone says at once, "Janie, are you home?" "Scamper" gives the listener, who is sitting in the dark (because his eyes are closed), specific cues. The teacher says to the listener, "Go to your favorite place in your house. Are you there? Don't answer, just nod your head." In "Scampering" no verbal response can be given, only an inner response. The teacher says to the listener, "Will you perform some action that is usual for you in this place? . . . Someone is calling you. . . . You answer—not out loud. . . . Open your eyes. Were you able to do all you were told to do? Who would like to tell us about it? What happened? What did you say?

Parent   I guess I really do see.

Teacher   We all understand that visualization is important for many reasons. And all of us in the arts have done something with it in relation to a variety of lessons. But to isolate it, to make it a technique, and to name it makes it available. It becomes another specific tool and a procedure. It adds another dimension. Perhaps it satisfies productively the need that day-dreaming, which is unproductive, satisfies.

Parent   I'd like to go back to your lesson with the card. That interested me, but somehow I'm not satisfied. Can you defend it beyond the obvious?

Teacher   Yes, briefly. What we focus on or pay attention to we relate to. Do you realize the importance of this? I used this lesson once with a group of teen-agers. A week later one of them said to me, "Thank you for the lesson with the card. I learned why I didn't like science." Curious, I asked her why. Her answer, "Because I never paid enough attention to it."

Parent   She was very perceptive. That was unusual, wasn't it?

Teacher   Yes. Ruth learned and was able to articulate the learning. Others may learn but at the moment are not able to state it. But if I work with students long enough, they will articulate because this is one of the acting teacher's goals. It is not enough to "know what you mean"; you must find the words to express it.

Parents   I am beginning to understand. You have identified for me some of the trees in what seemed an impenetrable forest. By the forest, I mean the abstract materials that seemed mysterious and vague. You have identified some of the practical learnings possible and also named some of the tools you use. You said "Scamper" is a tool?

Teacher   That's right. Brainstorming, doodling, and games are all tools used by teachers who work in the arts for purposes of growth and learning.

Parent   I expect your biggest challenge lies in the education of adults like me, who know only how to evaluate learning by the sum of knowledge put into a child's head.

Teacher   True. "What have you learned? What grade did you get?" Such questions are the only way the average parents evaluate their children's school and teachers. The concern is with input. They have difficulty under-standing that "output" is the only way input becomes meaningful to the child. When we can express what we know in our own way, to use for our own purposes, the knowledge is then truly ours. Strange that with all the emphasis on communication these days, few recognize it as a two-way street. It is not enough to understand. We must make others understand us. We want children to read and write because ability with language is essential to communication skill, but we do not see it as more than the decoding of words.

For years we have accepted the arts as therapy. All that is needed is to involve the patient in the doing. Involvement is the key to therapy. It takes a teacher with knowledge of the patient, of what he can and cannot be expected to do, of how to engage his interest and keep it going. In the use of the arts in education, we need teachers who "know" their students and who are working to develop many skills—not "how to" skills, but skills for living and learning. They need to know how to create new attitudes on the part of adults toward art *as* education. They need to know and name the specific goals and to identify the learnings possible. These lessons are not yet in the books. We who use the arts for learning have been guilty of vagueness. If we want to overcome this, we must dispel the mystique through clarity and precision. It is not enough that we know what we are trying to accomplish; it is our further obligation to communicate it to others.

REFERENCES

Scamper is available from the D.O.K. Publishing Co., Buffalo, N.Y., 14215.

Teaching Is a Dialogue by Grace Stanistreet is available from Adelphi University, Garden City, N.Y.

The Theatre: A Side View

Moses Goldberg

Moses Goldberg is director of Stage One: The Louisville Children's Theatre. He was granted a B.S. degree in psychology from Tulane University, a master's degree in child psychology from Stanford, and a second master's degree in drama from the University of Washington; he received his Ph.D. in the theatre arts from the University of Minnesota. Professor Goldberg, for many years a professor at Florida State University, has contributed numerous articles to professional journals and other publications. His most recent work is a college textbook entitled Children's Theatre: A Philosophy and a Method. *He is an exponent of involvement drama and is known for his innovative theatre productions.*

It is traditional to study the theatre from what I would call a "top" view. One looks at the particular forms of theatre that currently exist or that have existed in the past. Whether one is dealing with historical style, such as Elizabethan drama or the Peking Opera, or with a modern institution—Broadway, Happenings, Grotowski, Absurdism, etc.—the investigator in a top-view study is interested primarily in description and analysis. What was Shakespeare's stage like? What do his plays mean? How does Grotowski direct? What kinds of plays have made how much money on Broadway? What is the significance of sound imagery in Chekhov? All these questions view the theater and the drama as developed to a specific point. Since the theatre exists in such and such a form, they postulate, we can examine its form and the meaning behind the form. In studying form, we are studying the *surface manifestations* of the theatre—hence my phrase, "the top view."

The top view concentrates its attention on the artist's theatre. Most studies try to discover the intention or method of the theatrical practitioner. Those few top-view studies that do concern themselves with the audience are interested primarily in a discrete reaction by a specific audience to a single stage event, such as measuring the galvanic skin response of an audience member to a moment of tension, or analyzing the variables that produce a laugh at a specific line. Again, these are investigating a surface manifestation—a top view.

What I should like to propose—and this is certainly not intended to replace top-view studies but rather to supplement them—is that we also study the theatre from the side view. In addition to looking at surface manifestations of the theatre, we need to find out more about its developmental processes. I should like to see a major area of theatre research opened up under the general heading of Developmental Theatre. In this subfield we will take a side view of theatre. We will ask two major questions:

1. Why and how did the art of theatre emerge?
2. How does the theatre become increasingly relevant to the life of the growing individual?

Because this approach is built upon the fundamental assumption that both the medium of theatre and the audience's aesthetic sense are in a state of change, side-view researchers find it less meaningful to look only at a single manifestation of art or a single audience response. We must look at growth—at sequence; and this can best be diagramed as a view from the side. *Developmental theatre is defined as the study of change in theatre form or audience experience.* (Those few side-view studies that are being done today generally deal with the change in an artist's method; such as the development of Shakespeare's language through the various periods of his life.)

Since the side-view approach is comparative (i.e., it assumes two or more levels of related events), it suggests a need for relating levels of theatrical event to levels of growth in other areas—human development, economic development, spiritual development, and so forth. And this, in turn, suggests a need for an interdisciplinary study of theatre, particularly in dealing with the first question above. A study of the emergence of the theatre as an art medium may properly focus on an analysis of primitive people's changing psychological and sociological patterns. The significance of the interaction of magic, religion, theatre, and other now distinct but originally synonymous expressions of the human inner psyche may be investigated most appropriately by a team of researchers: a theologian, a sociologist, a historian, a psychologist, an anthropologist, and an aesthetician—all working together. Or, since there is much truth in the saying that "ontogeny recapitulates phylogeny," it may be reasonable to investigate the development of the theatre art by looking at dramatic play in modern children in order to discover why and how they evolve, for themselves, the elements of the theatre. Perhaps this is the true function of that activity that many have called "creative drama." Perhaps what creative drama is supposed to be is a process of guiding the child to create—for the first time and out of a basic human need—an art form, which can be conveniently called "theatre," since that is what all the other people who have created it—also for the first time—have agreed to call it.

By taking the creative drama approach to the study of the development of the theatre art, we are learning why theatre appeared, as well as studying the child as an emerging artist. It is also possible to study the second area of developmental theatre—the increasing relevance of theatre to the audience—by studying the child as an emerging audience member. It is not a coincidence that the field of developmental psychology (the study of changes in behavior) focuses most of its energies on the child. If we are to study change, we must go to where change is most noticeable; and that usually means to young people.

We can, I hope, hypothesize that the individual develops as an audience member; that is, he at one stage is an "immature" audience member, and at another stage—which is chronologically subsequent to the immature stage—is a "mature" audience member. I shall speak of this later stage as "aesthetic maturity." Aesthetic maturity may or may not be related to physical maturity, social maturity, intellectual maturity, emotional maturity, or spiritual maturity. These are all areas in which the development of the individual is recognized; and educators are aware that a person may be mature in one area and very immature in another. Maturity is hard to demonstrate, but immaturity is relatively easy to locate—in a young child. Therefore, the field of developmental theatre is committed to a study of children both as emerging artists—perhaps in creative dramatics—and as emerging audiences—again reminding us of an existing label: children's theatre.

Developmental theatre, then, can include both creative drama and children's theatre. But it goes beyond both. It is by no means confined to children. It is concerned with all theatre as it develops and evolves, and all individuals as they mature in aesthetic sophistication. Perhaps, as a concept, developmental theatre brings creative drama and children's theatre squarely into focus as part of the "real" field of theatre. Perhaps, in the long run, we would benefit if we forgot the terms "children's theatre" and "creative drama" and talked only about the development of artist and audience. How does the art of theatre emerge from our basic inner needs? How does aesthetic maturity evolve in the audience member? These are the two questions, slightly refined, which developmental theatre asks.

At this point in my own research, I am particularly interested in the second question—the one that deals with theatre from the point of view of the developing audience. I want to discover how we can help the individuals in the audience reach aesthetic maturity. I want to discover the sequence that each individual goes through in proceeding from immature to mature. I want to find or create the techniques and methods by which we as researchers could learn more about these concepts. And this means using the resources and methodology of the artist and the behavioral scientist to probe developmental theatre.

It means, primarily, creating a research laboratory that is essentially a theatre devoted to developing aesthetic maturity and that is equipped to experiment with various means of accomplishing this goal, and various methods of measuring its successes and failures. This laboratory must, of course, be a theatre that is fully artistic and entertaining. Otherwise, it will bore its audience instead of developing it. But it must also be a laboratory in which experimental failure is accepted as a necessary possibility, and in which artistic temperament and public recognition are subordinated to sound research methodology and audience development. Such a laboratory could study audience age levels as one major component of development, and would probably carry out much of its investigation with young audiences; but it would not be a "children's theatre." It would be a developmental theatre.

The creation of such a theatre laboratory would be a project worthy of a national funding agency with a public charge to develop aesthetic maturity—such as the Kennedy Center or the National Endowment for the Arts. However, it is most likely to result from a complex union of an educational research laboratory, such as the Central Midwestern Regional Educational Laboratory, Inc. (CEMREL); a regional theatre with a commitment to artistic standards and audience development; a major university, which can justify an experimental function for an arts unit; and, hopefully, the financial backing of the private and public foundations.

One of the key strengths of this new laboratory would be the ability of the researchers to manipulate variables, much as the behavioral scientist does, and to measure, in a systematic way, the changes that result. One example of the simplest kind of project that might be done would be an investigation of how the age of the protagonist affects any change in audience attitudes or feelings. Many have hypothesized that certain ages of audience will identify best with certain ages of hero, but never has this theory been tested reliably. Changes in audience attitude could reflect changes in audience identification, and attitudes can be measured statistically.

One method for approaching this problem might to be to choose a play—such as Harris's *Androcles and the Lion*—in which the age of the protagonist is not a terribly significant artistic factor; and then to cast the part with several actors of different apparent ages. In order to control for quality differences, the researcher might choose to use several different actors at each of three or four different age levels. Perhaps as many as twenty different actors would be rehearsed in the role of Androcles; but, in every case, the rest of the production and cast would remain as exactly uniform as possible.

The next step would be to develop a quickly administered measuring instrument—perhaps a questionnaire or adjective check list—that would find out the extent to which seeing the play had effected changes in the attitudes expressed by the audience, which in turn would suggest the extent of identification with the various heroes. Similar instruments exist in the literature of psychology and education, and would be usable here with some adaptation. Then, the theatre would present the play twenty times—or forty or sixty times to help remove extraneous variables such as a "down" performance—and measure the results.

Discovering the factors that influence identification would make it possible to go deeper and deeper into those variables which make the theatre experience a developmental one for the audience, and each new discovery makes finer and finer control of variables practical. Obviously, it will be a very slow process to uncover all the relevant variables. But, over time, significant information could be amassed with some confidence. Each study points out directions for further profitable research or closes the door on an unprofitable line of inquiry.

One could not, of course, begin to predict what the long-range results of such a theatre laboratory might be in terms of building a popular audience for the theatre in this country or in terms of enriching the lives of individual theatregoers; but it is hoped that such a project would have very tangible benefits as well as important scholarly ones. One goal of such a theatre would be to pinpoint the sequence of experiences most appropriate to the readiness level of the individual audience member.

For example, all other things being equal, it may be aesthetically unwise to do Molière for a particular audience before it has had a chance to see an example of commedia dell'arte. Perhaps the commedia experience provides, in some as yet unknown way, the "vocabulary" the individual needs in order to take the most from the Molière experience. And perhaps Molière, in turn, prepares the individual for Sheridan or Shaw? I have sometimes asked my graduate students to rank-order all the plays of Shakespeare in terms of the ideal sequence in which they would show them to an audience. Without my telling them why or how to make such judgments, they were still able to do it in a remarkably consistent way. Various students in various classes consistently rank *Midsummer Night's Dream* and *Macbeth* before *King Lear* or *Troilus and Cressida*. *Romeo and Juliet* is invariably seen as being more appropriate to a younger audience than is *Love's Labours Lost*. There must, therefore, be an intuitive understanding in these students' minds of sequential aesthetic experiences.

The Developmental Theatre student might begin by analyzing these intuitions, reducing them to possible categories, or criteria for judging one play more mature than another; and then proceed to test these criteria experimentally in the theatre laboratory. The result of such a study might have practical application to season selection, or curriculum planning in a high school and might even reliably inform the Broadway producer that he is making a financial mistake to do a certain play the season after another play has covered the same aesthetic ground.

The development of specific aesthetic concepts is another area for research and may lead to specific applications for the playwright, director, or producer. The audience member learns and changes by going to the theatre, and he also learns how to learn from his future theatre experiences. If we can find out how to maximize these kinds of learning, we are guaranteeing that the theatre will become more *useful* to the individual (without, of course, implying any loss of entertainment values).

For a ready example, let us look at the concept of "death"—surely one of the most personally relevant and yet difficult concepts in human existence, and, paradoxically, one of the concepts least prepared for in the traditional education and socialization of the child. In the theatre, the equivalent concept is "character death." "Character death" does not precisely equal real death, for a character has no life to begin with; but he has an aesthetic life, and can therefore suffer an aesthetic death. Perhaps the theatre should begin with this concept by merely teaching that there is such a thing as "character death." Perhaps this is done on the simplest level—as in a play for five- through eight-year-olds—by the witch screaming out, "I'm dead!" and then taking off her costume, revealing an actor whose role is finished. Of course, this is all hypothesis. There is no evidence yet to show that this, indeed, should be the first stage of introduction to this concept; and certainly no reason to attach this stage to the particular ages mentioned.

But, to continue with speculation, perhaps the next stage should introduce the individual, and perhaps ages eight through eleven represent this stage, to all of the various ways to conventionalize character death. In a realistic play, we conventionalize death with indications of pain and weakness leading to collapse and a lack of movement. In an heroic play, death may be indicated by rhymed couplets, or a spectacular fall from the balcony into the moat. In some Oriental drama, a red cloth placed over the face means death of the character. All these are equivalent concepts and all enable the individual who views them to learn the vocabulary of the theatre. In this second phase, the major emphasis is on learning how to learn from the theatre by learning how to translate its conventions into meaningful concepts.

Perhaps, in early adolescence, the individual next learns to cope with the significance of character death in terms of its relationship with the real concept of death. He begins to *use* his translation skills at this stage as he learns to compare the death of a major character with the potential (or actual) death of one of his own acquaintances or relatives. Perhaps, in a fourth, late adolescent stage, he learns how to deal with his own death by manipulating the character death of an identification model in his thoughts. A mature attitude toward death may simply require that he judge character death in terms of its necessity or appropriateness. Perhaps the aesthetically mature individual is the one who can say, "That was a good death, that a bad one, that a needful one, that a wasteful one." If the character deaths he has experienced through a series of plays can lead him to equanimity about the real ones he must experience, then the theatre has been useful to him. Obviously, it can be most useful if the particular concept is manipulated in the most effective developmental sequence; and my continual use of "perhaps" above indicates that we do not yet know what that sequence is. But we can discover it—in the developmental theatre laboratory.

The concept of manipulating growth, by the way, is a bit frightening, particularly when the manipulation is being done by people with whom we do not agree. But even more frightening, to me, is the concept of leaving a powerful developmental tool like the theatre unexplored—an unknown weapon in the hands of whatever naive practitioner might chance to put on a play. As the theatre becomes recognized as an educational force, public interest in its wise use will certainly replace the peripheral regard it now holds. Hopefully, the goal toward which the individual will be manipulated will not be political expediency, but rather aesthetic maturity.

The implication, of course, is that aesthetic maturity is a good thing; that fostering its development would benefit both the theatre and the audience. I

Peter the Postman by Torben Jetsmark. Courtesy of University of Minnesota Peppermint Tent Theatre.

see maturity—which can be defined somewhat inadequately as the ability to make the appropriate response—as desirable. Maturity in every area of human growth is important, and that should include aesthetic maturity. The arts are a powerful means of finding out about and manipulating concepts of the universe. I have spoken about "vocabulary" and "translation." The arts are a language system, a way of organizing knowledge and a way of expressing knowledge. Maturity is simply fluency in all available languages—verbal and nonverbal. The developmental theatre researcher and practitioner study ways in which the language of theatre may have come into being; how its referents evolved; how its syntax was developed; and especially, how each individual learns the language.

In conclusion, developmental theatre is seen as engulfing and replacing children's theatre and creative drama as subject areas. It is, after all, not theatre for *children* that motivates us, but theatre for *people*. We seek a way to make the art relevant to the human being, and we devote so much of our energy to young human beings because they are more educable and less isolated by psychological inhibitions, social contexts, or intellectual interests. We want to develop a nation of aesthetically mature human beings who will continue to use theatre in their lives as adults. In addition to bringing pleasure to the immature, our pupose is to bring them to maturity (through entertainment, always through entertainment). The developmental theatre seeks to open up channels of knowledge and communication to the individual. It seeks to teach him a new language with which he can reach out to the universe. It does not view him from the top—a "finished" product. It views him from the side—growing, stretching upward towards his fullest potential as a human being. In the last analysis, reaching that potential is the only goal worth having.

Smoking Chimneys

Lowell Swortzell

Lowell Swortzell was introduced to child drama at the Children's Museum of Washington, D.C., where as a child he participated in creative dramatics classes and attended touring productions of Clare Tree Major. While still a teen-ager he began writing plays, an area to which he has since made a notable contribution. His one-act plays and play reviews have appeared in a variety of periodicals and his anthology, All the World's a Stage: Modern Plays for Young People, *was hailed by the* New York Times *as an "outstanding book of the year." Professor Swortzell has taught at Yale, Tufts, Hofstra, the University of Wisconsin, and New York University, where he is currently director of the program in Educational Theatre. He and his wife, Dr. Nancy Swortzell, initiated this program, which includes substantial and innovative work in the area of child drama. His recent publications include* Here Come the Clowns, *a history of clowns and comedy from antiquity to the present;* The Arabian Nights, *a play for young people; and participation in the prize-winning* The New York Kid's Book. *He has edited a new anthology of plays for young people, which contains his dramatization of* The Little Humpback Horse.

In a review of *Children and Dramatics* that appeared in the *New York Times* in 1966, I wrote that Richard Crosscup's autobiographical account might rank among the most important statements on educational theatre since the pioneer work of Winifred Ward in the 1930s. While in retrospect my esteem for this volume in no way has lessened, I am troubled by the phrase "pioneer work," and wonder if I had any right to use it then or now in application to child drama.

Advances, to be certain, have been made since Miss Ward arrived on the scene to lead two generations of teachers through her courses, books, workshops, and lecture tours, and to spearhead the particular practice of educational theatre that came to be known in the United States as creative dramatics. Her students, in turn, joined by others who emerged independently, spread their knowledge and experience from coast to coast. So the geographical frontiers have been won, settled, even absorbed into much of the educational landscape, if not so far deeply into the cultural life of America.

But because "pioneering" means more than mere homesteading, we may wonder how far we have come in first discovering and then developing this thing variously labeled child drama, educational theatre, developmental drama, youth theatre, participatory theatre, children's theatre, drama-in-education, or whatever *you* may term it.

Historians speaking of the pioneer spirit in America like to recall a characteristic adage often attributed to the father of Abraham Lincoln, "When you can see the smoke from your neighbor's chimney, it's time to move on." When visible in our field, the smoke mostly emerges in puffs too small and too infrequent to suggest it derives from work securely sustained. Some of it seems more the result of fires of confusion than of certainty, some of it reflects eagerness to serve children unsupported by preparation to do so, and some of it appears to be screens sent up to conceal a lack of anything else to reveal. Certain reasons for this widespread obscuration are explored here, along with some of the currently popular forms it takes (instant theatre, audience participation, Story Theatre, Reader's Theatre, and commedia dell'-arte troupes). Yet genuine fires do burn, and vigorously in places, albeit their intermittent significance is too rarely noticed (and appreciated) and up to now seldom if ever causes neighbors either to move or to improve their own efforts. In time these fires, also discussed herein (some genuine experimentation here and in England), may come to be regarded as "pre-pioneering" efforts but for now they constitute signs of life that breed thought, generate productivity, and perhaps spawn creativity. Moreover, they invite criticism, which cannot exist unless significant artistic activity first exists to demand its presence; criticism is proof of both neighbors and their smoking chimneys.

A Place to Begin

No matter what aspects of educational theatre (and it is an enormous field) claim the services of teachers or the attention of students, nor whether together they strive for fully finished productions or for fulfillment of an exercise or class, everyone requires a philosophic concept or aesthetic principle to govern his operation. Creative teachers, like other artists, hope to develop their own theoretical positions through practice rather than accept ready-to-wear credos lifted from pages of books, even good books by established authorities. The best do, of course, and the rest must be encouraged to keep trying until they satisfy their own requirements for hypothetical foundations and structural systems.

Likewise, everyone, be he director, actor, teacher, student, participant, or observer, needs to locate a starting point from which to take up the experience of educational theatre. Can there be one place that appropriately applies to areas as diverse and complex as the playhouse, the schoolhouse, the playground, the community center, the street, and city park? Can there be a single position that launches young people toward an understanding of dramatic literature and theatrical performance? Indeed, can they commence collectively and simultaneously? For me, such a spot has been identified by Richard Crosscup in his observation that the validity of an activity resides in its meaning.[1] He is speaking of dramatic activities in the classroom while I am speaking of drama in general, in the classroom and everywhere else. Simply by substituting my word "action" (Aristotle's, actually) for his word "activity" we arrive at the essence of drama: the transformation of an audience, be it pupils or playgoers, when it recognizes the meaning of an action. Crosscup states the aesthetic process we experience when we lead children in dramatic play of even the most informal kind and it is the same process we undergo when we see a play: we establish the "relationship between *doing* and *meaning*, and between *meaning* and *being*."[2] The relationship of action and idea and idea and existence, our own and that of others, is the one we hope to establish when we write, direct, or act plays, just as it is the connection we attempt to make when we teach courses and conduct workshops in the creative arts. It is the *creative* connection, the one by which we can transform others as well as ourselves.

And it is one that frequently remains unmade or not fully completed both in education and theatre. Pressures to move from one activity to another in the classroom, as well as from one act to another in a play, or from one point to another in an improvisation, can impede, prohibit, or altogether destroy possible connections. This failure results from the harried teacher, unclear writer, insensitive leader of creative dramatics, careless play director, or the well-meaning but inept actor who has not carried the process through each of its essential phases to its comprehensive conclusion. Somewhere during a performance or dramatic activity an action is not communicated, experienced, or transformed into personal significance and the child remains unreached, uninvolved, unchanged. It is when the creative connection is made with regularity in the theatre and classroom that we best achieve artistic as well as academic goals. And the public now often confused about our activity, once convinced this modus operandi is central to children and dramatics, will no longer look upon us as surrogate babysitters filling idle hours with idle amusements, for they will witness actual creative growth in children; and if they also participate, in themselves as well.

Ancestors to Guide Us

If we wish to trace the aesthetic evolution of this basic creative procedure from its beginnings to the time of Ward, Crosscup, Hughes Mearns, and their more recent British counterparts, we sooner or later find ourselves contemplating Plato and Aristotle. We discover, for example, that such a twentieth-century sounding phrase as "memory is in the muscles," used today to describe the interdependence of intellect and action, goes back to the hills of Athens if not beyond. Aristotle, noting that action is motion and motion is always explicit, observes, "He who performs any action, not knowing what the action is, nor to what end it will lead, nor about whom action is conversant, acts from ignorance essentially, and therefore acts involuntarily." And when speaking of memory he argues, "No memory is a habit but rather an action," adding elsewhere that "those who are very young and very old labor under a defect of memory on account of motion." To Aristotle, man's ultimate happiness is found in an activity which he practices to his perfection and self sufficiency.

Philip Coggin in skillfully outlining the origins of drama in education notes the particular influence of Jean Jacques Rousseau on modern creative drama.[3] The eighteenth-century philosopher distinguishes sharply between professional theatre, not to be tolerated because it encloses people in dark caves, and participatory theatre, to be encouraged because it sets people free to express themselves in market squares where they dance, march, and sport their physical dexterities. "Turn the spectators into a spectacle," he says as progenitor of the creative connection, "make them actors themselves: make each one see himself and love himself in others so that all may be the better united." To accomplish this, one certainly must turn action into meaning and meaning into being. This advice is echoed in other words throughout the nineteenth and twentieth centuries. Goethe speaks of improvised drama: "I think this practice very useful among actors, and even in the company of friends and acquaintances. It is the best mode of drawing men out of themselves, and leading them, by a circuitous path, back into themselves again." The poet Shelley speaks of drama as the teacher of self-knowledge and self-respect: "Neither the eye nor the mind can see itself, unless reflected upon that which it resembles. The drama . . . is as a prismatic and many-sided mirror which collects the brightest rays of human nature and divides and reproduces them." Wagner speaks of dramatic action: "Without it, or without any reference to it, art representation is arbitrary, unnecessary, chancy, incomprehensible," but with it comes "the urge to bring the unconscious and the involuntary in life to itself as necessary to understanding and to recognition."

Martha Graham in introducing her 1974 company of dancers to New York City told her opening-night audience that to her "theatre was a verb before it was a noun; it was an act before it was a building," which of course is to say that civilization all along has made the connection advocated here in its development of the performing arts. First came the act, which required the verb to describe it; then the meaning, which necessitated the noun to name it; then the theatre in which to perform it and through which to interpret and communicate it to others. Certainly, had such acts not significantly affected his being, man would not have constructed theatres in which to re-create them and in which to glorify their meaning, century upon century.

The Process in Action

The creative process suggested here may be seen at work to some extent in every youngster. But for purposes of illustration let's examine an individual childhood that reveals its steady progression and undeniable power. Paul Zindel, the Pulitzer Prize dramatist of *The Effect of Gamma Rays on Man-in-the-Moon Marigolds* and author of several novels of marked appeal to adolescents, has delineated his own creative emergence and artistic self-discovery in a short essay significantly entitled "The Theatre Is Born Within Us."[4] Not until in his twenties did he attend his first professional play, and by then he already had written two of his own, a fact that leads him to believe that the seeds of theatre were inside him all the time, growing constantly from birth.

As a young child he became aware of his surroundings by exploring new neighborhoods to which he and his mother moved on Staten Island, each echoing a separate culture of distant lands as he roamed among heritages of Sicily, Ireland, the Near East, and Africa, observing their customs, hearing their languages, testing their foods, and sensing their varied values of life. By the age of ten, he says, he had gone nowhere but had seen the world. Long before this he had discovered marionettes and had constructed box scenes, those miniature depictions of cycloramic life constructed in a cardboard box that elementary classroom teachers fostered in the 1930s and '40s. He had gazed fascinated for long hours into aquariums, insectariums, and ter-rariums. He had discovered the local movie house, which claimed most of his Saturday mornings. "What a great love," he remembers, "I had of micro-cosms, of peering at other worlds framed and separate from me." During this time he discovered patterns of life as he watched thousands daily rush to and from the ferry and noticed the happy-go-lucky few who flew small airplanes on weekends. Then at the age of eleven he stopped what he calls "eaves-dropping on the world" and entered into it.

His first acts as a participant in life were to play a small role in church entertainment, to sing at school, and to be swung around by a roller-skating champion. Garnering no distinction or particular sense of accomplishment from any of these endeavors, he began writing for school assembly programs where his ideas were all borrowed and mostly bad from the start. Then tuberculosis removed him for a year and a half at age fifteen from the real world and he went back to observing, this time from the sidelines of a sanatorium. When he returned to school he wrote a play about cancer and for it won a Parker pen. In college he finished another; no Parker pen. And he saw that belated first play on Broadway, *Toys in the Attic*, which permitted one of its stars, Maureen Stapleton, to move him deeply enough to think that the theatre could become "my religion, my cathedral."

But one incident more than any other in this list of rather commonplace events transformed him. Late one evening in a Greenwich Village alleyway he saw as many as twenty people leaning out of apartment windows shouting and throwing money down to an old woman who was bent over several cans, eating garbage with her hands and ignoring the coins and bills that began to surround her. That graphic moment lodged itself permanently in his memory; he kept wondering why she did not take the money and buy food. When he later described the scene and how much it disturbed him to his friend Edward Albee, this playwright explained the act in the simple words, "She was doing penance." The essential connection was made. Zindel had found the missing meaning of the action and, in his terms, it "exploded" his consciousness, so that he never again would be the same person, or the same playwright.

Paul Zindel came to be a creative individual not by a unique path but by a universal one. With perhaps the exception of this last event, nothing extraordinary takes place in his chronology. Others may not grow up on an island of such diversity as Staten, but most towns and cities offer a mix of races and cultures to study and absorb. Today's children no longer are urged to express themselves through cardboard-box scenes but they are stimulated in far more creative activities. Some may not win early recognition for their artistic attempts but many, many do, and often in more encouraging forms than Parker pens. Few may find today's professional theatre a suitable vehicle for passions sufficiently strong to be termed religious but perhaps some still may be attracted and moved even by its momentarily waning glamour and talent, or, more likely, by the energetic and burgeoning imagination of the mass media. Not every youngster, like Eugene O'Neill and Paul Zindel, gets whisked off to a sanatorium at a critical point in his creative and intellectual growth, but most, if only for brief periods at a time, withdraw through sickness or by choice from the social to solitary life. They too observe the world before they enter and participate in it. They may not become playwrights or even members of a theatre audience, but this destination is not the essential aim of the creative process in action (although newcomers always are welcome to both ranks, of course).

In using drama our primary purpose is to bring each sphere through which a child passes in his development into its sharpest focus. By fully experiencing these microcosms in performance in the theatre and in direct participation in the classroom he can become a knowing person, able to recognize the meaning of his own and other actions and to be changed by their significance. Of course, if along the way he also becomes able to create experiences which foster this process in others, as Zindel did, so much the better for all of us.

Why, if the seeds of theatre are born within us, as Zindel believes, and if the creative process is part of every child's development, as stated here, are we only now pioneering the field of child drama? Why do we have too few Paul Zindels and too many others unable either to recognize the meaning of their actions or to be transformed by them? What halts the process and stifles creativity? Part of the answer to these complex questions obviously lies within our own ability as teachers and artists to complete the creative connection, to bring those spheres into focus, to provide the experience of the microcosms, and fully and truly to perform in the classroom and theatre. Once more we must acknowledge only fractional and occasional success. Even those most dedicated to creativity in education can be at fault if their class work merely outlines the process but does not embody it or if their productions only suggest but do not actually implement it. Yet we all know drama cannot describe an action but must do it, theatre cannot indicate an experience but must create it, and these same tenets are equally true of the creative process in child drama.

An examination follows of several popular practices and forms of performance that in my opinion often fail to communicate and connect a child's knowledge and being, and a look at several others that I believe are beginning to succeed with encouraging regularity.

Instant Theatre

Get-rich-quick schemes, forever a part of daily life, now pop up in child drama with the con-artistry promises of on-the-spot rewards. The seller claims that when the purchaser employs methods developed over long years of practice, he (along with mass consumers everywhere) is guaranteed instant creative success. The buyer of such hocus-pocus utopian systems should beware, remembering that inasmuch as there can be no such thing as infallible prepackaged creative drama or factory-made children's theatre, there should be no reason to get either wholesale. Nor in shopping for valid sources of information should we succumb to promotional labels and ballyhooing with which courses, workshops, and conferences sometimes are merchandised. Whatever a jacket may pledge, no book of "how to" rules or shortcuts delivers fully effective means to stimulate significant expression. All you have ever wanted to know about educational theatre is not between the covers of such a text or printed on cards in a kit awaiting purchase at a campus bookdealer. Those who deny the genuine creative process to young people by using secondhand and shopworn techniques withhold from everyone the joy of original and spontaneous collaboration.

Audience Participation

I have long possessed a desire deeply macabre (or perhaps worse, perverse) to just once have the enormous pleasure of attending a performance of *Peter Pan* at which when the big moment arrives to save Tinkerbell by appluading not one person can be heard to clap. "Say you believe in fairies," my ideal Peter pleads, and hundreds of voices in unison reply "No" or "Never, Never, Never," or better still, "Not on your life." How delicious to see the actress faced with this ultimatum forced to improvise to save her own life as well as to get offstage. As for Tinkerbell, she too, poor dear, would have to come up with some new way to recharge her batteries without troubling the paying patrons.

All this sacrilege arises not from Barrie's misuse of the device but from those who ineptly have imitated him decade after decade and coerced innocent spectators to perform to little or no dramatic purpose or theatrical effect. Audience participation often is required, like so much else in children's theatre, because the author or director thinks youngsters enjoy such moments, a conclusion arrived at no doubt from their own childhood memories of excitement in helping Peter to restore her/his friend to glowing health. So, time after time, Barrie gets the blame for having created a tradition that now has become an artistic albatross able to destroy the reality and beauty of an otherwise thoughtful production.

I almost had my wish come true in London at a Christmas performance not of *Peter Pan* but of one of its more feeble descendants. Printed inside the programs was a large solid red circle to which no reference was made until late in the second act. At this point we were told by the hero that the only way to stop the villain from taking over the entire city was to confront him (the villain was a fey witch in a sequined Folies-Bergère costume, played by a man) with red spots, the one thing in the world able to render his magic powerless. What red spots the audience wanted to know, having long since forgotten their programs. They had to be told where to find the spots, but this didn't bring the moment off either because by now they could no longer locate their programs. A mad (and decidedly maddening) scramble ensued during which children went through pockets, crawled under seats, looked in Mommy's purse, snitched programs from one another, or like myself said, "The hell with it!" The actors, mind you, unable to continue without red spots, became equally annoyed, saying in polite British desperation, "Oh, do hurry up!" Finally, enough battered programs were unfolded, pieced together, and assembled to destroy the evil spell, and the play limped forward, but no one felt he had participated in a victory, and there was no sense of triumph. Only a hundred or so messy programs.

The entire sequence was arbitrary, presented for its own sake, to be endured simply because the author/director felt it was necessary to the occasion but nevertheless failed to make it so. Why hadn't red spots been mentioned earlier and the moment properly prepared for? (Barrie skillfully set up both his scene and his audience when he did it!) And more important to ask, why does a director think he is entertaining a child when in reality he is only giving him the opportunity to move about, make noise, or in this case perform janitorial services for the management by tidying up the floors? None of these activities are what theatre is all about, in fact each is better experienced at home or anywhere else other than in a playhouse. Unless, of course, they can be made to relate to character or plot in ways that are clear, enjoyable, *and* essential.

But even then might not the time have arrived for a moratorium to be declared on audience participation in general? Each new attempt seems weaker than the last. Invention, it appears, has dried up; the bottom of the barrel, as the above instance illustrates, reflects faces of bored youngsters. Until some fresh and disciplined examination is made to revivify and justify this tired tradition, we look in vain for creative smoke here: the house and all that was in it burned down long ago.

Alas, the problem cannot be erased so readily, even if every director and playwright agreed it should be, for in the public mind (and this includes students taking college courses in child drama) loud and robust audience participation *equals* children's theatre. They think if we but cause audiences to shout advice to the hero, to come on stage and kick heels, or to play mass party games, and if we but bring this activity to a pitch of perspiration and exhilaration that demands upon arrival at home a shower and a nap, we have a good show, probably a great show, at any event a popular success. A critic writing in the *New York Times* claimed, "This is what children's theatre is all about." On the other hand, if we but leave young people in their seats to watch a performance at which they are expected to respond spontaneously as civilized playgoers, we may have a dull show, a flop, a decided disappointment to a large percentage of the audience. So determined are some directors to turn theatres into playgrounds that dramatists often turn scripts into handbooks for conducting physical and vocal sallies. All too few write real plays for children to see and hear, plays in which they may recognize meaning in the lives of the characters and apply it to themselves. Theatre can offer no better form of participation than taking part in the creative process of a genuine play genuinely performed. Yet at present child audiences often are denied this opportunity as they are kept occupied in revels appropriate only to celebrating New Year's Eve.

Story Theatre and Reader's Theatre

Story Theatre, an entertainment devised by Paul Sills working with a group of highly skilled actors, first at Yale University, then on Broadway, and finally in a short-lived television sereis, has encouraged a host of imitators from coast to coast. How many, I wonder, really know what they are imitating? How many have been attracted to this theatrical form because it seems to be a simplified method of production? And this it may be except for the actors who in their vocal and physical command must be multitalented and constantly personable paragons and for the director who in his stage cleverness must be both magician and genius.

Even the imaginative Mr. Sills did not always attain these distinctions, as his eager nonprofessional disciples might remember before following too closely in his nimble footsteps. While warmly received by critics and audiences, his first edition of *Story Theatre*, the one drawing largely upon Aesop, the Brothers Grimm, and contemporary folk music, was summed up rather accurately by Walter Kerr as a pleasant evening but scarcely a breakthrough in either theatrical technique or dramatic format. The second edition, based on Ovid's *Metamorphoses*, attracted less enthusiasm from critics and audiences alike and disappeared all too swiftly (indeed, it contained some lovely moments, most of which, again, resulted from the loveliness of the people performing them). The third go-round, utilizing documents and materials depicting events in the American Revolution, closed abruptly out-of-town after being declared an artistic shambles.

The published version of the first *Story Theatre* provides only the lines spoken in performance which are and always have been royalty free to readers of Aesop and Grimm; the style of performance is not free but neither is it described nor prescribed in the text. So, actors and director must begin exactly where Sills began, with the words. But the theatrical shape they are to be given can be constructed only in the disciplined collaboration that exists among actors trained in improvisation and long experienced in working together. If Sills and company couldn't shape and construct them with consistency, how many of the rest of us are apt to succeed? Yet largely because it appears to be a cheap means of mounting a show and, above all, because it looks easy to achieve, how many of us will try?

For many the real lure to Sills' work, as it is to Reader's Theatre, another worthwhile style of performance when carefully prepared by experts as able as Emlyn Williams, John Gielgud, or Michael Redgrave and the Royal Shakespeare Company, is the false assumption that productions can be undertaken in much less time than that given to regular offerings. Perhaps by the Royal Shakespeare Company they can, but when given by the second-year acting class of the local high school or college, they require more rehearsals precisely because the actor is *all* and without theatrical embellishment he must emerge better than he normally manages to appear. This means prolonged preparation periods that foster his technical growth and allow him greater mastery of vocal delivery and physical expression. And this means hard work, and lots of it for everyone concerned, which when accomplished and repeated on a long-term basis well might produce an artistic breakthrough, at least at the local level, and perhaps beyond. Both adult and children's theatres need more Paul Sills and more concepts like Story

Theatre and Reader's Theatre at their best but for reasons of authentic ensemble experimentation and innovation, not for purposes of saving expenses
of budget, creative effort, or time.

Commedia Dell'arte Troupes

Familiar today in college and community theatres is the actor interested in
improvisational techniques who decides to band his friends together to
troupe to schools, hospitals, homes for the aged, prisons, streets, and parks
and there in a reckless and sometimes self-centered manner to perform im-
promptu wares in what is one more instance of instant theatre. A nomadic
schedule and a lack of scripts delude such groups into thinking they share
characteristics in common with the Renaissance-and-later companies who
created a great popular theatre in the Italian commedia dell'arte. So popular,
in fact, they could be seen in their heyday as far away from home as England,
Scandinavia, and Russia, and enjoyed by everyone even when no one understood a word spoken by the immensely agile and communicative
comedians.

In the last two decades Italian companies carrying forward this illustrious
tradition have visited New York City to prove that good commedia staging
and acting still knows no language barriers. The bona fide mastery of this art
form obviously comes from long years of perfecting timing and physical
dexterity to make performances look spontaneous, effortless, and inspired
when in reality they are plain hard work. (We must face the fact there is no
escaping the term "hard work" however far back in history we may go in
search of extemporaneous theatre or however much freedom of expression
we may gain today.) But this very lack of work, tradition, and training results in
some of our current troupes, who if they entertain at all, amuse mostly
themselves rather than the young, old, hospitalized, or jailed audiences before whom they play the fool, or to be more accurate, before whom they often
simply appear to be foolish. Hamlet knew what he was talking about when he
forbade his clowns to enjoy themselves by laughing or setting others to laugh
by departing from their declared purpose: "That's villainous and shows a
most pitiful ambition in the fool that uses it." Yet many villainous and pitifully
ambitious young actors presently use precisely this philosophy of "anything
for a laugh" in the name of commedia and children's theatre.

Any actor who assumes to take up Harlequin's motley first should prove his
right to wear that long honored and most respected of comic uniforms
through rigorous training and enforced nonpublic apprenticeship lest we
produce a generation of spectators who mistakenly equate history's disciplined commedia players on tour with today's fun-loving commune playmates on ego trips. True commedia can enrich our being while carefree
imitations may lead us merely to wonder what our ancestors found to be
hilarious for three centuries. A serious loss of laughter in our lives will result if
slapstick is permanently replaced by slapdash.

The Tingalary Bird. *Courtesy of New York University.*

Genuine Experimentation

If the smoke spreading from improper improvisation and infirmed instant-theatre techniques is cause for critical pause in an assessment of the growth of our field, we must not lose sight of spontaneous and participatory activity that constitutes genuine theatrical experiences for playgoers and performers. In both children's theatre and creative dramatics the best new works and practices regularly result from experimentation and unremitting testing in studio, classroom, rehearsal hall, and the creator's head.

Anyone who has seen The Paper Bag Players knows to what original heights improvisation can be taken, although the Bags, as they call themselves, do not actually improvise in performance but rather in the long developmental stages of their individual programs. A child senses that the Bags' is a world wherein anything can happen not because it can (or does) but because theirs is a stage wherein simplicity forbids clutter and prompts freedom to move and to make-believe. Their selectivity of an action or an idea appears to be right and exact probably because it results from trying and discarding a multitude of other possibilities. Theirs is a style in which discipline imparts a security and confidence that in performance becomes the essence of spontaneity. To these considerable attributes the Bags display a grasp of teamwork and interplay exemplified in the title of one of their shows, *Group Soup*, a smooth and well-balanced blend of showmanship. They emerge in performance as a bunch of kids involved in playing imaginative games with one another and with spectators of various ages and cultural backgrounds but always with command of everyone's attention and interest. Now well into their second decade as the major professional company for children in New York City, they continue to develop new themes and techniques at a self-determined rate of artistic progress in a creative process that distills concerned experimentation into carefully prepared entertainment.

The long-running revue *The Proposition Circus* improvises routines from suggestions made by the audience, resulting in a cabaret style of production of appeal to both children and adolescents. Here informal techniques are the means and end of the entertainment and the instant creative process becomes the finished product. Even when performed by experts, as is here the case, the results are certain to be uneven but more often than not amusing to watch and sometimes exciting to be present at as unexpected or inspired events take place.

Our best directors have encouraged experimentation both in scripts and production procedures. John Clark Donahue of the Children's Theatre Company of the Minneapolis Society of Fine Arts created a highly personal style of writing and staging dramatic fantasy in his *Hang on to Your Head* and *Good Morning, Mr. Tilly*. Tony Steblay, head of the Outreach Program for the Minneapolis Children's Theatre Company, often has collaborated with students and production staff in the total creation of an original production, such as the spirited *The Capture of Sarah Quincy*. Others have mixed conventional-script elements with freer nonstructured components in the hope of achieving a dynamic form of production. At New York's City Center, for example, a group of professional players have begun a play or revue in a more or less traditional manner, then stopped the performance at a point of high interest to divide the audience into several groups, each headed by an actor who supervised the improvisation of a unit of action required to complete the story. After a short rehearsal period, the play proceeded with the children becoming the players for the remainder of the program. At the University of Massachusetts, the performance, at least on one occasion, halted several times to invite an exchange between actors and spectators on the choices open to the characters and to determine thoughts and responses to the actions performed. In this way, director Carol Korty moved her audience inside the play and its people to become part of its machinery and to contribute to its heartbeat, leading one observer to write, "What was stunning and exalting about this piece . . . was its directness in handling powerful and sensitive emotional material and finding an absolutely true tone throughout." Obviously, the creative connection can be made through improvisation and participation when experimentation takes place at this level of artistic achievement, which, the same critic noted, met not the needs just of children "but of everyone who wants to be his or her own person."

Of course, the risks and costs of experimentation are high and producing groups must be prepared to take and pay them. When the Program in Educational Theatre at New York University presented the American premieres of *The Tingalary Bird* and *Winterthing*, money was lost as both plays failed to attract large audiences. Yet these problematic but original works deserved to be seen in this country just as serious students of child drama needed the experience of producing them. Moreover, both plays merited full productions if to be properly tested, with special attention given by designers to their technical demands, and with utmost consideration given by directors to their fascinating pitfalls. If no great activity took place at the box office, every other area of the theatre bristled with the excited industry of creating new plays for children that in their exploration of unusual themes, moods, and images really were new. More of us working in child drama willingly must take this kind of risk and be thankful for the criticism, even negative, that results. However expensive a gamble, genuine experimentation is essential to progress.

The Young Vic

In 1974 the Young Vic made its first appearance in New York City, bringing with it three plays and a reputation as one of England's keenest repertory companies with a particular knack for attracting thousands of young people to its starkly plain cement-block auditorium to fill singularly hard and unreserved benches, which sell for one low price of admission. Since 1969 this company has won critical and popular praise at home and abroad for producing lively mountings with little or sometimes no scenery and only economy costuming. In this country the Young Vic played in two handsome theatres with prices increased five times above what young people pay in London. Public response was limited at first; even with a rave review from Clive Barnes, *The Taming of the Shrew* drew only a handful of spectators to its Saturday matinee. Fortunately, as enthusiasm spread, larger and larger audiences found their way to Brooklyn to see the spirited *Shrew, Scapino*, and a revival of Terrence Ratigan's nostalgic comic romance, *French Without Tears*. Soon some of the excitement that surrounds the company in London began to emanate in New York, especially for its contemporary staging of Shakespeare and Molière. *Scapino* (adapted from Molière's commedia dell'arte play *Les Fourberies de Scapin*, written in 1671) several months later was brought to Broadway to become a commercial hit at still higher box office prices.

The creative smoke rising from the Young Vic, both in London and New York, signals zippy direction, often by Frank Dunlop, who also administers the company, and stylish acting by a group able to move and to speak at rates of speed frequently Olympian in their record-breaking dash and dexterity. Jim Dale, one of the most facile of the actor/athletes, flourishes an original manner that wins audiences of all ages who at the end of a performance may find themselves willingly playing imaginary musical instruments in an improvised orchestra he conducts with audacious cheer. (Audience participation, kept to the curtain call of *Scapino*, could not interrupt the speed of this theatrical track meet, which although it appears to be improvised actually is precisely mechanized. Nothing, says Dale, can be added or changed in performance, not a word, not a beat.)

Hopefully, the success of this visit will spur our own directors and actors into forming American counterparts of the Young Vic. But because we have no Frank Dunlop to make productions young and no Jim Dale to make performances ageless, they may think it can't happen here. This is nonsense. Both men are major talents in the British theatre who maintain professional careers outside their duties at the Young Vic. And when they are away others take their place with equal success. Their gifted presence, though treasured, is not indispensable to the artistic life of the company. What is? Good plays, for one thing. The repertory of the Young Vic is filled with major works by Pinter, Beckett, Stoppard, Genet, O'Casey, Osborne, as well as by Sophocles, Shakespeare, and Molière. Dunlop and Dale, and all the others who are part of this bright company, give themselves the best material in world drama upon which to perform their popular miracles. In his rave review entitled "Molière Never Looked Younger," Walter Kerr wrote: "*Scapin* can take any kind of updating; he lacked calendar and wrist watch to begin with." Knowing how to select and then make so-called classics and modern masterpieces appeal to a wide spectrum of young people is the great success of the Young Vic, for on almost any night in London you may see youngsters in the company of older brothers and sisters and take satisfaction that *together* they enjoy the play.

Here the play *is* the thing, and directors and actors make this known to audiences by giving it their full energy and inspired but not sacred respect. Jim Dale in interviews that accompanied his elevation to Broadway stardom reminded reporters who think his Scapino is mostly his own invention that every word he speaks was written by Molière. If he brings the character to life in contemporary terms, it so happens those also are Molière's. Dale has connected the meaning of Scapino's action to modern being, much to the delighted surprise of thousands of playgoers, young and otherwise.

The Young Vic, of course, is not perfect, however worthwhile has been much of its work. As yet it has not evolved a satisfactory style of play production for young children aged five through twelve, although its experiments in this field are noteworthy from time to time. The unhappy incidence of audience participation mentioned earlier took place as part of one embarrassingly unsuccessful attempt to win and reward these children as the company has their dedicated adolescent audiences. Along with the rest of us, they must continue to investigate this need, and one hopes with that same rapture and determination they presently give to Shakespeare and Molière.

It would be ironic and tragic indeed if the field that wishes to pioneer sensory and social awareness in creative development should isolate itself by its own self-absorption and blindness to the work of others. This danger is very real today as we, for the most part, continue to grow inward rather than outward. In the theatre, despite exceptions noted here, we still retread familiar fairy-tale plays instead of testing new works. In the classroom, despite major changes in student interests and values, we still invoke proved activities of the past instead of attempting untried experiences. How many teachers put students through Viola Spolin's exercises year after year as if they and not she had written *Improvisation for the Theatre*? How many students talk about Jerzy Grotowski without reading *Towards a Poor Theatre* and relating its meaning to their own artistic development and lives? And perhaps more important to ask, how many of us pursue careers as teachers and artists without connecting child drama to every other field concerned with young people? Who draws upon the findings of specialists in child psychology, child development, child behavior, educational psychology, educational sociology and anthropology, linguistics, language development, creativity, and so on, to enrich our work and ourselves? Who has studied the forms of games children have played throughout history and world civilizations to see how they might illuminate child drama and children's theatre?

If we don't make these connections, or teach our students to do so, we may come to be characterized in the manner of that ancient prophecy: "The fish will be the last to discover water." Like fish, we guide children scurrying through a universe at once timeless and everchanging; but unlike fish, we must lead them to recognize both their surroundings and themselves. Theatre and drama most effectively provide this opportunity and challenge, which when completely met will end our pioneering with smoke in the chimney that can camouflage nothing because it results from a creative process that contains its own reality and validity.

Postscript

While an author rarely is presented with the invitation to revise and update an article written some five years earlier, I have decided to leave the foregoing pages largely intact and add this commentary in which the smoking chimneys just discussed are reexamined briefly and several new ones mentioned. Even though certain dangers alluded to above may have lost momentum in the interim, schemes of "easy and quick" forms of dramatic activities and theatre for children always are with us and must be guarded against no matter what guises they take in each new decade. Indeed "instant theatre" now seems less a threat even if a few publishers continue to make extravagant claims that their texts are able to turn readers into experts without stipulating the basic need for extensive practical experience and long periods of direct contact with children and young people. And perhaps audience participation plays also have declined in popularity; far fewer scripts seem to be published and produced in the 1980s than in the mid-1970s. And the quality of these new texts tends to be better, although enough exceptions still appear to belie any vast improvement as an established trend. With the notable success in recent years of traditional plays renewed hope has grown, at least on my part, for the script that tells a story in purely dramatic and theatrical terms without incorporating "activities" or once demanding calculated or manipulated responses from audiences. Of course I believe that in the ever-growing repertory of children's drama a place exists for good audience participation plays; my original protest was not intended to annihilate the form but simply to sound an alarm against a fad, which like all fads, has the potential power to sweep away the good work of the past in the name of being "new" or "innovative" without necessarily improving or advancing the field. Obviously, the greater the diversity represented in our plays, the more exciting the repertory will become, as long as the quality of each is genuine in its uses of theatre and drama and in its respect for young audiences. Let's hope the day never arrives when popular consensus either accepts one style as *the only* form of plays for young people or forbids any legitimate form from being heard.

Story Theatre and Readers' Theatre largely have receded from public playhouses to classrooms and studio workshops where they discover effective uses in the hands of participants who improvise scenes or read stories and plays, seizing upon their most actable moments and theatrical ingredients. Paul Sills' Story Theatre, as described here, has not reemerged on Broadway, nor has Readers' Theatre with the notable exception of Alec McCowen's impressive recitation of the entire *Gospel According to St. Mark*. On the other hand, a series of mono or solo dramas, that is, one-character plays, has appeared, portraying personalities such as George Bernard Shaw, Emily Dickinson, Oscar Wilde, Theodore Roosevelt, Harry Truman, and Gertrude Stein; it may be worthwhile to investigate this form of theatre to see what it offers young audiences.

In the realm of "genuine experimentation" it is a pleasure to report that the Paper Bag Players continue to be active and maintain their enormous popularity both in New York City and on tour and that The Children's Theatre Company and School flourishes vigorously in its handsome playhouse in Minneapolis. But others, such as The Proposition Circus and the New York City Center Company, sadly have disappeared; and their places not been taken by new faces, ideas, or productions.

We may take comfort from the fact that more and more tryout productions of new plays prove profitable to playwrights and to producers alike. When, for instance, The Washington Square Players of New York University produced *The Little Humpback Horse* in a new adaptation, all seats for the morning performances were reserved in advance, even though the title was unfamiliar (everywhere except in Russia where the fairy-tale epic is a classic of children's literature). Perhaps because it sounded like a promising story or because the design of the poster exuded excitement, the play lured schools to purchase large blocks of seats, and it outsold both Shakespeare and Ibsen in the series of mainstage productions. Artistic risks that sell tickets are doubly rewarding, to be certain, and we must be grateful that companies are willing to take and to realize them.

The later fate of The Young Vic is less happy to report than the early success story described here, for its visit to the United States failed to serve as a model for an American counterpart, and upon its return to London the company changed hands a number of times, always moving closer to disaster. No director since Frank Dunlop has made a strong or lasting impression, nor has any subsequent group of actors achieved the distinctive style of the first. The Young Vic has suffered enormous cuts in its subsidies and now operates only a limited season, the rest of the year accommodating visiting companies offering plays for adults. Dunlop later returned to Brooklyn to create an adult repertory theatre at the Academy of Music, which in spite of several promising productions soon vanished. Still, the original example of The Young Vic concept and its remarkable initial years should not be forgotten, either in England or America.

One chimney with smoke that has become significantly visible in the last five years derives from the appearance of more and more plays in print. I do not refer to those new titles in acting editions that publishers offer producers each year; these seldom are intended for young readers and almost never make their way into libraries or bookstores. I speak of hardcover editions issued by established publishers of juvenile literature who now include plays among their titles by distinguished authors such as Joan Aiken, Ossie Davis, and Madeleine L'Engle. Anthologies offer an ever-widening choice of plays of high quality rather than the standard adaptations of the past. In fact, so many good plays are available that when I prepared a university course in dramatic literature for young people, I faced the difficult decision of which among the many excellent titles to select for study.

Young people are writing plays as well as reading them. Each May in London The Young People's Scheme of the Royal Court Theatre stages a festival of plays written by young people. Hundreds of scripts are submitted in hopes of professional production, which British critics and theatregoers take seriously and support for a two-week run. Some of these plays display remarkable abilities among the young dramatists, who range in age from ten to eighteen years, and whose styles vary from theatre of the absurd to realistic depictions of daily life in school and community. Is it too much to hope that a university or regional theatre implement such a festival here and give life to the dramatic talents of young American and Canadian dramatists?

The widespread increase of theatre-in-education also must be hailed as a significant indication of greater acceptance and use of drama. Educational programs developed by regional theatres, universities, and drama specialists are welcomed in schools, hospitals, and recreation and rehabilitation centers, whereas only five years ago examples were limited to a few centers of activity. Today they also may be found at work in libraries and in geriatric and religious and civic centers, as well as in industry and business organizations. Young museum visitors who enact the story of a famous painting and are stimulated to create the movements suggested by a statue enjoy a genuine creative experience, one which could not take place as completely and effectively from merely passing through vast halls and only looking at the attractions on view.

The success of the Creative Arts Team, a professional theatre-in-education company in residence at New York University, has led to the creation of a second team and to extensive programs in conjunction with foundations and organizations such as the board of education and the New York Urban Coalition. These and other groups sponsor workshops for adults as well as young people and commission theatre pieces such as *The Tower of Babble*, a T.I.E. presentation on the dilemma of inadequate communication within a large public school system. The Director of the New York Urban Coalition, Lynn Gray, in commenting on the need for this show, stated: ". . . the Coalition wants to share its hope with you: that our energy can be constructive and creative, and that all of us can learn to see what is important to support and develop within our schools." Significantly, the Coalition has selected theatre-in-education programs and techniques to achieve its goals because, Gray contends, "the Creative Arts Team can talk clearly and powerfully. C.A.T. can help all of us learn to listen and to see. And so to grow."

Once these goals and achievements belong to everyone who brings drama into the lives of young people, we will see smoke emitting from even more chimneys in the coming years.

NOTES

1. Richard Crosscup, *Children and Dramatics* (New York: Scribner's, 1966), p. 7.
2. Ibid.
3. Philip A. Coggin, *The Uses of Drama* (New York: Braziller, 1956), pp. 222–25.
4. Paul Zindel, "The Theater Is Born Within Us," *New York Times*, 26 July 1970, Arts and Leisure Section, p. 1.

"Plees Make More"

Aurand Harris

Aurand Harris, author of twenty-five published plays for children, is one of America's most produced children's theatre playwrights. His plays have appeared in twelve foreign countries. He is the winner of a dozen playwrighting contests; was the first recipient of the Chorpenning Cup, the annual award given by the Children's Theatre Association to an outstanding children's playwright; and is one of the few children's theatre playwrights to receive a Creative Writing Fellowship from the National Endowment for the Arts. Born in Missouri, Mr. Harris received his bachelor's degree from the University of Kansas City and his master's degree from Northwestern. He has taught creative dramatics and directed productions in the public schools of Gary (Indiana), William Woods College, Teachers College of Columbia University, University of Texas at Austin, Grace Church School of New York, and at various summer theatres. He holds strong convictions regarding the function of drama in education, both formal and informal, but in this essay he addresses himself only to the question of writing a play for a young audience.

I was lucky. I was in the Chicago area when three great women were making children's theatre history in America. I was on the campus of Northwestern University when Winifred Ward was teaching her concept of creative dramatics and was starting the Children's Theatre of Evanston. To me she was an inspiration, and continues to be a critic and a friend.

Charlotte Chorpenning was writing and directing formal children's plays at the Goodman Memorial Theatre, showing her audiences and students what good children's theatre could and should be. I saw her plays, analyzed and

153

learned from her technique, and along with hundreds of children enjoyed her Saturday productions.

In Gary, Indiana, Mildred Harter Wirt was pioneering Auditorium in the public schools, using the elements of theatre as a pivotal subject in the school curriculum. My first experience in children's drama was under her encouraging supervision, teaching twelve classes a day in creative and formal drama. Winifred Ward, Charlotte Chorpenning, Mildred Harter Wirt—I started my children's theatre career at the right time in the right place.

Since then children's theatre in America has grown in quantity—more than fifteen hundred producing groups—and grown in quality—our productions at the recent international ASSITEJ meeting were first-rate. It is exciting to be a children's playwright in these expanding years.

I am often asked, "Why do you write for children?" A simple answer is that I like children and I like what children like in the theatre. When I write, however, I do not think, "I am writing a *children's* play." I write the best play I can, using the best characterizations, the best dialogue, and the best theatre techniques I can muster. I do not write "down" to a child. I write to please myself, an adult. I do use a child's theme for a plot. And there are certain adjustments—such as shorter playing time and quicker motivations, less dialogue and more action in developing the plot—but I do not find these limitations a handicap. Rather, they are a dramatic challenge and a good discipline. A children's play is lean and vigorous; it moves with an unyielding beat to a satisfying conclusion. If, as I write, all goes well, the finished play is one I like—and so do children.

I have continued to be lucky. Year after year I have enjoyed daily contact with children—teaching, observing, and learning. This consistent rapport, I feel, is essential in writing for children. Some writers, skilled craftsmen, do not succeed either in fiction or drama because they do not know, respect, or try to understand the world of the young. They have never shared or laughed or cried with a child.

The empathy a playwright has for a child's world is reflected in the first step of writing a children's play, the selection of material. Good plays have the same qualities that are found in all good children's literature—plots simple enough to involve the child, complex enough to challenge him, and emotional enough to satisfy him—all of which contribute to the revelation of a universal truth.

Many children's playwrights write only original scripts. One successful Englishman always devises his own plots because, as he confided to me, he finds doing research dull and adaptation hard work. It can be. But I find a good children's story can trigger my imagination and start me writing a play at once. While if I wait for a blinding flash of inspiration for an original plot, I may wait and wait and wait. Personally I enjoy doing research related to a situation that I find dramatic. From such searching I have learned a great deal about human behavior, social customs, and history in a profitable and painless way. It can also add interest to my conversation when I casually mention that Thomas Jefferson was the first President to wear long trousers, a historical fact that I found in my research for *Yankee Doodle*.

The time spent and the techniques used in adapting a story, I find, help me to organize my thinking, clarify the theme, and crystallize a dramatic concept. There are several ways in which one can treat a story in preparing it for the stage.

I have *dramatized* some stories, keeping faithfully to the text. In *Steal Away Home* I changed only that which was necessary to transfer the printed page to the stage. The characters were fully developed by Jane Kristof in her book. She also had written an exciting, straightforward plot. I had only to *adapt* it, to give the characters realistic dialogue, to make the scenes visual in action, and to give the play a mood and tempo which heightened the suspense of two boys, runaway slaves, escaping on the Underground Railroad.

I have written plays *suggested by* stories. Here it is the idea, the theme of the story, that is used and that the playwright treats in any manner he feels he can make theatrical and effective. Along with most children's playwrights I wanted to write a Pinocchio play. But the little puppet was already the hero of several scripts. I needed a new approach. In my research I discovered a second Pinocchio book, *Pinocchio in Africa* by Cherubini, which describes further adventures of Pinocchio. I wrote a play *suggested by* the book. I changed the locale from Africa to America where the same adventures happened to Pinocchio with the natives of America as did with the natives of Africa. He swam the Atlantic Ocean instead of the Red Sea but escaped from the same strange fish. I called the play *Pinocchio and the Indians*.

This was an early play written before I learned that many children's theatre people tend to be purists. (I include myself among them now.) Pinocchio is a familiar and popular hero. Children expect a play about him to follow the traditional plot. They want to see the scenes they have read and reread and loved. My departure from the cherished and expected was, I am afraid, too removed. Cinderella should always go to a fairy-tale ball, not fly to Mars. If you must write such a new treatment—and I am in favor of any original writing— don't call her Cinderella, but instead, perhaps Cindy. I did this, in fact. I used the Cinderella theme when I wrote *A Toby Show*. Cindy (she has a stepmother and two stepsisters) goes to a costume ball with the aid of Toby, the traditional red-haired, freckled-faced country bumpkin. There she dances with a modern prince and as the final curtain falls, flies away in his airplane.

Most children's plays based on stories are adaptations. Most of my plays are. This is a happy combination of using much of the story but fashioning it in an individual, dramatic and theatrical form. I *adapted* Phyllis McGinley's *The Plain Princess*. Her comments, accompanying her final approval, were to this effect: She liked the unity of the play—I had condensed it. She liked the individualizing of the characters—I had given each daughter a definite personality. She liked the theatrical stage effects—I had heightened each change in the Princess's attitude by a visual stage picture. She liked the spirit of fun and fantasy—I had only underlined the feeling of *her* book.

The most popular play I have written is *Androcles and the Lion*. It has had over six thousand performances, been translated into four languages, been given in such distant places as Nigeria, Czechoslovakia, and Midway, South Pacific. *Androcles and the Lion* is based on an Aesop fable, but I wrote it in a definite theatrical style. It is played as it might have been performed by a group of commedia dell'arte actors in Italy in the sixteenth century. So far is the content of the play from the simple fable that the publisher wisely describes it as "adapted very freely." I have even "collaborated" with William Shakespeare, giving him full credit for the lines I used in my *Robin Goodfellow* from his *A Midsummer Night's Dream*.

Whether it be an adaptation or a dramatization, I have found using a good story as the basis for a plot the best way for me to start writing a play. And I must admit I find it easier. The plot and the characters are there, even the title. If it is a good story the theme is usually universal and has a wide appeal. The title is known, which gives it immediate interest to children and parents. I feel more secure with a proven property. Instead of spending time and energy, or feeling doubt about an original plot, I prefer to start thinking in theatre terms immediately, outlining and *writing* the play. It may be a part of the director in me, but this is what I like and enjoy—taking a scene and making it come alive with actors for an audience. I feel if I can write a good play, one I like and one which children like, it doesn't matter if the plot is original or not. The important thing is that the finished play should be good theatre and entertaining to children. I might add it is also a comfort to know that Shakespeare usually used someone else's plot, and Shakespeare did very well.

The important thing is to start the writing. Original plays are often sparked by an idea, a character, or a dramatic situation. Stories and poems can be used as source material. There are two folksongs that I think have dramatic potential, but as yet I have not found a style, a concept that fits them and which I feel is right for me. Some scripts are written upon request. I began working on *Buffalo Bill* at the invitation of an American company that was to tour Europe. My problem in writing it was to make a hero out of a man whose claim to fame was killing off our native animals. The tour never materialized, but I *wrote* the play. Another play I might not have undertaken without outside stimulus was *The Flying Prince*. I was commissioned to write it by the Indian Embassy and the Washington Children's Theatre. It was given a gala and exciting premiere in the nation's capital during an International Theatre Month.

The most difficult part of writing for me is doing the outline and beginning the first draft. The joy of writing to me is rewriting and more rewriting. This can prove to be a rejuvenating experience if I feel I am making the script better each time.

I do not intend this to be an essay on how to write a play. Writing is a

From Androcles and the Lion *by Aurand Harris, produced at the University of Texas at Austin. Courtesy of Coleman Jennings.*

personal and unique craft. If I were a clock maker, after constructing twenty workable clocks I would have a certain confidence that the next clock I made would run. After more than twenty plays, I have no assurance that the next play I write will work. Each play is a new uncharted exploration that develops an inevitability of its own. When all goes well, the finished play can be a work of joy. But because it is shaped by fallible human hands and heart the result can be, and often is, disappointing for both the author and audience. There are certain general and elementary principles that are helpful to a play-wright—building entrances and exits, developing rhythm in dialogue, show-ing all the important scenes *on* the stage—but each writer has his own and best and eccentric ways of creating a play. I outline. I write with a pencil on a clipboard. I chew the pencil. I mark out, insert, draw arrows on the pages until I must type my scribbles to be able to read them. When there is a typed form, the play suddenly takes on a professional look which spurs me on to the next scene. No matter how or when or where—even in the bathtub where I have had some of my best ideas—it is only after I am so filled with the characters and the scenes that I feel forced to give them life, that I can start to write a play. Then I spend a long enjoyable time acting on my imaginary stage. And I fall in love with the characters.

In children's theatre there is a cry for more plays. Literature looks to the past and to many languages for its masterpieces. Children's drama in America is young and does not have a full library of native or foreign classics.

America is young. In its first century it fought for survival and built a nation. There was little time for the arts. Also, it is only in this century that theatre has become respectable, that America has started to overcome its early Puritan prejudice. In the early years, no lady or her children attended the theatre, and certainly they never performed in it. A theatre for children was inconceivable. This lack of cultural heritage is one reason there are so few plays.

However, children's theatre slowly has been building a library. A few American playwrights have been contributing consistently; a few forward-looking publishing houses have been printing more children's plays; and recently there has been an international interest in, and exchange of, plays with other countries. But as times have changed, so have theatrical styles and conventions. Children have changed; even the auditorium structures have changed. Older plays have begun to show their age. So more plays, new plays, which suit our changing attitudes, styles, and children are needed. An extending theatre must not only continue to make use of its past but also keep its doors open wide to the new works.

There is also a cry in children's theatre for "better" plays. This is the continuing cry on Broadway, in the movies, and on television. It is a cry I am sure was heard by Shakespeare and Sophocles. When I began to write for children, the cry loud in my ears, I vowed to myself I would try to write a "better" play. Of course I did not know quite what it was or how to do it. Several plays later, I discovered what others before me must have discovered: There is no perfect play for everyone for every occasion. There is a need in America not for a "better" play but for many kinds of good children's plays to satisfy the many different tastes, standards, and demands.

The demand for, and the receptiveness of children's theatre to, all types of plays is another reason I find writing for the young stimulating. I have experimented with traditional fairy tales, a modern barnyard comedy, a musical melodrama, a historical epic, a circus script with audience participation, a lyrical tale of the East, a dark comedy, an old-fashioned farce, a patriotic musical review, and my latest play, *The Arkansas Bear*, a modern fantasy with a serious theme of death. I have no illusions that any of these plays is a "better" play. I wrote each because I felt that particular story and style would produce good theatre and good entertainment for children. There has been a wide variance in the popularity of these plays which, I think, reflects in part the wide scope of needs and tastes in children's theatre.

A playwright does not write for himself alone, no matter what romances he may have at his typewriter. He writes plays hoping that they will be performed and be enjoyed by audiences. A production of a play is of necessity a cooperative effort, and the playwright as an honored parent slowly diminishes in importance. In the beginning he is almost a deity, having imagined a new world. He grows less important during rehearsals, and at the final performances he is looked upon as an outsider. This is as it should be. The actors have taken over the characters. The action and the dialogue belong to them.

Author? Who is he? The typewriter ribbon, the umbilical cord, has been cut.

The cooperative venture of presenting a play involves many people. Those who first read it and select it. Later those who interpret and mount it. These people may hold a variety of opinions. They may differ widely in their tastes, demands, and standards. America is not a small, homogeneous country. It is big. Accordingly children's theatre covers a wide spectrum reflecting different mores of different regions. Art is always controversial. It is healthy that in a democracy we can voice our approval and disapproval of theatre tastes. It also can make for confusion and disagreement in theatre practices and standards. Even as small and provincial as Broadway is, the critics often do not agree on the merits of a play. The playwright should be aware that there are certain questions in American children's theatre upon which people, respected in their professional fields and who will produce his plays, often disagree.

Should a play be acted by *children* or by *adults*? The answer to the question may dictate the playwright's approach. Because Shakespeare knew his female parts would be played by boys, he no doubt wrote fewer parts for women, fewer scenes, and often had females disguise themselves as men. If children's plays are performed by child actors, then it would seem characters should be written that lie within the acting scope of most children. I have directed plays both with an all children's cast (which is often a necessity in educational drama, ages seven to seventeen) and with a mixed cast of children and adults. It is my personal feeling that, ideally, any play is best cast with actors whose types and ages are closest to the characters they are playing.

Should or should not a children's play have audience participation? This directly affects the playwright. In plays for younger children, audience participation at times can be used effectively. But for older children watching a formal play, overt participation can often be a distraction, a breaking of the necessary dramatic contact. When the aesthetic distance is destroyed and the audience loses its belief in the world of make-believe, then it becomes a part of an informal happening. There are times when audience participation can be dramatic—the one time Barrie used it in *Peter Pan*—and it can give variety if it is used legitimately and sparingly. I have used it. It is one kind of children's drama. But I feel it can never be the "blood and bones" of children's theatre. From observing some children's plays, I feel that audience participation was not used legitimately to heighten an effect, but to cover up inadequacies in the script and production. It appears that audience participation is at times the only way some producers know to gain and hold attention. To me, in the theatre a party is not a play.

Which type of stage is best suited to children's drama? Theatre-in-the-round? The thrust stage? Or the proscenium arch? The physical stage on which his play is to be performed affects the playwright. Shakespeare wrote for the Globe Theatre. He knew the upper stage could be used for a balcony, the inner stage could be used for "discovering" scenes. He knew there was no scenery, so he could quickly change locales; but he also knew he must write descriptive passages to inform the audience.

The children's theatre playwright does not know upon what type of stage his play will be performed. Some plays, both adult's and children's, can be staged successfully in several ways. Some cannot. Since most children's plays are fantasies and a fantasy lends itself to imaginative and unusual staging, different kinds of physical stages can often be used. But to me, fantasy fades with proximity. The theatre by its nature is illusion, and to me, illusion is strongest when there is an aesthetic distance. Perhaps because I was trained in the proscenium-arch theatre, I usually write with a picture-frame stage in mind, carefully visualizing each scene with stage right, stage left, and footlights. Children are visually minded, and what they see is of utmost importance. As I write and as I direct, I try to visualize what the child will see as a stage picture, changing minute to minute, in scene to scene, and it is easier for me to see that the grouping, movement, emphasis, relationships, and so on are clearly and visibly pointed if the play is framed in a proscenium arch.

The in-the-round, or to a lesser degree, a thrust stage, makes for a closer physical intimacy between the actors and the audience. A rapport and an intimacy are important in a children's play. Certainly the upper balconies and the back rows of a large auditorium are bad and should never be used for children's audiences. But for me theatre-in-the-round has often been *too* intimate. I do not like to see the perspiration of the Brave Little Tailor as he strikes seven at a blow, the obvious makeup of the Cat Who Walked By Himself, or the sprays of saliva from King Oberon. A proper aesthetic distance can create the illusion that Pocahontas has built a glowing fire, although in reality it is only a light bulb covered with orange paper. Another problem is that the audience on the other side of the magic circle can become more entertaining—or distracting—than the play. Also, every movement in any play, especially a children's play, should have a definite and meaningful motivation. But too often the movement on the in-the-round stage seems to be motivated only to help the audience see most of the actors most of the time.

The stage with a limited thrust can be a happy medium between the arena and the proscenium-arch stage. Here scenes can be played closer to the audience, yet there are side entrances and a solid backing for scenery and lighting effects. For several summers I have directed on a modified thrust stage at the Harwich Junior Theatre, and I have found with some changing most plays can be effectively staged. In the thrust, as well as the picture-frame stage, Peck's Bad Boy can confide his thoughts to the audience with intimate asides, yet all the audience can see his pranks at the same time and laugh together.

Should children's plays have intermissions or not? Certainly this is a concern of the playwright. Intermissions are a theatrical convention that changes with the years. The adult theatre in America has in its short history gone from five acts to four, three, two and to an occasional long one-act. The popular children's plays of Charlotte Chorpenning were usually divided into three acts, which corresponded to the popular form in the adult theatre in her time. There is a tidy unity in three acts: Act I, exposition, introduction of characters, beginning of conflict; Act II, complications, with a high point at the second act curtain; Act III, short and with a satisfying resolution of the conflict. Intermissions can be used for various reasons. The dramatist may use an intermission to show a passage of time; the actor may use it to catch his breath; the audience may use it for physical release after a period of emotional concentration, or for a trip to the bathroom; and not least, the producer may use it to supplement the box-office by selling candy and refreshments.

Most children's theatre producers do not think of an intermission in terms of the structure of the play but think of intermission in terms of its effect on the audience. Can or will an audience of children sit still without a stretch? Can an audience of children be controlled if there is an intermission?

I have written three-act, two-act, and one-act plays—with prologues and epilogues, depending on the nature of the material. The average child who is old enough physically and emotionally to enjoy children's theatre is capable of sustaining attention for an hour and a half, and will if the production is good. However, I feel any audience needs "relaxers" during the performance. This can be accomplished by scenes devised for that purpose. I try to do this. And it can also be done by stopping the play—intermission. I also do this. In my opinion it is the play itself, as an artistic form, which dictates and determines when, where, and how many breaks there should be. These should be observed. But each producer has the choice of observing them with intermissions of several minutes or by simply closing and reopening the curtains and letting the play continue. The play then can retain its intrinsic form, and each producer can be true to his theory of intermissions. Those who want full intermissions can let the children wave and call to their friends or search for a lost glove. While those who want no intermission can get the audience out before the assembly bell rings, and have no worry of house-program airplanes flying from the balcony.

There are many more questions that affect the playwright. What length should a play for children be? One hour or longer? Should the cast be small for touring or large for a community project? For what age span, if any, should a play be written? Should there be less fantasy and more realism in style? Should children's plays deal with current issues and problems—segregation, divorce, women's lib? (Children's books have grown to include best sellers with such themes as abortion, drugs, death, sex, and war.)

The answers to these questions, as far as the playwright is concerned, should be determined not by outside opinions or pressures but by the material *he* selects and the approach *he* feels is right. The running time of a play should be as long, and only as long, as it takes to tell the story effectively.

There is no place in a children's play for extraneous padding.When I wrote *Circus in the Wind* I constantly resisted the temptation to insert theatrical circus acts; though entertaining, they would have interrupted the action.

The cast should include only those characters necessary to the plot. Too many characters confuse a child. There are, however, legitimate situations that can utilize "mob" scenes. This helps make a more flexible-size cast. When I wrote a children's version of Molière's *A Doctor in Spite of Himself* I included in the household (a rich one) several additional maids who, when they appeared together, caused one critic to mention them as a clever Greek chorus.

The story itself and its treatment will determine the best age of the audience for the play. Many good plays appeal on different levels to all ages. One reason I suspect for the enormous popularity of *Androcles and the Lion* is that the fun of the commedia dell'arte style appeals equally to the youngest and to the oldest.

The playwright will choose his subject—contemporary and realistic, historic or fantasy—intuitively. He will choose a theme to which he feels attuned. I have started and later had to stop writing on a theme to which I found I could not relate, while most of my best scenes have been the easiest to write because I knew them, I understood them, I felt them. Although writers should be aware that producers have different opinions, standards, and needs, and the writer may try to meet them as far as artistic integrity will allow, the playwrights who are giving the American children's theatre its vitality, its innovations, and its stature are the playwrights who are writing what they believe, who are following Shakespeare's good advice: "To thine own self be true."

A play is as good as its production. The first plays given for children in America were produced mostly by dedicated individuals whose sincerity and effort overshadowed their lack of training and professional standards. Slowly this has changed.

There have always been a few professional companies presenting, sometimes touring, plays for children. But until recently there have been but few, and those not of long duration. Bravely they have done, and continue to do, their best with the ever-pressing problem of inadequate financial support. Children's theatre, like most performing arts, can rarely pay its way. The professional children's theatre companies need the best talent to produce first-rate productions, but without sufficient money this is still a problem. Like the opera, children's theatre in America is a luxury. When it is recognized as a cultural force, as is the opera, and supported, as is the opera, children's theatre may also become grand.

The important growth in children's theatre, however, in both quality and quantity has been in the many regional groups. The best of these are usually located in university or civic areas where a pool of trained and interested people provide a reservoir of talent. It is their productions that have broken a vicious circle in which children's theatre was caught. Previously, because most children's plays were produced by well-intentioned amateurs, children's theatre did not mature in professional quality. And without artistic excellence, children's theatre continued to be considered an amateur stepchild. That has changed. A new circle is beginning. Because many children's plays now are being produced by trained people, children's theatre is maturing in quality. And as it proves itself in artistic excellence, it is attracting more talented artists, and hopefully the momentum will grow until the best directors, actors, technicians, and writers will become a vital part of children's theatre. And hopefully the circle will extend and include the best artists of Broadway, television, music, and the dance. Theatre complexes will be built for children's performing arts; and a large, regular audience will emerge throughout the nation.

Since in America there is no Little Broadway to give children's theatre a focal point, a place of national prestige, or to set high standards, the future, I believe, of children's theatre lies in the universities, the civic, and the regional theatres. They have trained theatre people, physical facilities, and a budget. I have been a playwright-in-residence at several of these types of theatres. Their enthusiasm, talent, and high artistic standards have stimulated me. If these and other regional centers continue to train, encourage, discover potential talent, increase the number of productions, and undertake tours of good children's plays, I feel that we can achieve a national theatre for the young that will rank high in the international world of children's theatre.

Born in the slums to do social work, growing rapidly enough in seventy years to be an invited guest as an educational and cultural force at the White House Conference on Children and Youth, children's drama in America is a twentieth-century phenomenon.

I am optimistic, although a bit impatient. I, along with others, will continue to write the best plays I can because I believe that good children's theatre is a child's rightful heritage. And I like my fan mail:

> I injoyd your play   I laft   It is real
> —like my dog   plees make more

If I am a bit impatient, it is because I would still like to be around when children's drama reaches a national standard of excellence in writing and production, when it is accepted and supported as an established twenty-first-century cultural tradition. I would like to be around when children's plays are regarded as dramatic literature, placed on library shelves, chosen for inclusion in the Ten Best Plays, even considered for the Pulitzer Prize. Then the time might come that I am waiting for, when a child, asked what he'd like to be when he grows up, answers proudly, "A children's playwright."

From Literature
to Drama to Life

Nancy King

*Nancy King is a member of the theatre faculty of the University of Dela-
ware. She received a bachelor's degree in movement and dance from the
State University of New York at Cortland and a master's in theatre from
the University of Delaware. Further study of dance and kinesiology took
place at the University of Wisconsin and Connecticut College School of
the Dance, as well as workshops in child drama, circus skills, the Alex-
ander Technique, massage, and nonverbal communication. She is best
known for her books,* Theatre Movement: the Actor and His Space *and*
Giving Form to Feeling. *She is the author of numerous articles and plays
for children's audiences. Her latest book,* A Movement Approach to Acting,
pursues the study of movement as it relates to the actor and his training.

*Professor King has held previous positions with community centers,
Head Start, Looking Glass Theatre of Providence, The Mary C. Wheeler
School for Girls, and Pembroke College. These experiences have been a
unique preparation for the teacher workshops and guest seminars she
conducts throughout the United States and Canada. She has also taught
in England and for the Scandinavian Drama Association in Denmark,
Norway, and Sweden.*

*She is an active member of the American Theatre Association, the
Children's Theatre Association of America, and ASSITEJ, the international
theatre association for young people. Her regular contributions to regional and national conferences establish her as one of the leading
younger members of our profession.*

The group of adults and children quietly worked at clearing a space in the
middle of the large classroom. Bits of furniture, clothing, and toys were

carefully placed in the empty space as people established life in a small fishing village. One child took a small toy, moved away from the group, and walked to the edge of the playing area as if to remove herself as much as possible from the main action. Suddenly, those not participating in the life of the village formed a huge wave, which grew in movement and intensity of sound. The villagers tried to flee, to protect themselves as best they could, but the power of the wave was too much. Soon everything was swept away and nothing remained but an empty, silent space.

As the lone child returned to the quieted waters she looked around in horror at the emptiness. Slowly the full meaning of what had happened penetrated her being, and she sank to her knees and rocked with despair. Clutching her small toy to her chest, she crooned a chant that was half sound, half sob. Then there was only silence.

This is what the group had planned to do to show their response to the book *The Big Wave*.[1] Each of the three groups had been asked to take the event in the book that had the greatest impact on them and physicalize it for the rest of the class. The group was preparing to discuss their feelings about the book when one member of the class who had been watching, an eight-year-old boy, suddenly got up from his seat. Without paying any attention to anyone else, he ran to the girl, knelt down in front of her, took her face in his hands, and said, "Come with me. You can live with me and my family. We will help you." The girl looked at the boy as if not fully understanding his words. "Come," he repeated. "Come with me to my family in the mountains. There you will be safe." The girl followed the boy, still holding on to his hand. She left the space in the middle of the room and sat down in a seat next to his.

In the discussion that followed, the members of the group sharing their work explained that for them, the moment of greatest impact was when the tidal wave wiped out the whole fishing village except for the child, Jiya, who had been in the mountains. The boy who came to rescue Jiya said, "The part of the story that made me feel the most was when Jiya is all alone and Kino finds her and invites her to stay with Kino and his family. Sometimes I feel a little like Jiya when my mother and father go out and I have to stay with a new babysitter. I feel all alone and terrible until I get to know the babysitter and I can stop feeling so bad. When I saw Sharon all alone, it reminded me of how I feel, and I just wanted her to know that she still had a friend."

Many in the group shared experiences of when they had felt lost or lonely. Some told what they did to make themselves feel better. One child said, "I always carry my bear with me, just in case I have to make myself feel better real fast." The children thought that was a very good idea, and as one child expressed her thoughts, "In case your house burned down at least you would have one toy left." When the sharing of experiences tapered off, someone suggested that they should read *The Wave*,[2] which was also about a tidal wave in Japan. Soon, many other books dealing with themes of loss, friendship, and coping with change were suggested for further reading. No one paid any attention to the level of difficulty of books. The whole emphasis was placed on the quality of the story told.

Working from the cycle of literature to drama to life provides children with a circular experience that starts by enabling them to enter someone else's world through reading or hearing a story, translating the meaning of that experience into another form (drama), which in turn gives rise to personal reflection, leading to a new or fuller understanding of life. The circle is continued as children read other books on similar or contrasting themes, which starts the process all over again.

Using literature as a source for making drama

1. Offers children a chance to explore a variety of books that preserve, explain, and/or question culture and tradition
2. Encourages children to go beyond books with controlled vocabulary or those designed for a particular age or reading level
3. Provides a way of looking at specific genres such as traditional tales, realistic fiction, fantasy, and poetry
4. Creates a common experience with which the group can explore ideas and feelings
5. Provides material with which to connect and transform personal experience
6. Enables children to recognize patterns in literature such as enchanted people; magical transformation, tasks or trials, magical objects, wishes and trickery, talking animals, fools and simpletons, and others, which can then become the basis for developing imaginative dramas of their own
7. Provides children with imaginative experience that can serve as the basis for personal reflection, critical thinking, and increased vocabulary with which to express thoughts and emotions
8. Expands children's notions of what is possible, to read about other people who have had analogous experience and consider ways with which these experiences have been dealt

Using drama as a way of responding to literature

1. Provides the child with the opportunity to physicalize, through nonverbal means, thoughts and feelings that result from reading or hearing the literature
2. Deepens the child's understanding of the story
3. Enables the child to understand the book from his or her point of view
4. Creates the opportunity to explore the story from alternative points of view
5. Provides the child with an understanding, through doing, of form, both story and drama
6. Enables children, as a group, to share comments that reveal differences in response without having to decide which idea is best or right
7. Encourages children to notice detail and ask questions while exploring motivation and action
8. Provides children with the opportunity to act as if they were other people behaving as children might not otherwise do or feel, and to imagine times and places other than their own

Using drama as a means of developing skills for living

1. Develops the child's ability to create solutions to problems when faced with unknown situations or incomplete information
2. Provides the opportunity to deal with different points of view, culture, and social skills
3. Provides children with the opportunity to develop new responses to old challenges
4. Acting as if you were someone else provides children with the chance to understand other people from their point of view, and to accept differences in feelings
5. Develops ease of verbal and nonverbal expression and the ability to interact
6. Develops ability to formulate and ask questions and to challenge ideas and attitudes
7. Creates alternatives for dealing with strong emotions such as anger and love, both in one's self and with others
8. Develops a vocabulary with which to express feelings and attitudes

One of the most common ways of using literature to stimulate drama is to have the children act out the story. Although this certainly demonstrates the extent to which the children know the story, it has several major drawbacks. The ability to accurately represent another person and situation through acting puts a burden on children who may not be able to remember dialogue or necessary details. There often appears to be one right way of portraying a character, and the child who isn't able to maintain credibility suffers. The teacher is often put into the position of becoming the director who shapes the work by focusing on the product, the re-creation of the story and the accuracy with which this is accomplished. Feelings, difficult to express under any circumstances, are submerged or ignored as everyone works to remember the sequence of events and dialogue. For many children, this approach is not as useful as those that place the emphasis on responding to the story rather than its re-creation.

Although there are many ways to use literature to make drama, in this essay I focus on three that I have found to be particularly useful when working with young children or those just beginning to work in drama. These approaches, *physicalization, point of view,* and *responding to emotional impact,* are also useful if a teacher decides to have the children act out the story because the experiences help the children understand what they need to know about becoming a character, determining motivation, creating action, and building relationships.

Specific stories are suggested as examples of literature that work well as a stimulus for drama. Very often these stories have boys as the main character, but unless the story *has* to be about a boy, girls can become the main character just as well. Good picture books and stories for children up through the age of ten are excellent choices to start with because these are read quickly, have well-thought-out plots, and clear characterizations. Bibliographies such as *Reading Ladders for Human Relations*[3] are excellent resources to facilitate literature choice.

When working with very young children, I often make group stories, that is, all the children become one character at the same time. The addition of new characters is treated the same way. With practice, some of the young children can work individually, but this takes a lot of experience and should not be a teacher's expectation at the beginning. Even if the children come up with clever ideas, I usually insist that they think up at least three so that, from the beginning, I am helping them to understand that there are many ways to react and respond to a story.

Some general questions for teachers to consider when making drama from literature are

1. What is the central conflict?
2. Whose story is it? From whose point of view is the story told?
3. Why does the story begin and end as it does?
4. Where is the crisis and the climax?
5. What would happen if the central conflict does not get resolved or is resolved in ways that are different from that which is written?
6. What is the most important aspect of the story to you? Why?
7. Why does it matter that you choose this story with which to work?
8. With which character do you identify, if any? Why?

Physicalization

The dialogue from a cartoon, "For Better or Worse," by Lynn Johnston illustrates one of the reasons why nonverbal activity is so often the best place to start when making drama from literature. In the four frames of the cartoon, the mother is cleaning up after a bottle of milk has been broken and is spilling all over the kitchen.

> *Mother* Look, I said I wasn't mad, Michael . . . it was an accident. (*Son looks at her with worried expression.*)
>
> *Mother* So don't stand there looking miserable because I am *not* angry. (*Son looks unconvinced.*)
>
> *Mother* I am annoyed, I am put out, but I am not ANGRY!
>
> *Son* Then how come you have all those wrinkles up here (*pointing to his forehead*)?

Much of what we think about how a person feels comes from what we see. If we observe a person who is hunched over, head down, and with little energy, we probably assume he is unhappy. Given a strong and clear context, this judgment can be even more certain. Therefore, the ability to physicalize, to make internal ideas and feelings external, can reveal motivation and communicate feeling. If words or sounds are used, the tone of voice and volume of sound also add to the emotional impact. When the verbal communication says one thing, and the nonverbal communication indicates another, those watching and listening generally become confused or uncomfortable, as in the cartoon, because the receiver senses the conflict. We tend to believe what we see more readily than we believe words, although the tone and volume with which the words are spoken are as affecting as the movement. We are generally more practiced at manipulating words, at hiding behind them, than we are at arranging our movement so that how we move deliberately hides our feeling. For example, a person who says she isn't angry in a tight voice with clenched fists is not likely to be believed.

To have children physicalize the emotional life of a character in a story requires that they move in ways that demonstrate how the character feels. Does the character move toward or away from others? Are his or her movements large or small, quick or slow? Is the movement toward or away from the center of the body? Is the voice, if used, loud or soft? Is the tone of voice hard or soft? Does the character voluntarily interact with others? Does the character invite or reject assistance? In order to check whether intentions and actions are matching, it helps to have those watching "read" what they see. This is not guessing, when children will call out answers until the correct one is chosen. The "reading" of a character indicates what those watching see and feel. If this is not what is meant, children watching should suggest ideas so that the character behaves according to how he feels.

Crow Boy,[1] a fine picture book that works well with young children and those who are just beginning their work in drama, is about a boy who is given the name of Chibi, "tiny boy," by his classmates. They virtually ignore him for their first five years of school, but in the sixth, a new teacher appears. He values Chibi and pays attention to him. The climax of the story comes when Chibi appears on stage to be in the annual talent show. His classmates, astonished at his presence, ridicule him before he starts to perform but react with amazement, awe, and then shame when they hear his ability to reproduce the sound of crows at work and play.

The story is easy to use because there are only two main characters, Chibi and the sixth-grade teacher. The rest of the children can be the classmates of Chibi. One way to begin working with physicalization is to have the children select pictures of interest to them from the book. These pictures are then enacted by the children as if they were posing for a photographer to illustrate the book. If the group is divided in half, so that part work and part watch, those watching can talk about what they see, to compare feelings shown in the pictures in the book with those illustrated by their classmates. It may be interesting to take pictures that can be developed instantly to enrich the discussion. The purpose of the comparison is to see if the children are able to show their feelings using posture and gesture, not to be criticized for the way they do it. The children may use ways to show feelings other than those used in the book because what matters is that the feeling tone is similar, not that the pictures be copied absolutely.

After making still pictures, the children can explore the feelings illustrated by the pictures, especially the interaction between Chibi and his classmates and Chibi and the two teachers. To reveal Chibi's sadness the children might move with small, inward motions and show little or no recognition of anyone else's movement. They might appear to be daydreaming, with little awareness of school activity. Chibi's classmates might participate in games during recess or classroom activities and respond actively to those around them. They would probably make no attempt to include Chibi except perhaps to ridicule and mock his behavior and habits. The children can switch from playing Chibi to being his classmates in order to explore the differences in feeling and find out how these feelings are physicalized.

In order to look at the difference the new teacher makes to Chibi, the children could start by being Chibi feeling sad and then consider how the attention of a teacher would make them feel. They might begin to move with greater self-assurance, taking a little more space, walking with a little more confidence. The talent-show scene is a fine event for children to explore a range of emotional activity from ridicule to astonishment to awe to shame and sadness. Once, when I was working with children on this scene I felt that they worked very believably until they pretended to cry in shame. I stopped them and asked, "You aren't really feeling bad, are you?" They grinned sheepishly and almost to a person shook their heads to indicate no. I asked them what they would do to apologize to Chibi and let him know they really were sorry for behaving as they did. One boy said, "I would say I'm sorry I hurt your feelings." Some of the children agreed; one girl said, "I would say, why did I have to open my big mouth?" Many nodded in agreement and repeated what she said. I asked them to turn to a neighbor and apologize for hurting her feelings. The children looked at one another quickly and then turned their eyes to the floor. I asked them what the difference was between pretending to cry and what they had just done. One child said, "If you cry, but you really don't feel it, you begin to laugh inside because it makes you feel silly. But if you really are sorry that you hurt someone's feelings, it's hard to look at the person because you know you should have been nicer and now you can see you made them feel bad." One girl said, "When you're pretending to feel something, it doesn't matter to you very much, but if you really feel something, then it stays with you for a long time and it makes you think about what you did."

The observant teacher will find many ways to help children go from drama to life. Practice and experience are key requisites. While working on *Crow Boy* with a group of first graders, I asked them to make a circle. One boy was left in the middle frantically trying to get his classmates to unclasp their hands to make room for him. No one would. Then I said to them, "It's a little like *Crow Boy*, isn't it?" Within seconds several of the children made a place for the boy in the middle. This moment of recognition is the primary way children learn from making drama. By using characters or situations in a story in which children find connection to their own lives and choices, they are much more able to understand what is happening than if they had merely been told. Telling affects the intellect, but *doing* connects intellect, psyche, and emotion to create an integrated learning experience. Sharing these experiences often reassures children that they are not bad, or that such experiences never happen to others. One lesson to be learned by working from drama to life is that all of us communicate feelings and attitudes through our use of physicalization, whether or not we realize we are doing so.

A part of nonverbal communication not generally considered is the use of tone and volume of voice. *Crow Boy* provides a wonderful opportunity to explore this aspect by having the children develop the sounds of the crows: those that are newly hatched, the mother crow's voice, the father crow's voice, the cry of the crows in the early morning, their cries when the village people have an unhappy accident, when the crows are happy, and when they make sounds in a far and lonely place. It is interesting for children to discover how they decide whether a sound is happy or sad, a mother's or a father's, made in the early morning or in a far place. If encouraged, children will probably remember times when they felt that the sound of a voice contradicted or emphasized the meaning of the words. Discussion of how this made them feel and what they did about possible discrepancies can serve as a springboard for new dramas.

Point of View

Every story is told from a specific point of view. *Crow Boy* is told by an impersonal narrator, who reports the events of the story by describing them without imposing judgment. How would it be if the story were told by Chibi? What would change if it were narrated by a member of Chibi's class, by his teacher for the first five years, or by his teacher of his last year at school? Would anything be changed or added if the story were told by one of Chibi's parents or by an older adult who lives in Chibi's village? Chibi is about a Japanese boy told by a Japanese author. Would the story be different if it were about a child from the United States, written by a person from the United States? It is interesting to have each child or group explore the same story at the same time, each working from a different point of view. When the group comes together to share what has been developed and consider what happens when you change the point of view with which the story is told, children develop an awareness of how perception is developed. This is a good way for children to discover that what we see and feel depends in good measure on the angle and place from which we see it, our feelings about ourselves, and our connection to what we are seeing. Even the amount of light, daylight or night, affects our perception, which, in turn, affects our judgment. Nothing is absolute; everything we hear, see, and feel is affected by our personal view and experience. Recognizing this tends to make children less judgmental and more able to hear what others have to say. They are, after all, only expressing their view of the world, just as we express ours.

One book that works very well as a stimulus for developing alternative points of view is *The Dancer, the Bear and the Nobody Boy*.[5] The story is told by the Bear, who tries to get the Dancer to notice him and become his friend. Up until the end of the story the Bear ignores the Nobody Boy's attention. When the story was told by the Dancer, we saw the Bear through her eyes. Children working with this point of view presented the Bear as dirty and bad smelling, who took up much more room than he thought he did and constantly knocked things over, breaking fine dishes and other fragile objects. When the story was told from the Nobody Boy's point of view, he presented himself as if he were invisible because no matter what he did, no one paid any attention to him and people talked about him as if he couldn't hear what they said. Each point of view was physicalized by taking the same series of interactions, which established the basis for comparison and then presented them in dramatic form without reference to specific dialogue in the book. In addition, each character did some basic activity such as walking and eating, which were then shown through the various points of view.

During the discussion that followed, one child jumped up with excitement and said that it reminded him of the difference between the way he saw himself and the way his parents saw him. He said they were always telling him to wash his face, change his underwear, brush his teeth, as if he were the dirtiest person in the world. He didn't notice any dirt or smells on himself and felt they were just saying what parents were supposed to say. Another child, a rather heavy, large girl, said that she felt like the Nobody Boy because every time her relatives got together they all talked about what they thought her parents should do to get her to thin down and become prettier. No one talked to her or asked her opinion, even though she was usually in the same room and often seated at the table, eating with them as they talked about her. Although few of the children had much sympathy for the Dancer, one child talked about how her parents were always taking her to lessons: music, dance, singing. She said that her mother had always wanted to be an actress, so she was trying to turn her daughter into what she (the mother) had always wanted to be. When this child played the Dancer, she played her as a person who had always been trained to perform but who no one really loved for her own sake. The child thought that it would be very difficult for someone like this to love someone because she felt so unloved herself.

The discussion left everyone feeling rather sad, so I suggested we try the story again and turn it into a fairy tale where everyone lives happily ever after. In doing this the children had to decide what each character would really want if he could have it. They were surprised to see that many had different notions of what each character's "good life" was. Finally, when they realized that there were basic disagreements, they created three different versions but agreed they could probably have made many more.

Responding to Emotional Impact

Although it is important for children to understand the events and information in books they read, it is equally important that they understand how they feel about a book and why they feel as they do, especially if others feel differently. To facilitate the discovery of personal reaction and response, teachers must respect whatever a child offers without passing judgment. Often what a child thinks he feels initially will change as he is encouraged to formulate his own responses rather than go along with a group.

One book that works very well with children who are nine or older is *The Lemming Condition*.[6] Bubber, the main character, tries to make sense of the trip all his lemming friends and relatives are about to take to the west. He is disconcerted by his friend the crow's questions, dissatisfied with his uncle's explanation, unmoved by another lemming's observation, and in awe of an old lemming's description of his thoughts and feelings regarding lemmings. How Bubber comes to think and act for himself makes for exciting reading and usually provokes strong feelings from readers.

I have found that it helps to have children isolate their thoughts by making a list of what the book makes them think about before they try to create any dramatized response. The following thoughts were suggested by a group of ten-year-olds:

> What it's like to ask questions of people who won't take the time to listen or who seem unable to hear what you are trying to ask
> Trying to warn people about something bad that's going to happen
> Feeling stupid because you are the only one who thinks a certain way
> Being ignored because people think you're stupid
> Being asked questions that make you angry because you don't know the answer or don't know how to find the answer
> Refusing to go along with everyone else's ideas because you think something bad is going to happen as the result
> Meeting someone who forces you to take another look at what you think you know
> Having strong feelings but no words to describe them
> Being unable to relate to your friends or family because they feel differently from you

I put the list up on the board, and the children got into groups according to the ideas on which they wanted to work. Some of the children used characters from the book while others created totally new people, places, and actions. Because they were working with the feelings that lay behind the ideas, there was a very high level of involvement. One child said, "When I started telling Bubber to do what I told him and never mind his foolishness, I felt just like my father. And then, I wondered if my father sees me as young and stupid, just bothering him all the time with silly questions." Some of the children were concerned about Bubber's isolation from friends and family. Most of them did not think that they could act as he did, that they would probably listen to their parents because they were older and knew more. One child summed up the group's feelings when she said, "I liked *The Lemming Condition* but it didn't make me feel good. I got sort of worried. I mean, parents are supposed to know what's right." We talked about the difference between lemmings and people, that the lemming adults were doing what they had to do, and that some lemmings did survive to start the population all over again. I suggested that the children make a play about making decisions, about what it is that makes you make up your mind.

The play they created involved two groups of people who find some children wandering around. Each group tries to get the children to come with them by offering them a variety of inducements, such as being able to sleep as late as you wanted or eat as much candy as you could. Both groups told the children they would have many friends, no jobs they had to do, and good places to live. It was interesting to see how the children at first thought something was wonderful, like eating a lot of candy, but then thought about what this could mean. One child asked, "Do you get cavities from eating so much sweets? Do you have dentists?" Most of the children could not decide which group they wanted to join because both sounded so wonderful. They seemed even more bothered by this experience than they had been by reading the book. I asked them to think about what was wrong, why making a decision was so hard. They talked about it among themselves, a long and lively discussion. What they came up with, which seemed to make the most sense to them was that they couldn't decide because they had no proof. All they had to go on was what each group said would happen, and as far as the children were concerned, it was easy to say something was true but much harder for it to be true. I wanted them to connect this idea with what they had read in The Lemming Condition, and so I asked, "What was it that made Bubber decide not to go?" One child said, "It wasn't any one thing, it was mostly that he couldn't make the trip make sense to him. He felt it was wrong and so he didn't go." Another child said, "He decided to listen to the crow and the old lemming because they talked to him and tried to answer his questions and nobody else did that."

We talked about what it took to trust your feelings when everyone else was saying you were wrong or crazy. We talked about people in this country who had done the same thing, for instance, Martin Luther King and Harriet Tubman. The children learned a lot from the experience, not the least of which was how much courage it takes to believe in yourself.

There is a passage in a book for young teen-agers, Is That You Miss Blue?,[7] that illustrates how even a strong passage from a book (rather than the whole book) can stimulate a dramatic experience that integrates intellect, psyche, and emotion. In the book, Flan, a young girl, has gone to boarding school and has not seen her mother in many months. Flan is angry at her mother and accuses her of not caring about anyone else's feelings. Her mother tries, without success, to make Flan understand.

> "Flan?"
> "What?"
> "You're going to meet a very old person one day. And when you do, you're going to have only her to answer to, and only her to be responsible to, and only

her to look back with ... and that old person is yourself. I hope you'll be prepared for her."[8]

I read the passage to some children of eleven and twelve and asked them what they would want to say, should they have a chance, to talk to the old people they will become. It was hard for them to consider what they would be like when they became old. To them, their parents were old. We got into a discussion of what the word *old* meant, and how a person decided something was old. Some children talked about grandparents who were active and others talked about those who were incapacitated. One child mentioned that old furniture and jewelry were more valuable than some that had just been made. Some talked about old paintings they had seen in a museum, which were valuable because they were old. Others mentioned that countries such as China, Greece, and Egypt were considered old in comparison to the United States, which is considered a young country.

The more we talked, the more upset some of the children became when they realized that old furniture, paintings, and jewelry were worth more old than new but that people were considered worth more when they were young than when they were old. One child talked about the arguments her parents had regarding her grandmother's coming to live with them. Another child described his feelings when he went with his parents to a nursing home to visit his great-grandmother. He spoke of how terrible it was to see people who seemed to be in another world and who couldn't make sense. He said he was afraid to get old. As if to counter this, one girl said, "My grandfather is eighty-six and he still rides a bicycle."

I gave them some books to read and then asked them to take one aspect of aging and create a drama that revealed their attitudes or feelings about what it meant to be old. I chose picture books because the group could read them quickly, but I also had a list of books they might enjoy reading on their own.

One of the groups chose to read and use *The Seeing Stick*,[9] which is based on a Chinese folktale. The children decided that old people are very much respected in China and thought they would work with this attitude. The story is about a blind princess who is helped to "see" by an old man who teaches her to use her fingers in place of her eyes. The group felt that people who *will not* see are as blind in their own way as those who *cannot* see. They created a scene where neighborhood children ask her father, the King, to let his blind daughter play with them. He says no because he is afraid that his daughter will get hurt. The children plead with him, but despite all their arguments, he refuses. One of the children brings her old grandfather to see the King. The King listens to the old man because old people are very wise. The old man tells the King that if he really loves his daughter, he will let her go and play with the other children, but that if he keeps her locked away from people, he is condemning her to a living death. The King listens to the old man and lets his daughter play with the other children.

Although the drama did not follow the book regarding the story line, it did develop from ideas and feelings generated by the plot. It also stimulated discussion about how hard it is to let people make their own decisions, that the reason old people are often wise is because they have made mistakes and now know what they should have done. The session ended with the children feeling much better about growing old than they had when they started. In addition to the children's reading books, some thought they should write letters to their grandparents. While aging is not a subject commonly dealt with by eleven- and twelve-year-olds, it is possible that this experience will affect the way they interact with the old people in their lives.

There are many ways of making drama, but none of them will have value if the children play-act rather than work "as if." People who play-act only pretend to feel something. They work at superficial levels that are often accompanied by giggling and other signs of embarrassment. When people act "as if," they are deeply involved, feel real feelings, and are supported by the level of involvement with which the whole group works. It is interesting to note that even young children usually know the difference between the two ways of responding and are often relieved when the play-acting is noted and they are helped to work at a deeper level. One child explained to me, "When you pretend to feel something, it doesn't get inside you. But if you really feel it, even if you know you're just making a play, you feel it inside you and sometimes it makes you feel real bad and you think about it for a long time." I asked her if it was only bad things she felt, and she said, "Oh no! The other day when we were doing *The Seeing Stick*, I felt so happy when the King decided to let his daughter play with us that we got real goofy and started laughing and jumping up and down and I felt nice the whole day."

Perhaps the cycle has no end. Going from literature to drama to life to literature is a continuous lifelong experience, one that helps us in very real ways to make sense of our feelings, our ideas, and our lives. If, at times, we can't talk about a troublesome event like death, perhaps we can talk about books that deal with it. If we encourage children to use their ideas and feelings to make drama, to bear witness to each other's experience, we can help them grow up into adults who have a clear sense of themselves and good access to their own thoughts and emotions. All of this is a prerequisite for understanding and appreciating other people.

NOTES

1. Pearl Buck, *The Big Wave* (New York: John Day, 1948).
2. Margaret Hodges, *The Wave* (Boston: Houghton Mifflin, 1964).
3. Virginia Reid, ed. *Reading Ladders for Human Relations* (5th ed.; Washington, D.C.: American Council on Education, 1972).
4. Taro Yashima, *Crow Boy* (New York: Viking, 1955).
5. Daniele Bour and Jean-Claude Brisville, *The Dancer, the Bear and the Nobody Boy* (London: Adam and Charles Black, 1975).

6. Alan Arkin, *The Lemming Condition* (New York: Harper & Row, 1976).
7. M. F. Kerr, *Is That You Miss Blue?* (New York: Dell, 1975).
8. Ibid., p. 158.
9. Jane Yolen, *The Seeing Stick* (New York: Crowell, 1977).

Drama in Education—
A Reappraisal

Gavin Bolton

Gavin Bolton is currently responsible for the study of drama in education at the master's and doctoral levels in the University of Durham, England. He was chairperson of the British Children's Theatre Association and is now president of the newly formed National Association of Drama in Education and Children's Theatre. He is widely known as an examiner of drama in British universities and has held many visiting professorships in European, Australian, and North American institutions.

During the 1970s Gavin Bolton made numerous trips to the United States and Canada, sometimes team teaching with Dorothy Heathcote, sometimes conducting teacher workshops and demonstrations of his own. His ability to articulate their methodology has contributed to his popularity with elementary school teachers.

Mr. Bolton gave the keynote address to the Children's Theatre Association of America Convention in Washington in 1975, on which occasion he was presented with the Phi Beta Award for service to the profession. His major publication, Toward a Theory of Drama in Education, *was published in 1980. In the essay that follows, he challenges some of the widely accepted myths as he describes the rationale and claims that have grown up around them.*

Myths Around Drama Education

Some years ago, Elliott Eisner[1] wrote an article challenging the rationale behind many cherished views of art education, assumptions that made up for him a "mythology" of art education. I shall try to do the same for drama education. Two points need to be made before I start. Exposing a myth is not a denial in absolute terms. One does not argue that something is not valid but rather that it is only partially valid or that its validity has been misunderstood, misrepresented, or distorted, or that circumstances have made it less valid. In other words, a kernel of truth remains unchallenged. Another point to bear in mind is that just as the creation of a myth is an event in a particular time and a particular place arising out of particular needs, so the erosion of a myth is a particular historical/geographical/philosophical necessity. Thus this brief study of myths in drama education applies, perhaps exclusively, to the English drama scene, both in the myths created in the early days of teaching drama to students and in the need in our present educational climate to reappraise our values in drama teaching. For America, past priorities and current challenges to the subject may be of such a different order that this chapter remains but of academic interest to American readers. I hope not. I have a hunch that because of that unchanging kernel of truth within a myth, I am bound to be raising issues of universal importance to drama teachers, even though my perspective is necessarily focused (if not blinkered!) by the development of the British educational system.

Myth 1: Drama is doing

The sheer relief with which pupils and teachers alike find a salvation from strictures of traditional school studies in the contrasting activity-centered happenings of a drama session is evidence enough, one might have thought, that drama, if it is nothing else, is and indeed must be *doing*. Wide disagreement among practitioners as to content, purpose, or method can be dispelled in seconds by the common understanding they all share that drama *is* doing. Nevertheless, I argue that this is only partially so and that it is the neglect of the part that is *not* doing that has distorted our understanding of the nature of drama and has caused us to underrate its potential for learning.

Of course the critical characteristic of drama is concrete action; it is this that distinguishes drama from other arts, even from its sister arts of movement and dance, which, also action bound, nevertheless are spatially and temporarily more abstract. It is not, however, the concrete action alone that carries the meaning of the experience. Indeed, in this essay I attempt to show that the meaning of a dramatic experience is not so much bound up with the functional, imitative meaning of the action as with a tension that is set up between the particularity of the action and the generality of meanings implied by the action. The meaning of the experience is both dependent on and independent of the concrete action.

Action, even imitative action, is not in itself drama. A child miming the action of posting a letter is not in a dramatic mode if his sole intention is accurately to imitate such an action. He is merely adopting an imitative mode of behavior, selecting an activity, the meaning of which can be denoted by the terms "posting a letter" and recalling in imitative actions precisely that function. There is but *one* dimension of meaning represented by the imitation: the denotative or functional one.

For the action to be considered dramatic greater significance of meaning must lie along other dimensions.[2] Such significance is determined by the combination of two contrasting sources: whatever is uniquely personal and whatever is more universally relevant. Thus posting a letter as dramatic action must arouse affective memories in the participant to do with posting letters sufficiently strong for the action significantly to feed into appropriate meanings such as "trust in a written message," "irrevocability of a decision to post a letter," "the anticipation of a letter's impact," and "the impotence of not knowing the receiver's reaction." These connotations go beyond the functional meaning and are what the participant in drama must be concerned with. In this sense, therefore, one can say that the meaning of the dramatic experience is independent of the action. On the other hand, the action of posting a letter is the vehicle through which such connotations are expressed. In that sense, the meaning is dependent on the concrete action. Thus the overall meaning is expressed in a relationship between the particular action and its more universal implications. Those teachers who are content to train their students in imitative skills are off target—imitating human actions and emotions is not drama. Likewise those teachers who, in their anxiety for students to achieve significantly thoughtful work, neglect the potential power of the concrete action at their peril, for the handling of abstract ideas, even in role, without some spatial/temporal reference is not in itself drama either.

In England we have large numbers of the former teachers who see the training of students in skillful miming actions as sufficient drama training. To these teachers one has to exclaim, "Drama is *not* doing!" To the second group of teachers, often found among teachers in the humanities who see the educational opportunities in holding discussions on some important issues in role, one says, "This is really an abstract exchange of views, which is fine as far as it goes, but drama *is* doing!" I hope my arguments have been sufficiently clear for the reader to appreciate that both forms of advice are misleading. Perhaps we should say, "Drama is and is not doing." Only with his sights ambivalently adjusted is a teacher likely to gauge correctly his priorities in teaching drama. We do not wish to limit our students to learning more precisely the functional actions of life; it is the significance of the universal implication behind those actions that learning in drama is concerned with. In attempting to challenge the myth of "drama is doing," therefore, I am not merely clarifying the nature of drama but, more importantly, showing that a teacher's priorities must inevitably become adjusted when its nature is properly grasped.

Myth 2: Drama is an escape from reality

Some play theorists see the make-believe play of young children as compensating for the "slings and arrows of outrageous fortunes," as the child's natural means of protecting himself from the cruel realities of living. Because drama is undoubtedly linked with play (perhaps another "myth" is that drama *is* play!), some practitioners see drama as an outlet for their students, either in the sense of "letting off steam" or as an opportunity to fantasize. The former describes a psychological disposition; the latter is concerned with drama's content. I now discuss these in turn, starting with the content.

The Content of Drama   To view make-believe activity as an escape from reality is, it seems to me, to ignore a critical attribute of both play and drama: The child at play, far from evading restrictions, actually imposes them. As the Russian psychologist Vygotsky[3] has pointed out, play is about abiding by the rules. The same applies to drama. However "unreal" the make-believe situation may be, the rules themselves objectively reflect the real world, even if it is an inverse reflection. If, for example, the rule is, to choose an extreme example, "all parents have to be punished and sent to bed early by their children," this merely (not "merely"—"significantly" perhaps) reflects a clear acknowledgment of reality, as does every piece of apparent fantasy. But a feature of play is that a child may give up playing or just change the rules when he feels so inclined. Drama, on the other hand, requires students to agree on the rules, acknowledge their parameters, and keep to them *even when it becomes uncomfortable*.

It so often happens that children choose a topic they do not fully understand and when they begin to perceive its implications subtly start to undermine the rules that are implicit in the situation. In other words, instead of facing up to the rigor of thinking, decision making, and coping with tension inherent within a topic, they prefer to slacken their grip on "the rules of the game." In this sense drama can be an escape from reality, where an unspoken consensus between class and teacher allows a drifting into a ruleless activity—immediately gratifying, eventually frustrating, educationally poverty-stricken. I can think of many examples: A class of nine-year-olds, in choosing to do their drama about hijacking, sought "fantasy" ways of solving the problem of being in the hijacker's power by suddenly producing weapons (one boy tried claiming magic power!) they had clearly not had in their possession when the hijack first took place. At an adult level, I recall a woman who in playing a role of a singleminded, determined person, under pressure from other people in the improvisation, "succumbed" in a way that was quite illogical for the character she was playing.

On the other hand, I also recall as teacher of a class of ten- and eleven-year-olds being *over* insisting on keeping to historical facts. The situation was about Florence Nightingale and her nurses, who were sent out by Queen Victoria to tend the many wounded in the military hospital at Scutari, only to find on arrival that the doctors running the hospital were refusing to allow women on the wards. "Nursing is a man's job" they firmly declared. Now the boys and girls in this class representing the doctors and nurses respectively explored many facets of this confrontation during four or five drama sessions, the girls successively adapting their tactics along a wide range of ploys from demands to requests, from blackmail to persuasion. By the fifth day the doctors went into private conclave and eventually whispered to me that they were going to offer a compromise: The nurses were to be given a chance to work on the wards for just one day—to prove themselves! I am sure the reader will agree that this was a mature decision for young children to take. Unfortunately, in my enthusiasm for historical facts, I would not let them do this, for *historically* the doctors did not give in in that way.[4] Even as I write I shudder at the harm that some of us as teachers do! It is obvious that I as a teacher was allowing myself to be controlled by a very limited kind of reality—a particular sequence of events—whereas the more important reality has to do with how people adjust to an impasse. What the boys wanted to carry out was *objectively valid* insofar as they had examined the various factors in the situation and made a reasoned judgment about them. This, then, is what is meant by the relationship of drama to reality: the perception, recognition, and appraisal of events within the fictitious context. The context may be close to a known social context or an apparent fantasy, but the rules that govern it must reflect the objective world for the activity to be worthy of the term drama and worthy of education.

Disposition Towards Drama   What people usually mean by "letting off steam" is a psychological release from tension so that participants are supposed to "feel better" after a drama experience. This represents a pretty crude view of the mental state of drama participants, but there is a more subtle expectation of our students' mental state that was first conceived in England by the great pioneer of child drama, Peter Slade,[5] and taken up staunchly by his disciples ever since. I refer to the quality of *absorption*.

It may puzzle the reader that I should include this admirable quality, which most of us as teachers have at one time or another worked to promote in our students among the "myths" of drama in education. I shall not argue that it is mythical in the sense that it doesn't exist (although some teachers working continually with recalcitrant classes may sometimes wonder!) but that we have been wrong to see it as a final achievement. Indeed I used to assume that if my students were absorbed, then that was a necessary and sufficient concomitant of learning.

But I want to suggest that this may not be the case; there is something about "absorption" that hints at "being lost" in an experience, thus escaping from reality. Now I know that the look of wonder on a child's face when he is so "lost" can be something to be marveled at, but I do not think it is moments such as these that we are working for in drama. We do not want children to "lose" themselves but "find" themselves.

Certainly we want a high degree of involvement and commitment to the creative fiction, but if it is to be a worthwhile learning experience for the participant, he must hold a dual perspective on the experience: an active identification with the fiction combined with heightened awareness of his own identification. So, far from escaping from life, the quality of life is momentarily intensified because he is knowing what he thinks as he thinks it, seeing what he says as he says it, and evaluating what he does as he does it. This reflection, concurrent with identification, leads to learning through drama. Sometimes, of course, students are not capable of so reflecting. It is then that the teacher, having attempted to discern what it is the student has experienced, can perhaps, after the drama, help him retrace the experience and reflect on it or, alternatively, can attempt to create a frame of mind in the student that will bring about a more heightened awareness when he enters the next phase of the drama. With such sensitive handling by the teacher the student can begin to use fiction to understand himself in the real world.

Myth 3: Drama education is concerned with developing the uniqueness of the individual

It is not insignificant that at the time Winifred Ward was establishing the term *creative dramatics* in America, here in England our Peter Slade was introducing the label *child drama*. The latter terminology was intended to imply that within each child there is a potential for dramatic expression that is important because it is personal. The teacher's responsibility lay in nurturing a person's individuality. Such a philosophical view of the child and of drama as being "within him" should be seen as part of a larger educational trend in Europe beginning with Rousseau, through Froebel and Pestalozzi, and culminating in our own Plowden Report[6] in 1967, which gave a seemingly final official stamp of approval to "child-centered education." It is perhaps true to say that whereas the "humanist movement" in America has been a counter movement to the application of behaviorism to education, the child-centered movement in England was seen as an alternative to the persistent image of children as passive recipients of an approved body of knowledge.

It is not surprising that when the child-centered movement was in the ascendancy in the 1950s and '60s that personalities in drama education emerged to pioneer a view of drama that was also child-centered. The message of drama as personal development was welcomed hungrily not only in England but throughout the Western world, for it bravely stood up to both the "body of knowledge" and "behaviorist" explications of education. Drama teachers were grateful to Brian Way[7] in particular for articulating a philosophy that emphasized the *process* of dramatic experience rather than the *product*, that saw drama as a means of approach to self-knowledge and even (as taken further by devotees like Richard Courtney) as the basis of all learning and growth. *Developmental drama* was the Courtney label that spread through Canada.

In England our interpretation of Brian Way's philosophy tended to be manifested by our concern with the importance of individual creativity and free expression often paradoxically catered for in practice by exercise se-

Factory simulation from On the Line *by Carol Korty. Courtesy of Carol Korty. Photograph by Akmal.*

quences for disciplined attributes like concentration or the puppetlike response to a signal from teacher's tambour; with a growing hostility to the
notion of children performing; with the assumption that there can be no
sense of standards in drama work because each child is his own arbiter in
this respect; and with the claim that "Drama is Life," thus effectively reducing
the activity to a meaningless catch-phrase.

But there is one aspect—our concern with promoting the uniqueness of
the individual—that perhaps more than any other manifestation goes against
the natural dramatic grain. Some art forms, painting in particular, are a
vehicle for individual expression, but drama by its very nature is a group
statement, commenting on, exploring, questioning, or celebrating not individual differences but what one human being has in common with another.

I have already mentioned different levels of meaning in dramatic action. In the example of posting a letter I suggested there are three broad levels of meaning—the functional (the imitative action of posting a letter), the universal (significant implications that posting a letter might have such as the irretrievability of the action), and the personal (whatever "posting letter" memories a particular child may recall). Now each of these levels of meaning is important, for the total meaning of the experience is made up of their interaction. But for the activity to be *drama* and not solitary play, the concentration of effort must be at the middle level of meaning; that is, it must have some significance related to the concrete action that all participants can *share*. If the context or plot of the drama with six-year-olds is, for example, to do with "catching a monster" the shared or thematic meaning might be "We dare not make a mistake" or "It is important to distinguish between evidence and rumor of the monster's existence" or "Are we to be destroyers or preservers of Life?" With ten-year-olds whose dramatic context is space travel, the theme might well be "Is our training good enough for what we have to face?" or "having to make a decision based on inadequate knowledge" or "the responsibility we have to all those who will follow." A group of sixteen-year-olds might be looking at "family" contexts where the theme might be "the dependence/independence ambivalence of the different generations," "the treasure/burden ambivalence of rearing a child," or "a family as a symbol of a past and a future."

Of course each individual will bring all kinds of personal meanings to the above dramas, some more relevant than others. Indeed they could vary from traumatic for the six-year-old who is scared at the very thought of monsters or for the sixteen-year-old whose family is breaking up, to the neutral feelings of the six-year-old whose mind is really on his new birthday presents or to the positively destructive attitude of a sixteen-year-old who is hostile to drama. But if the experience is to operate as *drama*, individual differences must be channeled into the collective theme. Ultimately, however, it is what the individual draws from the collective meaning that matters, a process of "finding himself in the meaning." In that sense the importance of the uniqueness of the individual is not a myth but, like a member of an audience, the individual has temporarily to hold his individuality in abeyance, sharing meanings he has in common with others in order that he may be personally enriched.

Myth 4: Drama is personal development

I do not wish to deny that drama, along with all aspects of education, can be an aid to personal development. Indeed I think I could argue the case that drama more than other subjects of the curriculum may accelerate the maturing process, especially for children who for some reason or other have had natural progress arrested. Why, then, have I placed drama as personal development among my list of myths? The reason lies within our past reluctance to distinguish between immediate educational objectives and long-term maturation. Enthusiasm for the personal development of their students has often led to an act of supererogation on the part of drama teachers who claim that personal development is what they were actually *teaching*. One cannot *teach* concentration, trust, sensitivity, group awareness, patience, tolerance, respect, perception, judgment, social concern, coping with ambivalent feelings, responsibility, and so forth; one can only hope that education will help bring them about over a long term. And as I have already suggested, it could be argued that drama brings them about in a special way, but the achievement of these admirable qualities is *not intrinsic to drama*; it is an important *by-product* of the dramatic experience.

Certainly a teacher can effectively structure to create opportunities for continual practice of many of the above attributes, but the drama must itself be *about* something. Sadly, it has so often been relegated to dramatic exercise in personal skills (just as in the old days poetry used to be abused in its usage as a mere vehicle for speech practice).

Among the many immediate objectives a teacher may have for a particular drama lesson or series of lessons, extending the students' understanding of the thematic content must be a top priority. Other objectives, such as effective use of the art form and satisfaction from a sense of achievement, follow closely. Now it seems to me that the students' regular opportunity for exploration of meanings within a theme through the effective use of the art form can cumulatively provide the very processes that will bring about trust, sensitivity, concentration, and the rest. But the teacher's and students' immediate concern must be with *meaning*. In England we have trained a whole generation of drama teachers to whom this would be a novel suggestion; drama lessons for them have been but a series of varied dramatic exercises that purport to train the students in life skills.

Myth 5: Drama is antitheatre

The relationship between theatre and drama is a complex one, the subtleties of which have been virtually ignored in the United Kingdom because of the historical situation that drove drama teachers into two opposite camps—those who saw school drama as the acquisition of theatre skills, training students as performers, and those who believed in child-centered education, the "progressiveness" of which was measured by the degree to which students were *not* trained as performers. The latter claimed that the educational reward came from the dramatic process, not its product.

Although the position I take on this is that the greater potential educational value lies in students' *experiencing* drama rather than *performing* it, I nevertheless regret that polarization into an either/or situation has occurred. It is not that I feel uncomfortable faced with alternative philosophies in education; I have no wish to marshal everyone into the same camp. My regret stems from something much more fundamental: that teachers have not been given a sufficient conceptual basis from which to make a reasoned choice between the two.

I propose to examine what I see as essential differences and similarities between drama and theatre in respect of *mode* and *structure* (other aspects, for instance, that theatre is normally linked with a *place* and that for many people theatre is a *job*, I shall not discuss here).

Mode By "mode" I am referring to the quality of the behavior of any participant who is consciously engaged in some form of make-believe activity. If we were to watch a child in a garden being a policeman, we would say he is "playing"; if we watched an actor on stage being a policeman, we would say he is "performing." We might agree that although both are "pretending," there is a difference in *quality*, or *mode* of action. It is useful here to attempt to determine at least some characteristics of these two behaviors. You will notice I have called them "playing" and "performing," apparently avoiding the term "acting." At the risk of offending those readers who have a very clearly defined notion of acting as something only an actor does, I intend to use the term as all-embracing, applying it to both the child's and the man's behavior. This allows me to think in terms of a *continuum* of acting behavior rather than two separate categories:

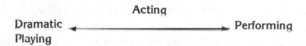

I have changed the terminology at the left end of the continuum to "dramatic playing" rather than just "playing." This is to distinguish it from much child play that does not involve make-believe or pretense—such as ball playing. I am now in a position to argue that the *mode* changes according to which end of the continuum the acting behavior orientates.

Let us look at the extreme left end first. It is not easy to find the words adequately to describe a child absorbed in dramatic playing; "being" or "experiencing" might well convey the right qualities. It seems to be both active and passive in the sense that the child is responsible for his own playing and yet is at the same time submitting to the effect of his own contriving. Thus he could say, "I am making it happen, so that it can happen to me," and he could add, "And it is happening to me *now*." Thus the experiential mode of dramatic playing can be distinguished by (1) both a deliberate devising and a spontaneous responding, (2) a sense of "nowness," and (3) *me* in the experience.

If we take our child playing a policeman, the three features are demonstrated as follows:

1. In order to give himself a "policeman" experience he must contrive to recall and imitate policemanlike activities, at least, as we have discussed earlier, insofar as they are relevant to the *personal* meaning he is exploring.
2. He must achieve a sense of "policeman" things happening to him as he plays, for example, visualizing that traffic is *now* whirling around him under his control.

3. The experience, while ostensibly about "policeman," is really about him in a "policeman" context.

I have discussed earlier the heightened awareness that increases the chances of a child's reflecting upon and learning from the experience. A feature of this awareness that is relevant here is that whereas a child can say, "It is happening to me now," he also knows it is fiction. This paradox that it is happening and yet not happening ("psychical distancing," a term employed by Bullough[8] in relation to audience attitude in particular, might be appropriate here) provides us with a fourth essential characteristic of the *mode* of a child's dramatic playing.

Now if we move to the extreme right of our continuum, it becomes clear that all four features—contriving/responding, sense of "nowness," sense of "me-ness," and psychical distancing—although essentially present for the actor, are significantly reduced or overshadowed by a new set of intentions to do with interpretation, character portrayal, repeatability, projection, communicability, and empathy with an audience. Heightened awareness, not to mention entertainment, must ultimately be enjoyed by the *audience*.

Child drama, creative drama, creative dramatics, educational drama, or whatever we care to call nonperformance drama in schools, seems logically to be placed toward the left rather than the right of the continuum, for the ultimate responsibility, intention, and skills of the actor must lie in his ability to give someone else an experience. In other words, the fundamental difference in the *mode* required lies not just in the skills employed but is a matter of *mental set*. This difference seems to be so decisive that one might wonder whether indeed the notion of a continuum should be scrapped and replaced by distinct categories, thus validating the antitheatre attitude among drama educationalists, a view that in practice one sees painfully reinforced by those many occasions in schools where young children are directed into a totally inappropriate mental set of taking responsibility for entertaining adults. The harm lies not just in demands made on the children by the particular occasion but in the subsequent attitude of those children who, feeling inadequate, are put off drama by the experience or those who, finding a flair in themselves for entertaining, continue to view drama as an opportunity for furthering facile techniques, which teachers, also unfortunately deceiving themselves, persist in encouraging.

Nevertheless, in spite of evidence of some appalling examples of children thrust into harmful theatre experiences, in spite of the distinction that logically can be sustained of alternative mental sets, I now propose to argue that there are enough occasions in children's play, student's creative drama and theatrical performance, when the acting mode in terms of the participant's intention or mental set is ambiguous and not purely one thing or another to justify the image of a continuum rather than separate categories.

There are a number of instances when child play, dramatic activity, and performance seem to shift their position along the mode continuum. I propose to list some examples of these.

Child play Sometimes a child playing on his own, absorbed in make-believe—let us take our "policeman" example—will say to his mother when she enters, "Look, Mummy, I am a policeman." Now this implies not only a shift in intention (he was up to that point doing the actions for himself only) but a possible change in meaning. For whatever *subjective* meanings the "policeman" action expressed may now be held in abeyance for the sake of communication. Just as language has a private and public function, so *action* has both connotative and denotative functions. Although to a hidden observer the child may be repeating the same "policeman" actions, it might well be only the public, functional meaning that the child is now interested in sharing with his mother. This does not of course become a theatrical performance, for the actor's responsibility is to make sure the audience identifies with all levels of meaning.[9] But the point I want to make is that using fictitious action for the sake of communication to someone else can start early on in child behavior. To put it another way, a change of *some* kind in the quality or mode is well within the capacity of a child, even a young one.

Dramatic activity We rightly claim that students in "experiencing" drama are not concerned with communicating to an audience. And yet this does seem to ignore three features:

1. They often as they participate adapt the quality of the mode in order to communicate a variety of levels to each other.
2. The use of constant intervention by the teacher, in inviting them to reflect on what they have just done or are about to do, also invites them to see their work very much as a series of products to be evaluated rather than a process to be left undisturbed.
3. In spite of the concentration on "experiencing," when the quality of work is aesthetically satisfying to the participant, the many layers of meaning communicate themselves to an observer *even when there is no intention so to communicate*.

I think the above three points sufficiently illustrate that *within* the process of experiencing with its overall orientation toward the left of the continuum there appear to be contrary pulls in the other direction. Similarly, when we now look at performance we can detect a less rigid position.

Performance The obvious examples of a different orientation:

1. Those times in rehearsal when an actor is drawing on his own resources to find meaning are very close to what a child goes through in a drama experience.
2. Those performances where spontaneity of interaction among the performers themselves is deliberately kept alive so that fresh meanings can emerge for the actors. In other words, the actors are operating at a double level of both communicating preconceived meanings and at the same time generating (actually experiencing as in drama) new meanings.

I hope I have established that in terms of quality, or mode of acting, the forms of behavior one might expect of a child at play, a student in drama, and an actor in theatre have at times sufficient in common at least to blur the edges of distinctions between them. Let us now examine the drama/theatre dichotomy in terms of form.

Form   When we examine drama and theatre form, we find not just similarity but a considerable overlap, enough to justify the argument that structurally drama and theatre are indistinguishable. The basic elements of both are focus, tension, contrast, and symbolization. It seems to me that just as a playwright working for theatre is concerned with using these elements to convey his meaning, so a teacher working in creative drama is concerned with helping students to explore meaning through the use of these same elements.[10] So in a curious way, when even young children are working in creative dramatics, they are working in a theatre form. The teacher's function can be seen as an extension of a playwright, sharpening and deepening that form.

Let me now summarize this long section on the relations between drama and theatre. I have claimed that one of the myths about drama is that it is antitheatre. Even as I write this I am aware that this is a dangerous thing to say, for people will assume I want a return to the old "train children to perform" days, so let me first spell out what I do *not* mean: I do *not* want drama to be seen as training in acting techniques. I do *not* want to encourage large-scale spectacular productions of the kind that require the teacher/director to be brilliantly inventive and the performers to be conforming automatons. Unfortunately, such presentations can be impressively polished and slick, and the loud prolonged applause can convince parents, education officials, teachers—and, of course, the treasurer—that they must be of educational value.

On the other hand, I am convinced that there are firmer connections between drama and theatre than we have in the past acknowledged, subtle connections which, if better understood, would allow us to *harness* the notion of "showing" drama instead of either despising it or using it superficially. Different kinds of performing, varying in the degree to which they are formal/informal, audience oriented/audience ignored, finished product/incidental to a dramatic playing process, lasting an hour/lasting a few seconds, a script interpretation/a group's dramatic statement, a collage of scripted excerpts/a whole play. Whichever of these dimensions is selected, the potential pivotal relationship between "experiencing" and "showing," which we have tended to ignore, can occasionally sharpen the work at the dramatic playing end of the continuum and always enrich any move toward the other end.

Comment

In this chapter I have outlined what might be called the mythology of drama education. The "myths" I have selected are Drama is doing, Drama is an escape from reality, Drama is concerned with the uniqueness of the individual, Drama is for personal development, and Drama is antitheatre. Having argued against all these, I perhaps need to remind readers what I said at the beginning, that in important ways they *are* viable: Drama in a narrow sense *is* doing; drama for some children can be used as an escape from a reality that is painful to them; drama education is ultimately concerned with the uniqueness of the individual and his personal development; and drama, although not antitheatre, does offer critical differences of emphasis that we ignore at our peril. My aim, therefore, has been to extend the conceptual framework so that we have a firmer basis from which to examine these important issues.

NOTES

1. Elliott Eisner, "Examining Some Myths in Art Education," *Student Art Education* 15, no. 3 (1973–74): 7–16.
2. Sadly, many drama education "packages" seem to rely heavily on the one dimension of imitation, even to imitating *emotions*!
3. Lev S. Vygotsky, "Play and Its Role in the Mental Development of the Child" in *Play: Its Development and Evolution*, ed. J. S. Bruner et al. (New York: Penguin, 1976).
4. For those readers who are interested, the doctors at Scutari capitulated, not from choice, but because after a particularly severe battle, there were more wounded than the male orderlies and doctors could cope with.
5. Peter Slade, *Child Drama* (London: University of London Press, 1954).
6. Plowden Report, *Children and Their Primary Schools* (London: Her Majesty's Stationery Office, 1967).
7. Brian Way, *Development Through Drama* (New York: Longman, 1967).
8. Edward Bullough, "Psychical Distance as a Factor in Art and as an Aesthetic Principle," *British Journal of Psychology* 5, pt. 2 (1912): 87–118.
9. It is relevant to refer here to the form of drama, popular particularly in our Secondary Schools, where students are required to improvise in their groups 'making up' a play to show the others at the end of the session. In such circumstances the teachers, unwittingly, may be inviting the students merely to prepare the denotative meanings for the sake of easy communication.
10. For a detailed discussion of theatrical elements, see G. M. Bolton, *Towards a Theory of Drama in Education* (London: Longman, 1979).

Drama as an Aid to Fuller Experience

Peter Slade

Peter Slade is best known in America for his book Child Drama, *published in 1954 and now in its sixth edition. He is also the author of* An Introduction to Child Drama, The Experience of Spontaneity, *and* Natural Dance *(1977). His influence has been felt not only through his writing but through his thirty years as drama adviser to the Birmingham Education Authority and his directorship of the Educational Drama Association. His Children's Theatre Players provided theatre for primary school schildren in Birmingham almost continuously during this period of time.*

Peter Slade's professional career began with experience as an actor in repertory, the West End, and the BBC. In 1945 he founded the Pear Tree Players, the first professional company devoting full time to educational work. Three years later he developed the Rea Street Drama Centre in Birmingham, a prototype for other centres in various parts of the world. Here he conducted courses in drama in education, taught dance, and developed experimental adult theatre. He was one of the first persons in England to work with retarded and disturbed children and served as drama therapist in the army during World War II. In 1977 Peter Slade was awarded the Queen's Silver Jubilee Medal for his contribution to education and youth theatre.

Peter Slade believes the root of child drama to be play; therefore it is with play that the teacher must first be concerned. The words love, joy, *and* enjoyment *occur often in his writing. This emphasis is one of the ways in which his approach differs from those of his contemporaries.*

After returning to England from the university town of Bonn, where I met some of the great minds of the world, I went on the stage, working in repertory, the West End and the BBC. It was at this time, 1931, that I started professional theatre-for-children companies. Here I found a marvelous opportunity for observing humanity and children at play. What I saw during those years altered my life and, incidentally, my way of producing theatre-for-children with adult actors.

Having indulged in just such activities myself as a youth, I now espied (but consciously) what appeared to be a new world, very different from the theatre of my time. In order to be precise, my remarks have been scaled down to a number of headlines. Please forgive the fact that this may make them sound more dogmatic than is intended. I believe there is a child drama and that it is an art form in its own right; but this belongs to the early years and is largely unconscious. Later, as the child grows, he becomes more conscious and in adolescence stumbles, almost, into the adult art of theatre. This wonderful, difficult art form, which we have painstakingly built, is like a bubble floating on the sea of civilization. Underneath is the deep ocean of the unconscious. The child's unconscious drama is the way he tests, reexperiences, and proves life; the way he comes to terms with fear, and sometimes with failure. (I think we train too much for leadership and success. Most of us fail much of the time. We might better spend more time training for the courage to go on.)

No teacher can be good without the power to observe. This is a special quality, and we should cultivate the ability to see what is revealed. We must first note the phenomena of human behavior, then be able to read the thermometer of where a person is in life, and then evolve techniques for furthering a promising situation or compensating for an apparently poor one. For this, one must, of course, know what is expected, roughly what is normal. Here child drama gives us valuable information, for it is directly of the emotions.

Among the many things we are being clever about these days, with our sorting out of social structure, finding apparatus for helping backward children, building up masses of figures, we are still far behind in the training of the emotions. I personally feel that this is the most important factor in education.

Now for a headline: *I do not believe in everlasting free play.* I do not think all children profit by it. I think they grow bored and need help so that their play will not fizzle out. I believe we should engage in guided activity. This is not the same thing as interference, and for such guidance you must know the various stages of human development. In my first book, *Child Drama*, I drew attention to the wild drama of the streets and the difference between that (which can at times be violent and dangerous) and drama, which is the nurtured product of a good school. People sometimes say child drama is not necessary, that children will engage in it outside school anyway. Of course they do, but it can go wrong; and if drama reveals the way that a child ticks, then we should use it in a constructive manner and not throw away so important an aid.

I once heard a lecturer mention that "house play" dies and that something ought to be done to encourage its continuation. My own feeling is that of course it will die because it is far too narrow a view of the whole process. Child drama is an empire; house play is one tiny county in one country. It is largely materialistic, and there are vast tracks of imaginative experience that it actually obstructs. Despite the importance of using objects, there ought to be frequent occasions for imagination without them, for some of the best of child play is of the spirit and has an aesthetic quality. It should not always be cluttered with riches—far happier the child with fewer toys and, ultimately, far more steady and secure. Not that beloved objects are not important; they are. But there should not be too many of them. The doll with one arm and no eyes may be more beloved than several whole ones. Incidentally, after dealing with many distressed children, my conviction is that this early love for a doll or toy, particularly a damaged one, is connected with some inner feeling of loyalty and to take the toy away or replace it can damage an important quality in the character.

There are the two main sides of activity in humans: *projected play* and *personal play.* Each one of us at certain times needs a different admixture, though eventually circumstances may press us into a type indulging rather more in one than the other. For instance, when even an adult spends too much time at organizing in an office job and writing memos (projected activity), a doctor may say: "Drop it all for a bit, go out and play games." Or "swim" (personal play) or "take a holiday." There is a lot of projected play nowadays in school, with apparatus and sand trays, but still not nearly enough personal play, where the child must take on a role and test out the responsibility for moving and communicating as in life. We should sometimes think of apparatus as impedimenta, for it often impedes this activity. In the projected sphere the child invests objects with significance as an extension of himself. Later he discovers that other objects have been invested with mysterious significance by adults, like the symbols we know as letters, words and numbers. This is the realm of the three Rs. The child may not be able to invest them with what we consider the appropriate significance. In other words, he does not always understand; then he experiences a sense of failure. What do we do to compensate him for this?

One way is to use child drama in the form of personal play. For in the realm of drama all feel more equal, and to take on a heroic role can give a feeling both of purging and of overcoming difficulties. There is a sort of psychic bank account in all of us, whereby too many failures bring an overdraft with mounting interest. Some people can never pay it off without the help of an extra bonus or dividend or outside person, a sort of "bank manager." Dramatic play has much to offer here, and one cannot help feeling that there comes a moment when the number of successes equals the number of failures—if only in the realm of imagination—and then the account is even again. The task now is to build it up. I have often seen a sort of candle lit behind the eyes of a child after he has received such guided compensation, and only then will he start to learn again. (In the sphere of numbers one can also help some children by letting them be, say, five, in a group and experience it in three dimensions: letting them feel plus and minus by going forward and backward).

We talk a lot about communication these days but not nearly enough about its practice nor its basis, which should be the love of sound. Children love sound when they start school; I'm afraid they don't always love it when they come out. What have we done? We may have taught them about reading books and reading music—both good in themselves—but what a loss if they do not love the sound these symbols represent, for only then is the meaning rich and the emotion aesthetically stirred.

Incidentally, for the backward reader, we can compensate by using imaginatively what I call "the constructive lie"—a period when he may be allowed to read a book that isn't there! This is very important, for you can read an ordinary book but the child cannot. However, he can read out loud from his imaginative book, whereas you can't. And the child can tell you so! He can be "right" for once, and you can be corrected. You do not leave it here, though; you guide things into reading a sort of "free translation," perhaps, and thence into reality. But the defenses have not been destroyed, and for a disturbed child this can be an important slow transition.

One must know enough about the phenomena of behavior to espy the techniques needed. In the realm of speech, do not let us underestimate the barrier that can build up inside any one of us because of circumstances preventing sheer practice in expression and communication. Having a bad tooth, a sore throat, loneliness or shyness, can all be detrimental, as can being ridiculed, criticized, or ignored. I have written elsewhere about language flow. It can be encouraged, and it can also be dammed up. I therefore often use "jabber talk," particularly with immigrant children, just so they can speak at all. Sometimes everyone in the class uses it because the dragon understands, or the men from Mars teach us. When we are all jabbering away in invented words, I suspect that Pakistanis, for instance, sometimes speak their own language. Occasionally I invite them to do so—anything to keep the "flow" and the will to speak going. Then they can and do jabber, jabber, jabber talk and include their one English word. Wonderful that they can speak English now! Of course they just did it, didn't they? Incidentally, this is a useful way of teaching British children French or other languages. Have them include whatever words they know; but above all, have them speak!

As an island race, we British are a bit lazy about learning languages. We have taught children to pass examinations (projected when writing) rather than to speak. We seldom use enough actual speech through personal play, which gives living purpose to the event. It is important to use the emotions as well as the intellect and keep alive the love of sound. Incidentally, I have always used something of this for training adult actors (both amateur and professional) to release emotion and convey something through the use of happy, joking, and, finally, sympathetic or sad jabber sounds.

I think children divide sound into three main compartments: time-beat, rhythm, and climax. Time-beat is a dead *bam-bam* sound; rhythm is based on time-beat, has a repeated pattern, may veer away from that pattern and return (as in jazz). But rhythm also includes a magic quality, perhaps growing faster, louder, more exciting, in a way that can be shared with an audience. In rehearsal, production of music or theatre is based largely on time-beat, but by performance time should have moved over into the magic of a rhythm of its own. The audience may not know it, but this is what holds it. There is a sort of shared mental agreement when at its best. The third child division of sound is climax, a building to a peak. This is what all children want to do, and this is what we spend all our time stopping them from doing. Do not misunderstand me, I am not preaching anarchy; I am merely stating a fact. We must find a compromise, for adults need peace. But then so do children. It is hard enough for us to find it, but I am convinced that in this violent world children are unable to find peace without our aid. We all suffer to some extent from speed anxieties. I therefore add one other use of sound and give it the name "de-climax." It is not the same as anticlimax but is an intentional bringing down from loud to soft and then to silence. How often do children have to stop actively listening because teachers talk too loud—and too much?

Just a point about vertical grouping, which is mentioned often these days. I have always advocated a closer approach to a personal timetable. If vertical grouping aids this, good. If the spread of ages in the grouping is not too great, all will be happier. We should stop trying to teach so much at one level so that the clever ones can go ahead and the backward take more time. I have some reservations here, however, for the child is a mental, emotional, physical, and spiritual being and needs to go through the developing patterns of man, as shown in child drama, without hurry. It is essential that he should have some experiences and work with his peers. Younger children are not always welcomed by older children; they can be rebuffed when in need of help just as older ones can be kept back by a younger "nuisance." Finally, it is often valuable for a child to get away from the family and the bossing of an older brother or sister. This situation can be unwittingly repeated in school and the personality development of the younger child impeded, for he can be deprived of the experience of himself being the boss.

In all drama activity in the very young it is important to help them do their very best and use the utmost energy for short periods of time. Often, stories in infant schools are far too long; the children "fill in" and do not do their energetic best. I believe this ultimately affects all their work. In guiding child drama we should often ask them for ideas to build into a story, but occasionally we should add our own. The result is then "our" story (all of us) and carries with it a sense of security. Because of the love of sound, I often say,

"What does this sound remind you of?" I have taken noises to school and asked children to make their own musical instruments. It is important to do all we can to help them notice the riches of simple things in feeling, hearing, and expressing. At about six and a half years of age comes the "dawn of seriousness." As the "gang" starts in the infant school, it is clearly much better that the first gang leaders should not be the toughest, largest, or loudest children in the class. It is noticeable that where drama is properly guided, those who have had their dawn of seriousness often become leaders, taking responsibility with respect and recognition. Society is thereby far richer. Much delinquency can be traced back to the type and character of an early gang leader, yet how many teachers are *really* conscious of their responsibility and influence in this area of education?

In the first years of junior school, particularly between the ages of seven and nine, we find the important cathartic element of spitting out experiences, which occurs in their little gang or in group plays during child drama. There is a lot of cartooning, a way of using humor in a courageous search for ways of facing up to life. But valuable playing-out is also present, particularly the violence we allow children to see on television. This is important. One notices that older delinquents frequently return to the pattern of play normally associated with these early years. It is possible to get into a rut of role playing an evil character. This must be watched carefully and guided by a sort of challenge: "Today see if you can do a story with no killing" or "different killings." Or "You've had your play several times, now it is my turn. Let's have a story about *this*."

You will do them no psychological harm whatsoever! They may not succeed, but they will have tried, and this is the beginning of drawing them out and away from repeated roles and themes. I cannot overstress the importance of this stage of development. So many teachers do not realize their task here. But if the "drawing out" has been well timed and successful, children may become dissatisfied by what they do on their own and feel the need for more gentle infusion. This is the moment for a great march forward. The need is for richer characterization and plot, so it is worth using the great stories of the world, myths and legends, upon which to improvise—stories that have stood the test of time. This is a move closer to what is obviously theatre rather than unconscious creation. The teacher's task is to act somewhat in the manner of producer, gently suggesting neatness and precision but being careful not to destroy spontaneity. I would not rehearse such creations more than about six times myself, but would watch for neatness of entry and exit, eyework across space, contrast, clarity of speech, sound of the footfall, use of music, and special "golden moments" when time is made to stand still. These productions (using costume and light) or somewhat "polished improvisations" would, of course, not be on a stage but in an open space, using the shapes that belong to child drama in the grouping and the journey.

At this time and at various other moments, arising out of the best of their drama, which is a sort of creative wisdom built together by teachers and children, there is a particular atmosphere that I can only describe as innocence. I believe the world needs this innocence today; then the adolescent could look back on experiences, which would stand him in better stead, were we able to help provide them more consciously and more often. As so many people ask for the details of putting this philosophy into practice, I now include some of my personal notes on working sessions in drama with a study group of teachers at a conference on Compensatory Education and the Infant School, held at University College, Swansea, in March 1969.

Notes on Practical Sessions

My task was to fit the work of the drama group into the framework of the conference, showing how it could act as compensatory education.

It was necessary first, however, to establish a premise, so I outlined some details about the findings of Professor Cizek, who first proposed that there was a child art, an art form in its own right, and that it had fallen to me to suggest that there was also a child drama (and incidentally a child music and a child poetry and a child dance), for the child does not change its whole being and attitude by going from one subject to another. My next few points were somewhat autobiographical, showing how my attitudes had grown from experience, partly by being forced into a position of an outlaw at school, which gave me sympathy for the less fortunate, finding "ways through," absorbing psychology at a university abroad; then observing humanity while walking about the streets of London in the early 1930s. This close observation taught me so much.

We then went into the main division of play; that is, projected play, where a child projects the dream out of his own mind into, onto, or around objects outside himself and makes them significant unto himself. My point here is that this realm of play has to do with symbols, which ultimately grow into such things as understanding letters and numbers and thus the three Rs. Anything in fact, from sand play and art to building cathedrals and building sentences and equations. The less able or disturbed child is not always able to invest these symbols with the necessary significance. Indeed, he may be precisely the one who cannot. He then has a sense of failure. Fortunately nature provides another realm, where he can succeed or imagine he succeeds (which is almost as important), and that is personal play. In personal play he gets up and enacts people and situations; he moves about and relies less on the use of objects and dolls, toys and puppets, than on his own body, energy, emotions, and imagination. He takes upon himself at this time the full responsibility of playing a role for practice in living and doing.[1] He becomes the conquering hero.

Audience joins actors in celebration dance. Courtesy of Peter Slade. Photograph by C.N.A. Photo Service.

DAY 1

I put some slow music on the phonograph. Members of the class were asked to walk about the room feeling furniture, curtains, walls, tables, radiators, and so on, to try to rediscover a joy in the sense of touch. (*Reason:* We lose this joy as we get older and periods of reinvestigation help us understand the young child's delight.) Then we moved about the room, discovering elementary sounds by gently tapping different things—metal, wood, and the like (to use the child's division of sound and also to try to enjoy simple noises for their own sake, listening to differences in quality and tone).

We did some humming and then used the noises we liked best to a phonograph record, beating in time.

We discussed at length the fact that children can grow a skin over their ears and have to be helped along a slow path in order to listen again. Listening itself has in it intellectual meaning but also emotional response to sound, which is often forgotten, if an adult is lax, so that "no" can have a certain indefinite "yesness" attached to the sound of the word. Much more should be done to encourage sensitivity and love of sound in developing music, drama, and speech. We then did exercises that may look unusual in print, but which, in fact, built a believable situation and were proposed as two examples of training in use: (*a*) energy, (*b*) gentleness (for discovering different ways of behaving as a basis for (*later*) discovering appropriate behavior for the given situation). For *a* we pushed wheelbarrows full of heavy things. For *b* we imagined that bubbles were bouncing on fingers and backs of hands. Very quietly to Debussy music we picked up the bubbles and put them in a pile in the middle of the room. This brought the action to an end in "de-climax" (to show how to induce quietness so that children can go to other activities without being overexcited). Absorption in the task and sincerity about doing it were stressed throughout.

DAY 2

We talked a little about the preschool years, about attitudes and the role of parents, and about the circle of power around each one of us, which we try to master. Sometimes these overlap and can be the cause of aggression in either projected or personal play. We discussed ways of building a sense of security.

Speech exercises: obtaining ideas through discussion. The teacher builds a short story from them and the group acts the parts as we go along. Here is a suggestion: "Try telling a secret to a rabbit in his burrow." (*Reason:* Children who won't speak to us or each other will sometimes talk to an imagined rabbit in this way.) Try conversation in pairs, buying and selling things in shops. Then reverse roles. Telephone a partner across wider floor space. (Notice how one becomes progressively more shy at first talking over a greater distance. Children react the same way).

We then attempted groupwork. We started as individuals, then worked in pairs, finally in groups. This is a natural pattern. We discussed the different forms of casting before individual and separate role playing, and I warned them about too early casting. We experienced exercises in

1. Group casting—for understanding, shared responsibility, when a number of young children play the same person
2. Conglomerate—for understanding how children hold on to each other, conglomerate, and make a bigger thing or animal of themselves
3. Tribal—for understanding a family or tribal experience, though each member is a separate character

Suggestions were given about guiding, not dominating, and about teaching with purpose. Doing short exercises with energy. The more backward the child, the more guidance is needed, but with constant opportunities for short free creation to test growth or a sense of responsibility. I gave some pattern but said that ultimately we all must work in our own way (artist as teacher).

DAY 3

Building a story together with ideas from the group. (*Reason:* Progression, to put more responsibility on the group and away from the teacher through question and answer. Where did the man go? Where did he live? Whom did he meet? What happened then?) Using noises as inspiration for stories, we discussed liberation of speech particularly for immigrants and backward children and practice jabber talk. We imagined going to Mars and talked in "their" language. Heard one or two separate conversations of jabber talk.

Suggestions were given for blowing off steam and calming down. We became cavemen talking in grunts (to get back to completely primitive first efforts), then came up again to full English sentences to note the difference. Then we broke into groups and each made a little improvised play. Finally, we acted in separate groups and shared our results with all. (Normally, scenes are built first by ideas from the teacher, then slowly full responsibility is given to the children). This was all part of the guided education, including the known and likely pattern of human development.

Additional exercises were suggested for developing a visual image of one-self, investing the symbols of letters and numbers with significance. To music: Paint the shape of words on the floor with your feet. Paint your name in the air; try some numbers in the air. Try a secret in the air. Speak the same secret down a rabbit hole to a bunny, in case he is the only one you can tell.

Three-dimensional mathematics exercises   Discover the feeling of plus and minus by imagining that you are on a ladder and you climb up by going forward, come down by moving backward. March about, feeling the domino shape of five and four, add ourselves together, look around and notice the feeling of five and four, then count nine, divide the groups away again and feel the personal three-dimensional significance of subtraction. Do not forget that in all speaking and in all action, for the tiny child to receive compensatory education, it may be necessary for him to do very simple things; and just as he scribbles in art, he must have time to scribble in movement and use elementary sounds that will one day become speech. This may be for him the wonder of language. We talk so much about the importance of reading that we forget the importance of speech.

Finally, spiritual education and concern for others. We did some movement based on individual style, helping a baby dragon with a cold (teaching sympathy), and we finally thought of a Christmas present we would really have liked (as adults) but we brought it and put it in a pile (like the bubbles on day 1), left it there, and slowly retreated so that the presents could all be sold to help children starving in other parts of the world. Everyone sat quietly in complete de-climax. I then spoke quietly about the purpose of the course. It was not theatre, but the doing-of-life. Our main task is to release energy and build confidence in each child so that he can communicate and "do" well.

Secondary School

In secondary school I would advise seeing the drama as divided into three sections: imaginative, social and theatrical, roughly in that order, though as in all things pertaining to human nature, there are no rigid boundaries.

After the experience of junior schooling, which has become much warmer and more understanding in this country, it can be a shock to find oneself in a large secondary school, perhaps a comprehensive school, with different attitudes toward learning and discipline.

Friends may have been left behind and a respected teacher, perhaps; and one has to try to relate to large numbers of strangers when many psychologists believe that it is possible to relate to only a limited number of people at one time. To counteract this, it is important for a class teacher, and particularly a drama teacher, to try to build a feeling of family as soon as possible in order to establish a sense of security. I would also advocate at such a time (which may contain some bewilderment) the improvised playing of different characters in many different situations, not only to show the teacher where children *are* in life, but to help discover who they are *not*. Sometimes it is important to be able to play a character whom you have become aware you are not. Again, it is important for young people not to get into a rut of repeated role play, particularly that of bad characters.

At about twelve or thirteen years of age there comes a change on the unconscious level. Child creation begins to die and a rapid move toward adult consciousness takes place. Indeed, the consciousness may come so swiftly as to be an actual cause of the self-consciousness we so often see in adolescents. If oversophistication has been imposed too early, the stages of inward growth are more difficult to detect, but they are going on underneath, and the drama teacher should be aware of them. At this stage many young people do not wish to be in school. Feeling like adults makes for an interest in out-of-school things and situations. This is the time for social drama, by which I mean preparing for life after school; time for discussing relationships; preparing for events before they happen. I would avoid using the words *drama* or *dance* or *movement* now, but try to start a discussion. Out of the discussion may arise a scene or situation they want to play, after which further discussion can take place. The art is in such remarks and questions as "You were wearing a fur coat, because it was cold?" "Yes." "What do you think about fur; is it a good thing to wear?" Keeping our own minds open, strong discussion can follow.

Staying out late is another good theme. Reversal of roles, with the child becoming the "parent," often brings a different viewpoint. Welcoming a customer in a shop, being polite, knowing the price of goods, loyalty to an employer, or taking your first love out to a meal are all possible themes. Some people cannot "telephone" each other face-to-face in an improvisation. If not, try back-to-back first. (Having faced a person) the difficulty of lifting the voice may come next. Try moving people only a few feet apart at first, then try "phoning" someone on the other side of the room. This takes more courage. So also does standing up and being seen by one person, then by more. Then going up on steps or a stage and addressing the whole room. Purpose 1 is to overcome shyness gently; purpose 2 may be to move toward clarity and more concise expression. The need for this cannot be denied when we see on television so many "heroes" who are unable to communicate even simple elementary thoughts, yet they all come from our schools. What have we been doing with them all this time?

When helping young people to overcome shyness, speech may be poor; but when shyness has been somewhat overcome, louder, clearer speech should be encouraged. This is what is meant by *purpose* in the lesson. You may have to do only one thing at a time. As to reading aloud, this might follow the use of improvised speech (to get used to speaking out loud at all); and importance should be placed on learning to read one or two words, or at least syllables, ahead of what is actually being spoken so that people understand (or at least sound as if they understand) what they are reading. It sometimes seems as if reading were becoming a lost art, but it is closely linked with theatre, for one often has to read a part at sight and infuse it with meaning too.

Social drama could rate a complete book of its own, but I will finish with a remark made by a young lady after a course I was giving with a colleague for personality development in industry. "When I first started doing what you asked, I thought it was daft, but then I was tied in a knot, and now I'm not."

We are moving slowly toward the art of theatre, for large groups at first and possibly for selected groups later. A step on the way is the feature program; that is, a show based on a theme or featuring a subject. I differentiate between features and documentaries. Documentaries are more concerned with facts and are suitable for more experienced young people. Feature programs can include variety talents and, if desired, large numbers of people; in expressing the main theme, there can be choral speech, selected pages from a play for those who can learn words, improvised scenes for those who can't, mime or movement or dance for those who do not speak well, all linked together by music and a narrator. To give examples mentioned elsewhere (*Experience of Spontaneity*), I have directed such themes at universities or summer schools giving them titles like "The World, the Flesh and the Devil," "Sprite," and "Kings and Commoners."

When serving on the Ministry of Education National Drama Working Party years ago, I advocated small studio rooms for drama. I would still like to see more of these in schools for detailed drama work and for the teaching of English and other languages. Such things as clarity of speech, contrast, pause, and atmosphere are often lacking. These could be taught in a small studio, then applied in a larger hall later. Also there is training of the emotions and the effect of light on speech. I have conducted interesting experiments on this for a number of years and have worked on the blending of light with music. Detailed floorwork, stage movement, and the difference between exterior and interior acting could best be started in an intimate atmosphere. Small classes of about half a dozen selected sixth formers; a space 20 feet by 20 feet, with a good record player, half a dozen lights connected to a movable dimmerboard, and a few rostrum blocks is what I have in mind. We are concerned with quality, sensitivity, and artistry, taking a few pupils who are more interested than the average and possess understanding and ability to perform. One sees some productions that are fine; others appear to be superficial, rather like provincial repertory of the middle 1930s. Some of the best productions I have seen in recent years have been produced, not by drama departments or English specialists, but by musicians. This is an interesting and somewhat unexpected development.

Finally, there is the full-length stage play. If an audience is going to honor us by coming to see our show, we should do everything we can to see that it is as good as possible. Apart from the technical points already mentioned, there may be a two-way building of wisdom between young actors and producer. Sometimes the young have intuition regarding shape of production; sometimes the adult can help to widen the possibilities. My feeling is that one should not do a show in the round, or anywhere else, just because it is fashionable, but only because it seems the best way of presenting that play and sharing its message with an audience. Only then does one avoid gimmicks and ensure integrity. I did not produce *Our Town* at Wentworth Castle in the usual way; I turned a whole room into a street in order to get the close-up feeling I wanted. My play *St. Patrick* was done extended-arena style, with the audience on three sides. In Obey's *Noah* I had a group of little lads in boots running around on a wooden floor in the hall under the auditorium floor, to suggest animals. This gave the sound and shaking experience of being actually *in* the ark. In theatre-in-the-round it is better to try to train people how to act in the round first, that is, acting outward from the center of yourself all around the body. Children do this naturally, and that incidentally is one of many reasons for understanding child drama. Adults have to relearn this ability; otherwise they tend not to act in-the-round but (perhaps unconsciously) in four proscenium forms outward. The basic shapes of child drama are essential to know also—particularly the diagonal, which is half of the cross; the *S* shape, which is half of an 8. In the *S* shape an actor shows himself twice: in front face and profile, to all members of an audience grouped around. A conscious sort of kindness and giving must be in the actor's mind so that sympathy, hate, despair, love, and cheerfulness can be given off almost from the back of one's ear. If this does not happen, the theatre does not convince me, and I have no emotional experience. If it does happen, a vital exciting "something" takes place, which not only thrills at the moment of enactment but remains in the memory long afterward.

Theatre for Children

I always feel that this should be based on a knowledge of child drama, the shapes fully understood, and that it should be in the form of a polished improvisation, at least for juniors, so that if a member of the audience does something unexpected, the actors are not "thrown," but by training are able to bend a bit and come back to the story in a comparatively smooth way—as when one of our characters at last found the lost voice of a lady in a bottle but hadn't money enough to buy it.

A little boy jumped up, crossed the arena, and pressed a penny into his hand, It nearly altered the plot, but the actor managed it somehow, and the child and he played the rest of the show hand in hand. The moment of the voice coming out of the bottle would be suspended in time too, in my production, and perhaps there would be an extra spotlight to make the bottle shine. There would be pin-drop silence and then the voice would fade in very gently as it came back to us in a sort of golden fulfillment. I am prepared to risk a lot in this sort of theatre, but then I am not afraid of beauty. Actors should understand fear, too, and know how close to go to audiences of various ages and how loud to speak.

If audience participation is used, it should not be as a fad but because there is a genuine task to do. There might be windows to open, imaginary balloons to burst, cloud parcels to blow, or magnets needed to get the chap down from the sky after offering breakfast, gently, to the morning star. A common mistake is to say, "Who would like to . . . ?" without some preparation. You either get none or far too many offers, and so have to disappoint some. It is better to go straight to one or two children and say, "Please help." If they are shy, pass on quickly to others. Make sure, when the task Is done, to thank them, and they will go back to their seats.

Middle Schools

A word here about the middle school. It seems to follow a general pattern of education for children from eight to thirteen years. If my suggestions about the importance of the early years have been understood, it will be seen that the middle school age range cuts into the 7–9 years gang stage, and this can be a serious disruption. The fruition may come later or not at all. On the other hand, there is a clear run-through at the top. To go up to thirteen years means finishing the unconscious art form of child drama. But, oh the teachers! How should we train them for so wide a range? They will have to be very clever and adaptable people to understand in full the mind of a junior child and its needs yet know enough about drama and theatre to gain respect at the upper level. I see little recognition of this, but one does find a number of delightful teachers in this type of school, so there is hope for the future.

Movement and Dance

For many years, much of this work has been of imposed forms of technical accomplishment based on an analysis of movement, which in theatre terms, at least, is demonstrably inaccurate. I used to do a similar thing by imposing my own method of drama—athletic—movement on all professional actors who joined my companies. Later I saw different needs, particularly in education, and I started to harness natural grace and the beauty of the child's imagination to the process to avoid copying. There is also the importance of individual style of movement. In the personal-play realm of dance, individual style is the parallel of character in hand writing (projected realm). By using imaginative ideas as a basis, pupils of every age see purpose in the lesson because an understandable task is being undertaken and they are not merely doing a thing because the teacher says so. This is true aesthetic education. Unless there is inner motivation, the resulting action is surface effort or artistically dull and dry. Overpolished dance dramas are often dry and dull to watch because they are concerned with what the theatre calls exterior technique. On the other hand, we would not rush into dance dramas with insufficient preparation as they bring an excess of emotional involvement with repetition resulting from a paucity of gesture and vocabulary. It is also important for everyone to go through his or her "personal dream stage" in dance, before he can make full use of (or sometimes even accept) the impact of technical instruction.[2] While developing a deep appreciation of music and the detail of phrase and interpretation, the balance and the art of guiding is to maintain a standard without destroying spontaneity. On the whole, I think it is the job of the physical education department to teach formal and traditional dance, as well as technical skills. It is the job of the drama people to develop inner creativity. When both of these have been developed, we can decide what to do with them. The answer may be dance drama.

Religion

Many young people these days have strong social consciences yet reject the formal dogmas of religion. One finds, however, that some become keen about creating modern psalms or religious folk tunes—much as David did—and we can learn about tolerance and sympathy from those among us who have come from countries far away. The change from star performer to group message in theatre training, and the whole realm of sensitivity training in dance, has to do with concern for and duty toward our neighbor. It is possible to bring an experience of this reality, rather than mouthing familiar words that may have lost their meaning. And, of course, in certain isolated moments during dance, creation may be found to be so crystal clear that it appears and feels like a form of prayer. For those who understand this, and the young often do, it is a form of playing before the Lord, as our forefathers did. Dance may yet again enter the churches, not in a decadent or salacious manner, but as a proud form of praise.

Finally, in training teachers, I would always want to give them much imaginative, active, three-dimensional experience and work in drama and dance so that they can get back to a recognition of the world of imagination and fantasy. To reinvestigate the dream world without actually pretending to be a child; to develop a sense of humor and perceive more clearly the difference between dream and reality; and to investigate their own behavior and reactions at these levels, perhaps to become more mature. I believe young teachers would be much more confident if they had this training in depth. We should guard the qualities of child drama, which are absorption and sincerity (deep absorption in the task and a sincere way of going about it, both of which can become good habits), and, wherever possible, keep a respectful and pleasant relationship with children. This does not mean that we must not be firm. We should have concern and objective, thoughtful love for all human beings, smaller or younger than ourselves, rather than merely wielding the rod of power.

I look upon all drama people as potential brothers in arms; therefore I very rarely criticize anyone. But this I must say. There seems to be a cynical attempt by a few to debunk all the knowledge that has been gathered regarding children and their needs. They disapprove of words like "absorption" and "sincerity." Is it that they do not know how to get a child absorbed, or don't they recognize it when seen? As for "sincerity," they go purple in the face. Have we in the future to do without this civilized quality?

In a sort of stubborn ignorance these educators are putting the clocks back forty or fifty years. How out of date to still be raising the old arguments against things that have been proved over and over again down the years! I myself observed over thirty thousand children in one year alone in order to be sure of a single movement before writing a word about it. Have they done the same? It would be much better if they really digested what has been learned and went on adding to our wisdom from there. It is much easier to destroy than to build; perhaps they find that less hard and more fun.

Here I must also put in a word against the overuse of drama games. All of us have used some in our time, but they should not be the only things we use, as they tend to lead to superficial work, and drama should provide a deep emotional and aesthetic experience. What is the purpose of it all? Remembering the difference between theatre as such and drama-as-the-doing-of-life, it is for us to find ourselves as we grow up, to make the best of ourselves; for the young to develop balanced personalities, with confidence in themselves and the ability to use words; to be physically fit and able to communicate with their fellows; to have lively imaginations; to be able to stick to a job because their absorption in a task has been encouraged; to be honest in their dealings because sincerity has been nurtured; to be interested in the needs of others; and to be blessed with a poet's eye and ear so that everyday sights and sounds in this beautiful world may be as fully appreciated as possible while there is time, in case Man suddenly decides to blow it all to pieces.

NOTES

1. Further explanation in *Child Drama* (London: University of London Press, 1954).
2. This and many other details in Peter Slade, *Natural Dance* (London: Hodder & Stoughton, 1977).

Drama—
A Study of
Underachievement

Ian Bowater

Ian Bowater's impact on drama and theatre in education in the London Borough of Newham identifies him as one of England's outstanding younger leaders. The excitement generated by his program has resulted in an extraordinary spread of activity for young people and outstanding teacher workshops. Ian Bowater was born in Sheffield and educated at Bretton Hall College of Education. He taught English and drama in Birmingham, became head of drama at a comprehensive school in Essex, and was appointed to the Advisory Drama Team in the Borough of Newham in 1973. As senior visiting drama teacher, his work today includes all aspects of advisory work from preschool to adult education. In collaboration with the Monega Team, he has devised and performed in over twenty theatre-in-education (T.I.E.) programs. One of their most effective presentations, The Biggest Nursery Rhyme Book in the World, *involves five- to seven-year olds in the tasks of reading including how a book works, reading activity for the first time, phonics, and sequencing. Most important is the fact that youngsters enjoy and become involved in the process of reading through a theatrical device, which stimulates learning.*

Ian Bowater has written a children's play, The Princess in the Clocktower, *and most recently, a touring program called* The Money Show, *which examines world economic history between the two wars. In the following article he takes a critical look at current British attitudes toward drama, as well as the curriculum it supports.*

Of all the questions asked about drama in education, the one that concerns me most is why, after twenty years of drama in schools in Britain, are we still fighting for a place in the curriculum, still pleading for facilities, and still seeing drama cut when the economic going gets tough? I do not understand it; it's a relatively cheap subject to run—all you need is a large empty space. I was also led to believe that it was the most radical way of teaching ever to hit the curriculum. I still believe this, but is that just because I have a vested interest? If I sold micro-chip technology, would I believe that to be the most radical way of teaching? No, because computer learning is largely old methods with flashing lights. Drama puts the child at the center of the learning experience; computer learning places the child on the rim of a big wheel with the computer at the center. Drama develops the child's thinking in response to various stimuli; computers organize the child to respond to pre-programmed thinking norms. With computers, children jump through hoops; with drama, children build their own bridges of understanding. So why is there so much talk about spending millions of pounds on computer education, while drama is left to die?

After twenty years of growth, drama could disappear by the year 2000 because there has been no real move to persuade those who are skeptical about drama of its value, and those are the very people who make decisions on curriculum matters—head teachers, inspectors, and chief education officers. Well-known names in the drama in education field give sessions that are littered with acolytes who formulate supportive questions in talkback periods. If questioned in a critical way, they "smokescreen," sidestep, or just cave in. And, unfortunately, most drama practitioners have delegated their thinking to these so-called gurus. Drama is no longer in the education marketplace; it is stuck up some cozy back alley, serving old customers.

In my view, there are three major areas at fault in drama in education:

1. It has not found a role in the curriculum.
2. It has done nothing to develop new areas of the curriculum.
3. Its main technique, improvisation, is becoming tattered by too much bad handling.

During one of her recent sessions, Dorothy Heathcote described the work as "low-key drama, high-key curriculum." People nodded sagely at this pithy little epigram; few in the room saw that epigram as a potential epitaph for drama. In the wrong hands, however, that phrase could be the signal for the winding down of drama in education so that it eventually disappears in its own accountability.

After the heady days of the 1960s and the rapid rise of drama in the curriculum, there came a period of accountability. It was an obvious progression; authorities had poured large sums of money into the subject, and coupled with cuts in public spending in the early 1970s, they were looking for favorable reports on their investment. Similarly, the 1980s are going to do the same; only this time it will be falling rolls. If a teacher goes, he will not be replaced; the pupil/teacher ratio is maintained regardless of the value of the subject area lost. Of course, in areas like math, English, the sciences, the places are maintained; but if an arts teacher is lost, we are lucky if we are even allowed to exercise our accountability argument. And if we are? All we can come up with is that drama is a useful and lively way of teaching other curriculum subjects. We have faithfully carried out the predictions of the best-known thinkers. As far back as 1969, Dorothy Heathcote, John Hodgson, and Gavin Bolton were all saying that the direction, indeed, salvation, of drama in education was as a teaching method. Consequently, drama has been largely dealt with as a process rather than having aims and objectives of its own.

What is wrong with this point of view? The answer is twofold. It weakens the inherent strengths of drama, and I, for one, am not entirely happy with the curriculum we are so eager to support. For example, if we in our imaginative and dramatic way get a group of children to draw maps of the world and research the flags of nations, it does not mean that this is necessarily a vital and useful activity for the group to be doing. We have just wrapped up in colored paper and silken bows the same old geography syllabus we as children had to endure. The late A. S. Neill pointed this out early on; for while he saw drama as "a pleasant enough activity," he was sure that in curriculum terms, it merely sugared the educational pill. The curriculum we are eager to support is exam conscious; even at its early stages it deals with blocks of knowledge, not learning, and it reveres memory rather than thinking.

Drama can offer much more than the development of those areas of the curriculum. It can, in the first place, offer an alternative curriculum. As yet we do not have any program of social welfare in our curriculum other than in the rather clinical "how other people live" humanities sort of way. There is no syllabus designed to develop a concept of self or personal role play in large and small societies, nor to build up ego strength. These are left to house football matches and after-school chess clubs, which tend to build up ego rather than ego strength. It is often called "character-building" and manages to construct some pretty evil characters. Whereas, in a drama syllabus, these areas are, or should be, planned in a less haphazard way. Drama is about people and how they act and react to themselves and other people and differing situations. To have an understanding of drama requires an understanding of self and others. There has never been any serious promotion of this aspect of drama simply because there is no place for it in the present curriculum, and there has not been enough curriculum analysis to suggest its inclusion or any significant changes in approach.

In the area of intellect and the development of thinking drama is once more at odds with accepted practice. Where thinking is encouraged among children, logic is lord and master. Carefully considered straight-line thinking is promoted at the cost of any other approach. This is because our curriculum deals with right answers rather than with possible solutions, and with straight-line thinking it is possible to be right so far. In drama, however, the way participants are asked to think is almost diametrically opposed to straight-line logic. In the first place, drama is not always carefully considered; spontaneity is promoted, a wit is developed that is able to respond to any given situation. Second, thinking in drama is not progressive in the same way as straight-line thinking; instead of working step by step, processes are sometimes repeated, having had their elements changed, and a person who has developed one point of view is often asked to consider the same elements from another viewpoint. I am not suggesting the wholesale abandonment of the former mode of thinking for the latter, but considering that in further education the assertive thinking engendered by the straight-line approach is discouraged in favor of the more tentative lateral approach, which considers many more possible solutions (if only to discount them), what I do suggest is that the thinking promoted through drama should gain more cognizance.

Obviously it is not easy to overthrow traditional educational values in favor of the "young upstart" on the curriculum—drama. We have not made suitable efforts to prove its value in curricular terms, and without proof, we cannot expect change. Nevertheless, in one area there is a substantial build-up of evidence to suggest that drama has an educative value beyond simple curriculum integration. In several universities in the United States there have been some experiments conducted on the effects of different learning groups. Working from the hypothesis that the most effective agent for learning is the group itself, they have tried to make the learning group more efficient. This is a small start, but an important one. It seems that a good deal of the activity engaged in by the group was very similar to the kind of activity we call drama. For a long time we have made claims on the efficiency of drama as a teaching method without explaining why; perhaps here is an answer—drama is a good learning medium because it is a corporate activity.

It would of course be foolish to cast drama aside as a teaching method. Out of any drama that we create there can be drawn the strands that connect it to other learning areas. To leave it with that raison d'etre, however, is to sell drama short. It could be a curriculum innovator rather than a curriculum supporter. But in our search for a suitable compromise we try to marry the two, even though they are incompatible. One cannot change a curriculum by supporting it. Drama should exist in the curriculum in its own right without trying to ape other subject areas.

Drama could develop its earlier claims concerning its value to interpersonal relationships. I believe this to be the curriculum growth area over the next twenty years if we are not going to educate for employment. Whatever happened to "personal development"? Not long ago this was one of the great claims of drama in education. We were led to believe that the teaching of drama in schools had a strengthening effect on the personalities of its participants. They became more "aware"; some even claimed that it made us all "better people." The reason that it has drifted out of our credo is that there is no real evidence to support such claims. By what calibration does one measure the betterment of people and on whose terms? Far from becoming more aware, there is evidence that some participants suspend their critical analysis for the sake of the drama or the group. The notion that drama is an effective learning tool for use in curriculum expansion has not, on the other hand, gone out of fashion because there is actual evidence that drama techniques do significantly affect the learning process. Similar tests cannot be run to assess aspects of personality, although it may be possible to formulate exercises to assess group response and interaction. I suspect, however, that the results of such a program would be disheartening to the believers in personal development because of the power of conformity within the drama group (a subject I will return to later). Because of the lack of significant evidence, is "personal development through drama" a hopeless cause? Of course not. But what must be done is to apply conclusions of related fields of study to our drama operation in order to test our hypothesis.

In endless discussions on the nature of drama, I have noticed two distinct schools of thought. One, the interactionist, who believes drama to be a result of conflicts between people and situations; and two, the individualist, who believes drama to be the internal response to those conflicts. In truth, the answer is probably somewhere between the two. There is both a sociological and a psychological connection in drama; I am drawn, therefore, to the area of social psychology. As a discipline, social psychology is itself in its infancy, but it has already raised some interesting questions. Like drama, it is largely concerned with the operations of both the group and the individual; but perhaps what is more interesting to the drama teacher is that it explores these in terms similar to ours: play, games, role, acting out, theatre, audience. Indeed, Goffman, a respected social psychologist, went as far as to expound a dramaturgical theory, which likened every individual's operation in a social context to a theatrical performance. Now some of these theories may seem rather slick, others hopelessly inadequate; but they deserve our attention if we want to understand more fully what is happening in our own drama lessons. There may not be the evidence to support the personal development theory, but social psychology may help define our areas for possible research.

Let us look first at the group, for it is vital to drama. We set up whole-group dramas, we split up into small groups, we are constantly aware of group dynamics. The group in itself, however, is an abstraction; it is neither the sum of its individual parts nor an entity greater or less than the sum of its individual parts. That needs some explaining. The earliest work done on the group was called "crowd theory." This suggested that a large group of people is capable of a collective behavior that is not attributable to individuals within the group. It became popular during the nineteenth century, and it conveniently explained the social upheaval of the time. There was a good deal of public demonstration by the working classes, and this relatively new discipline of psychology offered an excuse for such unusual political behavior.

More recently, the now unfashionable crowd theory has been given another airing with studies of soccer hooliganism and crowd behavior. But it has been noted in soccer crowds that far from generating new behavior, it regulated existing behavior (its social acceptability is an issue quite apart from crowd behavior). It has been observed that groups produce conformity.

This is significant for the drama teacher; for, far from advancing the group's awareness, it is possible that the group encloses its thinking. The group becomes introverted, then begins to form a subculture. Instead of teaching at risk, the experienced drama group is cozy and safe. It is up to the teacher to break those habits with changes in teaching style and method. Long before the dangers of conformity set in, the most valuable aspect of group interaction takes place—negotiation. This requires the creation of social models, fields of operation in which opinions can be applied and tested. In a drama lesson it happens in two ways: first, in the life of the drama, where characters establish relationships; and second, in the planning, when groups begin to explore their own ideas. In these early stages it is possible to see the group as a collection of individuals.

In observing the individual, we come across the idea of "self" and "self-concept." Again, the idea of self is an abstraction. Most displays of self in the drama session are manifested in terms of roles, both within the drama and without. The outward image of the individual is only that which is permitted. It is noticeable that more is permitted within the life of the drama, but only very rarely does the presenter lose control of the role.

Roles are useful masks to hide behind, for they are safe. Through them we can look at others' reaction to us, and at situations; and if they do not work, they can quickly be changed. Brecht's theory of acting is useful here as the Brechtian style avoids the entrancing of the actor so that the performance is presented by intellectual comments of the outer role by the inner self.

It seems that there is an inner self, which is private to the individual and is best described as a self-concept. In the normal person no amount of deep-searching drama can reveal the inner self; what is usually presented is a carefully chosen objective view of life. Only in certain mental disorders is the inner self revealed, and even then it is rare for someone not to present an outward "mask" of some kind. This is important if one's justification of drama includes, at any level, the therapeutic aspect. People do not allow themselves to be stripped completely bare, nor is it necessary for a loss of control in order to begin therapy. Perhaps the best description of such an inward analysis is Stanislavsky's "psychotechnique." It provides useful exercises for delving into the self. But it must be remembered that even this method is really exploring only an external role.

Obviously, in the space I have here, I cannot expound any theory of personal development or the relationship of drama to group and self-concepts, but it is an area still open to drama. Nothing in current drama practice has suggested that it is not still heavily committed to interpersonal relationships and personal development. Perhaps there ought to be more "high-key drama" with "low-key curriculum" content.

Perhaps the one area of drama in education that *has* developed over the last few years has been the study of methodology. This is understandable because most of the writing about drama is concerned with *what* to do rather than *why* we do it. Role interventions have become very popular; the study of dramatic form in the drama lesson is looking at new ways of "finding the metaphor" for a learning experience. One area that has been overlooked, however, is improvisation.

Improvisation, in its various forms, appears in so much of our work as a practical method that in investigating the nature of drama, one might fall into the trap of thinking that one has studied the nature of improvisation. Inasmuch as it has gained such a lofty position in our methodology, improvisation often goes unchallenged; and not being challenged, it underachieves and sometimes fails. Through gaining a position of strength, it has become weak. This fault is common wherever improvisation is used.

Whether we like it or not, improvisation comes to us from the theatre; it is a theatrical technique that we have adapted for educational purposes. In varying forms, like the Italian comedy, the Moscow Art Theatre, the American method school, and the theatre gamesters of the 1960s, improvisation has come to us as a complex method of analyzing and discussing aspects of the human condition in a manner that confronts us with the truth in an uplifting rather than an alarming way. But even the theatre seems to have lost sight of this goal. There seem to be three attitudes toward improvisation in the theatre: (1) it is done because there is a supreme virtue in doing it; (2) it is a contemptible obstacle to the real work in hand; (3) at worst, it is a series of games done before, and having no connection with the real work in hand. Of these three attitudes, the second is perhaps the most productive because it at least puts pressure on improvisation to turn up with the goods. In short, the protagonists of improvisation in the theatre have pushed it toward insignificance so that it hangs about the stage and the rehearsal rooms like an inert gas.

Similarly, in schools improvisation is becoming rarefied. Not that it would ever be attacked in the drama world as an obstacle to the real work (since most other drama activities are even more theatre-based), but simply because improvisation is not attacked. This is not because its supreme virtue but because it is difficult envisaging anything else being done. The philosophy of drama in education is based on the educative value of play, and this had led a good deal of our work in improvisation to be a mere extension of play. Now we might be able to get away with that, even with the most discerning adolescent, but it would be foolish to think that any learning was necessarily going on. An alarming percentage of improvisational work that I have seen in the last three or four years in schools has involved sending children away in a group to make up a little play. Some of the results were *very little* plays indeed. The teachers suggested in many subtle ways that success was coming back with a little play. Improvisation as a technique was restricted to thinking up a story, handing out parts, "making it up as you went along," and "sharing it." All human life was there: drugs, birth, death, parents, nuclear war, and so on.

Now I am not saying that this is wrong; a great deal can be learned from observing life in this way. What is alarming is the extent of this process.There are now being created, in drama studios up and down the country, improvisation stereotypes—the improvisation pregnant sixteen-year-old, the improvisation junkie, the improvisation wicked parent, and so forth. Not only is the subject matter always the same, but the outcome of the improvisation is always the same. Why is this? I think the answer to be threefold. First there is, as with most teaching, a sense of moving toward preconceived ideas and solutions; the teacher covertly suggests what he is prepared to accept as an answer, and the children obligingly work toward that. Second, sharing work is always presentation, and teacher-inspired patterns of success produce formulas to be repeated. And finally, this type of improvisation work leads to the creation of a reality that exists only in improvisation; because the work is success-bound, it repeats previous success regardless of the truth or even the task in hand. So, in a simple problem-solving exercise, the father with a problem adapts the problem to the "improvisation father" we know and love. This neither offers insights into the character and motivation of the father nor discusses the problem. The intended areas of learning are avoided through improvisation.

How does the situation occur? Most likely, insidiously. No drama teacher openly tries to avoid learning through improvisation, and if the children were manipulating improvisation in this way, it would suggest a sophistication and understanding of the process that would lead one to believe that effective learning had already taken place. No, it happens through a slow wearing-down process in which early values and standards of teaching are eroded. In the early sessions, we choose a topic that is modest in its horizons. We create exercises, games, tasks for improvisation that toss around and open up our topic. When this is successful, we put more and more pressure on improvisation by taking larger issues, by reducing improvisation tasks to the single technique of playmaking; and in our search for success, we create stereotypes and a reality that exists only in improvisation. Far from being the radical way of teaching we all claimed it to be ten years ago, improvisation is most reactionary in its outlook and methodology.

This immense change in the fortunes of improvisation would perhaps have seemed inconceivable fifteen years ago, but we must bear in mind that it is not the nature of improvisation that has changed but our application of it. I cannot stress enough the importance of an early reappraisal of the use of improvisation since, if we allow improvisation to create a world of its own, we may soon reach the sinister position in which an examination of its nature would only be valid within the reality improvisation creates. Such a study would have little value to the outside world and even less in educational terms.

Very often teachers in schools have low expectations of drama, even those with some experience of it. In my job as an advisory drama teacher in London, I am fortunate in seeing a wide range of drama teaching. I find that a good deal of the time it suffers from its own mediocrity. Because it appears to be more efficient than "chalk and talk," very often it is not extended in any way and simply remains *only just* better than "chalk and talk."

A good case in point was an experience I had in a primary school working with a teacher who, for some time, has been using drama as part of her teaching. The basis on which I went into her classroom was to help with a session she had chosen to do. She had agreed to provide the topic and suggestions for ways of exploring it through drama. The topic was the Emergency Services (police, fire, and hospital). She had worked hard beforehand, and when I arrived, the children were divided into three groups and had done some research on one particular emergency service. What she suggested the drama should be about was a street accident that would involve all three groups arriving at the scene. In short, a straightforward story—the drama, a little play about an accident. In my experience that sort of drama leads to chaos; some of the children are fully motivated, others do not have a clue of what they are doing. Young children especially (these were nine- and ten-year-olds) have difficulty developing a corporate identity quickly in such a loosely structured exercise. Also, the exercise needs space, and so the drama teaching has to be geared to timetabled "hall time." What I proposed we do was hold the drama in the classroom and have that story in mind, but structure the session very tightly so that we looked only at particular moments of the situation.

The first activity the three groups were asked to do was to set up a tableau of an ordinary working day. We saw policemen writing reports, eating sandwiches; doctors phoning their families; nurses making beds; firemen playing table tennis, snoozing, and so forth. We then listened to some of their thoughts; some were thinking about their jobs, others thinking about anything but the job. This meant that we had quickly created a set of characters who were going to be central to the story but who existed outside the story. Next, we decided to find out more about each group. Again, using the tableau idea, we asked each group to set up a tableau of the moment when an emergency call was received. The class found out that each group operated in a different way. We noticed that the firemen began each line with "Quick!" "Hurry up!" or "Come on!" suggesting they were very much an action group, whereas the policemen were an operational group issuing a series of commands. Then we found out about their private thoughts: a nurse worried by the sight of blood and a doctor worried about being late home for tea.

We spent an hour or more doing that, looking at specific moments of the story; some high points, some low points, sometimes stopping to decide the next part of the story, on other occasions letting the action paint the direction of the story. All the time we heard both spoken and private thoughts of the characters the groups were playing, so there were complex people dealing with the accident. As the story advanced, more and more private thoughts were about the job in hand. Then these took on a different purpose; by having these thoughts heard by everyone, the group could react to individuals rather than individuals conforming to group norms. So often in a free drama a participant can only guess at what is going on in the others' heads.

The session was completely teacher-directed, but the children still remained free to choose the story, the characters, the essential moments of interaction, the outcome. The point of the teacher's directions was to maintain the high level of investigation, constantly pressuring the group to find out why things happened and to use the knowledge their teacher had so skillfully given them beforehand. Very often when teachers talk about curriculum, they mean syllabus; the topic they have chosen to look at. There is no earthly reason for studying the emergency services other than that they interest children. But since they *do* interest children, we can use them to look at such things as the "caring society," the human response to crisis, cooperative ventures, and the problems created for society by setting up these public agencies. None of these things was considered by this teacher before choosing her topic, but for me they are the only reason for choosing it.

If structured properly, drama is forced to open up areas of learning not covered by any current curriculum pattern. It is wholly concerned with the human condition and therefore is about learning for the future rather than learning for now. There should be no need for retraining in life skills if the drama curriculum is fully implemented, and the adults of the future should be able to adjust to the crisis of their current skills' becoming redundant.

Another area that the above example illustrates is that of the ability of drama to elucidate concepts and promote understanding of complex issues even with young children. I am sure I would have had great difficulty in explaining the quality of operations as seen in the police, fire, and hospital. Indeed, before the session I had not even thought of it. It seems obvious now that a fire department is an activist group, the police are an organisational group, and the hospital is a caring group in that situation. However, at the time I had no thought of it, and *the children were able to tell me*. So, in a sense, drama creates new areas of learning as it develops new understanding. It is important, therefore, for teachers to be ready to respond to these opportunities as they are presented in the drama.

Of course, this is not the definitive lesson. All these operations can be facilitated by other techniques and sometimes "going away and making up a play" can raise similar issues; however, I do feel that it incorporates a great deal of the beneficial aspects of drama in education. First, it questions what is meant by "curriculum," and for drama we see that it is rather more than simply a topic for improvisation. Second, it suggests areas that could form a new curriculum that is peculiar to drama, especially in the area of social health, personal development, and interpersonal relationships. Third, if we are going to promote drama as a learning medium, then it should be as a means of understanding and concept forming rather than a "bright lights" memory aid. And, finally, if we are going to continue to use improvisation, as we must, then we should see drama as an investigative process and improvisation as its chief implement. Drama will survive only if it can avoid being wasted away by its own complacency, so perhaps the investigative process should first be turned on itself.

To Play or
Not to Play

Donald Baker

"To play or not to play"—that is the question.

Donald Baker was awarded his bachelor's and master's degrees in English language and literature from the University of Birmingham, his master of philosophy degree from the University of Southampton, and his doctor of philosophy degree from the University of Bristol. He has taught on every level from nursery school through college. At one time head of the English Department of the Wesley Teacher's Training College in Kumasi, Ghana, he has also conducted courses for teachers in Jamaica, Uganda, Cameroun, and Togo, where he did research on traditional festivals. He is presently principal lecturer and head of English and drama at Dorset Institute of Higher Education in Weymouth, England.

Dr. Baker is a Hardy scholar whose play, Hardy, *was presented at the Hardy Festival in 1968 and 1978 in Dorchester. He is the author of* Understanding the Under-Fives: How Children Learn through Play, *as well as numerous articles for scholarly journals. He serves on the Publication Committee of the Association for Childhood Education International and has led workshops for national conventions of this organization in the United States, where he has lectured at several colleges and universities on various aspects of the theatre. He has always worked closely with schools in the use of education through drama and is an advocate of the value of play and drama as the basis of all learning. In the following article he focuses attention on the importance of play in the development of the very young child.*

"Theatre is play" declares the Dutch theatre historian Benjamin Hunnigher in a definition that raises more questions than it answers.[1] For one thing, we probably know that *ludus* means "a play," which we watch in a theatre building, and is loosely related to "ludicrous," referring to a fantastic or ridiculous act or object having little or nothing to do with the earnest and serious business of life. Consequently, when applied to education in general and creative dramatics in particular, it is hardly surprising that play is regarded with suspicion, if not total antagonism, by those who wish to evaluate and measure every aspect of learning, especially in these days of accountability. In fact, we need to define play and its relationship to drama much more precisely if there is to be any chance of convincing the skeptical of its educational as well as its potentially aesthetic value. I believe that a study of the ways in which very young children play will help justify play as an educational and social force. In this chapter I attempt to outline a theory of play and demonstrate its importance, not only for creative dramatics or child drama in particular, but also for the education of preschoolers and kindergarten or first-school children in general.

In the first place, drama for very young children is synonomous with play, though not in the sense that Hunnigher uses "play" to define "theatre." "Playing" and "the play" are certainly related concepts, but they represent different modes of activity and response, which Peter Brook, the British theatre director, has clearly pointed out: "It is not by chance that in many languages the word for a play and to play is the same."[2] The distinct yet related attitudes of those watching a play and those actively participating in it imply a scale of involvement and range of response and judgment that depend entirely on the aims and intentions of what is being done. In short, there is an implicit and explicit difference between playing and nonplaying; understanding the theory and the practical outcome of this correlation between what I call "drama" on the one hand and "theatre" on the other helps clarify the various activities somewhat broadly and vaguely described as "improvisation" in Britain and "pantomime" in the United States.

Although the distinction between theatre and creative dramatics or drama may seem no more than a semantic quibble to those who work in the professional theatre, the practical implications of theoretical definitions are crucial for teachers, children's theatre groups, and commercial companies engaged in theatre-in-education, or T.I.E. Quite simply, if we fail to distinguish between the respective aims and claims of drama and theatre, we may generate an event that is neither aesthetic nor educative. Even alternative or fringe theatre companies could clarify their genuinely experimental work by taking note of the psychology and philosophy underlying drama, especially of the drama being done with preschoolers and the under-sevens. For it is with very young children that the differences in the content and intent of drama and theatre are seen in perspective, and sharply focus on the particular attitudes we adopt toward the nature and function of play itself. In short, "to play or not to play" is the question to be answered if we are to deal effectively not only with child drama and educational theatre but also with early childhood education in general.

For *playing* and observing *the play* demand a clarity of definition in theory to give precision in practice. Two examples from the British theatre will illustrate the confusion of response when these fundamental distinctions are not made. The first relates to a performance by the "fringe" Joint Stock Company's production of *The Speakers* based on Heathcote Williams' book *Speakers' Corner*. The production assumes that the performance area is Hyde Park in London where the orators provide not only entertainment for the tourists but humourously and satirically criticize and comment on current social ills often identified with politicians and potentates whom we may dislike.

The piece requires both participation and observation, and seeks to transform the performance area into the park where the "audience" is directly participating in buying tourist postcards and tea from an actual tea bar. But when specific scenes are staged, as, for instance, when a speaker makes an actual speech, the actors and audience have to be clearly differentiated. Participation becomes performance. In Belfast, when *The Speakers* was produced, the line between participation and observation disappeared, and the policemen of the play were thought to be actual members of the Royal Ulster Constabulary with such dire results that the show was abandoned.

A similar though less violent outcome occurred in the Royal Court Theatre's production of John Osborne's *A Sense of Detachment*. At the final curtain the actress Rachel Kempson leaped into the audience and attacked two men who had been interrupting the performance. The play, however, invites the audience to participate directly, and two "plants" sit in the auditorium to offer comments on the action. Consequently, it was not really surprising when unsolicited interventions made life difficult for the actors. They, or rather the director and playwright, were at least partly responsible for their difficulties.

Everyone who has worked in creative dramatics or some form of children's theatre will recognize the problem of defining the response expected of the audience, whether it is to be participatory or observational or both. And unless this problem is resolved by clearly defining, signalling and maintaining the attitudes expected of those present, the result is often a chaos of confused reactions providing a legitimate excuse for an emotional orgy. Defining drama and theatre, with particular reference to work with under-sevens in terms of who is to do what, why, where and when, is the major concern of what follows.

Play, Drama and Life

The equation of play, drama, and life, which can be confusing for adults, has been made by many authorities. Peter Slade, for example, says that "... the root of Child Drama is *play*,"[3] and Richard Courtney claims that "drama is a doing of life."[4] The equation is clearly seen in the learning and behavior of very young children. However, play itself defies precise definition; there are probably as many accounts of its forms and functions as there are psychologists, zoologists, and philosophers. Nevertheless, to understand the relevance of drama for preschool and kindergarten children, and indeed to make drama more meaningful in a general educational and social sense, we can make a few points about the nature and function of play.

 In the first place, very young children do not always seem to separate life from play; for instance, they seem to slide imperceptibly between actually living in their own home and playing at home in a corner of the classroom or under the kitchen table. We cannot, of course, prove that children adopt this ambivalent attitude; nevertheless, what appears to be "playing" to us is quite likely "for real" to the player. Watch a four-year-old carrying buckets of seawater to fill a ditch he has dug in the sand and then try to decide whether he is working or playing. The distinction we make in our minds is linked with our adult concept of work, which has profound implications for our approach to educational methods in general. As adults we know that work is not play and, therefore, by the same token we may argue that drama is not an essential part of a child's serious learning process. Nothing is further from the biological and psychological truth. This particular point is succinctly put by D. W. Winnicott, who, claiming that play is the basis of all human experience, asserts:

> No longer are we either introvert or extrovert. We experience life in that area of transitional phenomena, in the exciting interweave of subjectivity and objective observation, and in an area that is intermediate between the inner reality of the individual and the shared reality of the world that is external to individuals.[5]

 For young children, that "area of interweave" embraces their whole world so that play, drama, and life are experientially inseparable. Ask a four-year-old about the lump of clay he is using, and he tells you it is a car. A few minutes later, ask him how the car is getting on, and he informs you he has a lump of clay.

 For the under-fives especially, drama is really a form of play, and providing we surround them with potentially stimulating experiences in the form of dressing-up materials, a home corner in which to play out the events of everyday life, and objects associated with different crafts and professions like building, painting, dentistry, medicine, and cooking—in fact anything that will stimulate play or dramatic sequences—there is no need to have a set "drama" time. An old cardboard box is much more likely to generate imaginative play than is a manufactured bicycle. Life to the under-fives is always playful and "dramatic," and through play they are learning about themselves and other people, as they venture into the world around them.

The Teacher's or Playleader's Role

 The teacher's or leader's function in preschool drama is to stimulate *play*, not to direct *plays*. Indeed, children may not always allow an adult into their fantasy world, and we should never force an entry. Often it is enough to sympathize with the situation by accepting it in complete seriousness, so that if we are asked to join the tea party and eat the imaginary sandwiches and drink invisible tea, then our eating and drinking must be absolutely sincere. During these sessions, it will always be possible to extend children's langauge as we talk to them and encourage them to talk to each other. Thus drama, in which children are using not only their bodies but also their voices, is a vital cooperative instrument for the development of language. And experimenting with language is a specific form of play.

Whereas a three-year-old usually pursues his solitary playing, around the age of four, cooperative play emerges clearly, and we notice children in the home corner spending long periods of time in play which, if we like to describe it as such, is "drama" in embryo; for these children are deliberately playing at life. In group or cooperative play, children often consciously play out events they have witnessed or heard in order to master the puzzling and sometimes frightening new experiences, and subsequently learn how to come to terms with them, to cope with the new sensations, new ideas, new people and things, and so forth. The playleader's role in both individual and cooperative play, which approaches the stimulated or induced play of drama, is to provide an environment of toys, objects, dressing-up clothes, boxes and barrels, and all manner of junk material that children can explore in a more or less undirected way. The teacher or playleader adopts an attitude of general but self-effacing interest, occasionally entering into the children's world of play through conversation. She should suggest but never impose; she is always present as a focal point of security, not as director of operations.

As children grow older, the mental separation of fantasy from reality, of play from life, and of animate from inanimate objects begins; eventually a child is able to make abstractions, form concepts, and ultimately to think. To illustrate this process, I cite an instance that occurred when a four-year-old member of my wife's play group remarked on seeing her in the street: "So there's two Mrs. Bakers!" A young child views each experience as an isolated event; only gradually are these separate pieces of information about the world absorbed, modified, and connected to one another. Eventually the concept of a person who exists independently of a specific location is formed.

Play is the process by which this ability to conceptualize and make abstractions—in short, to think—is encouraged. Consequently play, especially for the under-sevens, is the dynamic of learning, and if we concede that play is fundamental to intellectual and emotional development, then some means must be found in preschool education to motivate it. Moreover, if drama is to be a synonym for a young child's play, then it assumes even greater importance than it does for older children. In play, children learn about themselves and about their world by testing their physical, emotional, and intellectual capabilities on what they find in it.

Two important functions of play are the exploration of oneself and one's environment. Exploring new experience inevitably involves improvisation, a process of trial and error in which we discover that some sounds and certain actions satisfy us and are also acceptable to other people, whereas some do not. By repeating the satisfying sounds and movements, we begin to establish behavior patterns to organize the chaos of impressions into structures that are relevant to our particular culture and that are, in effect, the product of the interaction between the personal and the social. Etiquette and morality are examples of such patterns; ceremonies and rituals the practical expression of them. Through play children begin to relate personal to corporate life by discovering the mutual acceptance of social conventions.

Some Functions of Play

All play is a process of exploring and structuring. A. H. Maslow, the American psychologist, claims that play is both expressive and coping,[6] which is another way of saying that all playful activities fulfill two major functions: We reach out to the world and then try to make sense of what we find there. So from spoon banging, which merely shows that a child can cause things to happen, he develops the activity into a purposive sequence eventually recognized as a rhythm, which can be beaten out on a drum as a ground base for movement and dancing. Hence, drums, tambourines, and percussion instruments like shakers and rattles are useful means of inducing the exploration of sound and organizing these sounds into meaningful patterns. Indeed, these sound patterns and rhythms are the basis of speech, so that, quite incidentally, a child picks up the sound, pitch, tone, and rhythm of language in what are effectually motor activities. Tapping out the names of children is one method of learning to pronounce and, eventually, to spell words. Although this may be an induced response to an external stimulus, it can not strictly be called drama or creative dramatics; it is a function of play in which mastery of movement and the specific gesture of speech is the inherent though unconscious purpose.

A second function, and following from the use of rhythm, is the significance of movement itself. We know that young children engage in what Piaget has aptly called sensorimotor learning, which simply means that we learn by moving. The young child must actually *be* an airplane, identifying himself with the object. Eventually he realizes that objects are not part of himself, and so he is able to *think* about the plane. But this does not happen all at once. Play, because it involves movement, helps learning to take place as the attributes of things and people are explored and organized into meaningful patterns. In their play children imitate what they have seen and heard, and they also need the physical space to investigate the properties of the objects and the persons by "doing," which, as we shall see later, is the original meaning of the word *drama*, namely, "a thing done."

Third, and more specifically, children experiment with adult life styles and occupations. Role playing is familiar to sociologists, who now recognize its value in developing individual personality and social awareness. We all play roles, but young children have to discover the range of roles available to them. Thus, by playing mothers, fathers, teachers, doctors, cowboys, spacemen, nurses, and so on, a child creates a personality. This takes time and there have to be numerous experiments before the individual personality emerges. Not only are these roles related to behavior, but also to occupations. So children are learning what it is like to be someone else. These activities are stimulated by dressing-up; as noted earlier, there should always be a supply of old clothes, shoes, hats, curtains, and clothes available—in fact, anything that potentially extends the imagination and creates a character from the raw materials of experience. Thus, by trying out different roles, children structure the particular traits they have observed and subsequently play them out until they have formed meaningful patterns of behavior, just as they have organized other experiences into systems of information, or "schemas," as Piaget calls them.

Fourth, dressing-up enables a child to play out fears, anxieties, and other puzzling aspects of life. For instance, parental disapproval occasioned by some minor misdemeanor may cause children to have guilty feelings. But disguise in animal suits helps them master antisocial behavior. The superb narrative and sound psychology of Maurice Sendak's *Where the Wild Things Are* illustrate this point about restoring parental approval in the field of stories and is paralleled in this following anecdote of children's play.

One morning, a four-year-old girl played at being ill. She was attended by several other children, who listened with a stethoscope to her breathing, gave her various pills and potions, and administered injections. This sequence lasted for about half an hour; we can call it role playing, drama, or just play. The important points to notice are that everything took place within a secure framework of the play group and that the girl who was "ill" wore a rabbit suit, thus effectively distancing herself from the unpleasant event. It was the rabbit, not she, who was regarded as being ill. Disguise of some kind, like masks for adults or hats for children, always offers a sense of protection from the feelings and emotions being explored. Moreover, the shy child frequently finds it easier to express his inner and half-understood experiences when wearing a disguise like an animal costume or a hat. This kind of activity undoubtedly verges on drama, but it still remains a form of play for pre-schoolers.

For very young children, then, drama is a function of play and does not have to be artificially induced. All life is drama, play, a "doing of life." As Desmond Morris, the British zoologist, observes: ". . . virtually every action is a new invention. . . . Each bout of playing is a voyage of discovery: discovery of itself, its abilities and capacities, and of the world around us."[7] In practical terms, we shall see a three-year-old playing entirely on his or her own. Children of this age talk to themselves a great deal, exploring linguistic and manipulative skills as they move from what Piaget calls their "egocentricity" to self-awareness. At the same time, they are beginning to differentiate them-selves from the world of objects around them. Ultimately they are able to make abstractions, and by shuffling the concepts and mental images, learn to think. To summarize with an example. A three-year-old hurtles around the room actually being a car and mimicking the noises associated with it. A year or two later, he plays with a car sitting in the seat of a wooden toy vehicle and going through the motions he has observed and now imitates. Later still, he projects his ideas onto a miniature car and eventually is able to think about any car without a physical replica of the object being present. This process occurs through sensorimotor activity and is a major function of play. More-over, as this process develops, children are becoming ready for drama. But in order to pursue the respective forms and functions of play and drama in more detail, we need to note their difference and similarities.

Play and Drama—Similarities and Differences

Two factors are common to play and drama. The first is improvisation, which is, in effect, a spontaneous response to any situation real or imagined. The process of life itself consists partly of improvisation, for whenever we are confronted by a new experience, we improvise, responding in a novel and untried way. Whether that response is built-in, programmed by our genes, or depends on reflexes consciously learned from birth or even earlier are

"Is there anybody home?"
Four-year-olds. Courtesy of
Donald Baker. Photograph by
Richard Hearne.

questions for the biologists and psychologists to answer. Quite possibly, the explanation of any given response is not a matter of simple alternatives; but whatever the reasons may be, "play," like "drama," is essentially a means of discovering how to make effective responses and adjustments to life situations and to make them in such ways as provide feelings of personal satisfaction and communal acceptance. The only difference between play and drama in this context is apparent to an observer, who sees the former as an aspect of actual life and the latter, to use current terminology, as a "simulation." To the children who play, however, this distinction is irrelevant, for it is impossible to conclude that the one who plays is consciously aware of playing.

In passing, we may draw a parallel with the theory underlying simulation techniques in the training of airline pilots and astronauts. Whether they are always aware at the moment of simulated crisis that they are involved in a piece of pretense—a "drama"—would be difficult to determine. The less aware the subject is of the simulated quality of the program, the more likely he is to respond effectively in actual moments of crisis and emergency. Plainly, the ideal simulation is one in which the participants are completely identified with the situation, and although an external observer will be assessing their reactions to the various crises presented, the participants under test will no longer be conscious of the artificiality of what they are doing. Play has become, at least for them, truly a "doing of life," a "drama."

A second factor common to both drama and play is repetition or rehearsal of improvisations. Although two situations in life are never exactly the same, we recognize certain features in a sequence of events that have appeared on previous occasions, and we respond accordingly. In the play of very young children, we notice events that are not properly understood, being repeated. Thus, indiscriminate pieces of information are organized into behavior patterns. The process depends upon the predictable quality of events experienced—that a specific act will always produce more or less the same result. In this way, a child's actions assume shape and meaning as their purposive nature emerges with increasing control over them. For instance, children learn that a particular inflection of the voice requires an answer, whereas a different inflection does not, and so they begin to distinguish between question and statement.

A similar repetitive, predictable quality appears in children's rhythmic stamping, when a three- or four-year-old rotates on one spot while beating his or her feet on the ground. The movement probably reinforces a feeling of mastery over the movement of feet, which makes a predictable noise. It is therefore very helpful to use a strong rhythmic marching beat for young children, since the rhythm of the march is almost exactly that of the heart, namely, seventy-two beats per minute. The predictability of the rhythm, which allows it to be mimicked, provides children with a sense of security, a sense that is echoed and reflected in the repetitive quality of folk and fairy stories as well as refrains in songs and lullabies. Spoon banging, table tapping, jumping, and hopping are movements that apparently rely for their effect on the discovery that a feeling of satisfaction is derived from the physical expression of those rhythms fundamental to the body's functions, the heartbeat, breathing, and so on. Disruption of any pattern, whether it be of a story, a song, or a movement sequence, can cause concern, and what we also note here is the quality of ritual, the ancient function of which is to secure a community within a familiar and predictable structure affirmed in verbal and acted expressions. And these ritual forms are related not only to the functions of the body but also to those of the turning year with its recurring seasons.

The second element in play, then, is that of security and order in the young child's world—and possibly our own as well—which are reinforced as children repeat in play the events of their own lives. Often their play re-creates the life of adults—playing house, for example—or by playing at the potentially frightening visits to doctors and dentists they may eventually learn how to cope with them. Loss of parents or pets is also played *at* and *out*, consequently revealing a great deal about the thoughts and feelings of the young child in the process.

There is, however, one aspect of deliberately stimulated play that approaches the idea of actual drama, and this may be introduced with children of four-plus who are intellectually and emotionally ready for an extension of cooperative playing. In this simple form of drama, the emphasis is on discovering the body in relation to other bodies. "Body awareness," as it is sometimes called, helps children realize how much space they occupy so that they begin to learn to respect the rightful claims other people make on space. I describe this respect for other people as discovering "mental space," which each one of us takes up. Just as we have to learn how much space our bodies take up, so we have to learn that our mental attitudes and ideas have to be modified in order to come to terms with other people's. It is what one psychologist, Arthur Jersild, describes as "life space," and a growing awareness of what life space means, together with increasing physical skills, suggests what might be done with four- or five-year olds, as definite pieces of "stimulated play," which I call "drama." Two examples will show what I mean.

First, children engage in a "growth shape" sequence based on electronic or synthesized sounds that can stimulate movement that interprets the growth of a seed into a tree. The "trees" can then be shaken by the "wind" as another group of children, interpreting different sounds, move among the trees of the forest. The trees shake and move gently or violently, depending on the strength and direction of the movements by the "wind"—children who learn how to cause a reaction, though never actually to touch or tumble the others. The sequence can be controlled equally well by a tambourine shaken softly or loudly by the teacher. This is a very simple example of play that becomes deliberately stimulated dance drama, the purpose of which is threefold: to help children listen for the quality of sound, to interpret it in a sensorimotor sequence of learning, and to discover something about body awareness in terms of one's life space.

A second example that illustrates cooperative play and shows how information is taught through simple improvisation is based on the fact that Eskimos fish through holes in the ice. With five- and six-year-olds, the playing is really "drama" suggested by the teacher who has previously done some craft work on making paper parkas with the class. Simple improvisation of fishing with hook and line, useful for the development of hand and arm movements, with the children working in small groups, has informational material as well as social development in group play as its educational aims. Play has now become distinctly "drama."

A final interesting and, in one sense, purely technical similarity between play, drama, and, incidentally, theatre for the very young is the natural shape of play, which is the circle. Most traditional dances are based on this figure, and it is significant that the circle seems to characterize a child's physical activities from the first crawling movements to the more sophisticated singing and dancing ring games of older children and adults. In fact, it is possible to interpret a child's growing awareness of the world as a process represented by expanding concentric circles. Years ago, Jung drew attention to the *mandala* as a fundamental symbol in mythology and dreams,[8] and though we may be reluctant to regard all circular play structures in Jungian terms, it is nevertheless a curious fact that the circle is a recurrent figure in children's running play, dancing, and rhythmic stamping whether it is done by individuals or groups. Thus, in purely practical terms, the space for play, drama, and, indeed, theatre should offer opportunities for working "in-the-round," especially in the case of the under-sevens.

To summarize: In play there is both improvisation and rehearsal or repetition of improvisations, characteristics that also appear in drama. The implications of this summary are that we should be providing young children with the opportunities for exploring what the sociologists call "roles" within the secure framework of the group or class and focused in the sympathetic relationship between teacher and children. The raw material for this "role playing" may come from directly observed events, or by the stimulation of a child's imagination visually, aurally, or by any means the teacher considers appropriate and effective. With the preschool child this work will be in the category of play; with older children it will be the contrived play of drama; but irrespective of whether we call it play or drama, children are experimenting with roles, discovering pieces of information about their world and exploring and establishing their own and society's behavioral patterns. As Richard Courtney puts it: "The child *plays out* his own view of the world as he sees it. To an extent he can learn emotional control to tolerate and to consider others."[9]

Whatever theories we hold about the form and function of play, there is no doubt that at some point in the development of children, a distinction between play and nonplay becomes clear, and it is then that drama as distinct from play assumes relevance in early childhood education. Having discussed the equivalence of drama and play for young children, we turn now to the specific characteristics of drama and theatre and the contribution that each makes to the median activity described as "theatreless drama."

Defining the Terms

In the original Greek, *drama* means "a thing done" and *theatre* a "place for watching." These comments are familiar enough, but to oversimplify even more grossly we can also say that *drama* is "doing one's own thing" and *theatre* is a place for watching other people do their's; though we must qualify the latter by adding "significant things," for many events occur in life that, though undoubtedly meaningful to the doer, are insufferably boring to those who have to watch. It seems to me that a great deal of "performance art" or "happenings and events" fall within this category of nonsignificance, and while having intrinsic value, cannot hold the interest of those who adopt the traditional posture of an audience. Participation and observation are two distinct responses that derive from different attitudes to *play* and *the play*.

"Drama" I regard as equivalent to what Peter Brook calls "play," in which there is total involvement and absorption in the event, and participation is the key to its method. In conventional theatre, a play is performed to the audience, who observe actors distanced or separated from them. Nevertheless, although "play" and "the play" exhibit different modes of activity and response, they correlate on a sliding scale from participation to observation. Between these two extremes, there is a median phase where participation and observation alternate. This is the commedia dell'arte style of playing, the genre of the folk play, and the basic working premise of much theatre in education or, as it is sometimes called in Britain, "theatre of participation." I describe this phrase as "theatreless drama," a phrase that seeks to preserve the major characteristics of both theatre and drama in a distinct mode of operation. It is, for instance, the method of the African storyteller as well as the folk play, in which vocal and actual participation is not only encouraged but expected. The ease with which young children slide from fantasy to reality, from play to nonplay, demonstrates the existence of a continuum from playing to the play that separates into distinct modes only with a child's developing self-awareness. For older children, and adults who have become conscious of a self-identity, the difference between play and nonplay is usually clear; it is therefore necessary to define the boundaries in practice between the attitudes of participation and observation that characterize "drama" and "theatre" respectively. Failure to do so may cause confusion of response referred to earlier, and this could be avoided by companies working for and with adults in a professional playhouse as well as educational theatre groups involved with older children.

For under-sevens, however, theatre is not entirely relevant, because their mental development has not reached a point where psychic distancing, the distinction between play and nonplay, has very much meaning. Drama, then, is one form of self-expression; theatre a form of art that communicates an experience to those who are not directly in or immediately involved in the actual means or precise moment of its experiencing. As Brian Way observes: ". . . theatre is largely concerned with communication between actors and an audience; 'drama' is largely concerned with experience by the participants, irrespective of any function of communication to an audience."[10]

If drama and theatre lie at the extremes of a spectrum of activities ranging from participation to observation, between the two, and drawing on both for its inspiration and intent, is "theatreless drama," because it is neither completely theatrical nor entirely dramatic. It hovers between play and the play and defines an area of response in which those involved are both spectators and participants, observers and creators. It depends on a group of actors working a prearranged plot structure within which there is room for improvisation by and for those present, whose role alternates from observers to participants. Much theatre-in-education is based on this participating style or method. Perhaps this explains why young children find this commedia style easy to comprehend, because their own development has not yet reached a point where such differentiation is either possible or meaningful. Consequently, I use this method a great deal. Among other advantages, it introduces the observational attitude of theatre, but does so within the context of the all-embracing imaginative world created by the children and teacher. I can illustrate "theatreless drama" briefly here by referring to one of my own events—I use this the term "event" to avoid the implication of either drama or theatre exclusively and also to escape the connotations of the experimental "happening."

My example is based on the Breughel picture *The Medieval Fair*. It included sequences in which children actually watched a "booth theatre" production of a mummers' play at prearranged moments and also participated in improvised buying and selling at market stalls. In this way, we move almost imperceptibly from the direct, participatory play of "drama" to the distanced, observational watching of the play in "theatre," though the whole event is contained within the imaginative world suggested by the picture. Plainly, in describing this piece of commedia style playing. I am assuming that drama and theatre or any combination of the two manifest certain quite specific characteristics, and in order to justify the assumption we must now examine each of these in turn, beginning with drama.

Drama

We have discussed drama under the heading of "play," which is much more relevant to young children, but for drama to exist in the sense of total physical and emotional involvement, certain conditions must be met. For instance, we have to assume the existence of a community based on classroom or school group, which reflects some of the characteristics of traditional societies in many parts of the world where the culture is indigenous and localized and the numbers sufficiently small to allow the whole community to celebrate events of a personal or communal character in a public manner. In Africa, for example, a death or marriage is a festival in which everyone spontaneously participates. But participation on this scale is motivated by a sense of community and arises from an experience of shared living in which individuals, though retaining their individuality, are absorbed and secured within the extended family or tribal group. For effective drama, we presuppose this temporary and somewhat artificial community in a class or school, whose ethos permeates the playing together, the "doing of life" that we call drama or creative dramatics.

Theatre

Theatre, on the other hand, I regard as institutionalized drama, that is to say, drama transformed into an experience re-presented in purposive and communicative form. Theatre is vicarious playing to which we refer as the performance of a play. Theatre depends on a degree of dissociation from the world, a mode of distancing or separation of the experience itself from reflections about it, the doing from that which is done. It follows from this that a conventional actor/audience relationship in the theatre has little relevance for young children, who tend to relate the world wholly to themselves in what Piaget, referred to earlier, has called "egocentrism," which is not to be confused with egotism or selfishness but describes a state of mind in which inner and outer realities are fused. In practical terms, this appears when children are so completely absorbed in what they are doing that they do not distinguish between play and nonplay.

For this reason, very young children are not audience conscious. They are, in effect, both actors and audience, and seem to have no difficulty in assuming this dual role that stems from a continuum of play modes within a child's experience. This leads us to discuss the important phase of theatreless drama in more detail.

Theatreless drama

In the five-to-seven range of the British First School, which spans the period during which a child's "egocentrism" gives way to "decentered attention," the separation of the "me" from the "not me," it is essential for every teacher or group leader to recognize the distinction between drama and this second phase on the drama/theatre spectrum. If she understands children's changing attitudes toward play, a teacher will be able to distinguish between drama, which is expressive, frequently therapeutic, and often a once-only means of exploring experience in movement and speech, from one that demands some form of psychic distancing or mental reflection from what they are doing. Theatreless drama, while retaining some of the elements of drama itself, yet moves distinctly and deliberately toward theatre at clearly defined points.

In some respects, theatreless drama is similar to the style of commedia dell'arte, which came into prominence in Europe during the sixteenth century and which has reappeared as a fundamental modus operandi of much theatre-in-education. Commedia methods are especially relevant to work in schools, for as Allardyce Nicoll observes:

> Unlike other dramatic works they offer no dialogue for the characters introduced; all that the author provides is a series of entries and exits, with indications of the "business" (the lazzi) of the various scenes. The "business" involves not merely what the characters are to do, but also instructions as to what they are to say.[11]

Three characteristics of the commedia style have significance for theatreless drama. Firstly, a troupe of actors is used; second, the dialogue they speak, though partly improvised, has certain key lines that serve as cues; and, third, the *soggetto*, or scenario, provides the structure of the narrative within which improvised speech and prearranged dialogue take place. There is little doubt that a sixteenth-century audience participated vocally, but in theatre-in-education, the audience of children is deliberately encouraged to participate physically as well as vocally, and this has led to this median phase of activity being called "theatre of participation."[12] Children seem to accept this pattern of participatory programs quite easily, providing there is an intimacy of relationship between actors presenting the scenario and the children, who are to be both doers and watchers. Two examples will illustrate the mode of response expected and the methods of working.

Examples of Theatreless Drama

A program based on Longfellow's poem *Hiawatha* was introduced by a discussion of American Indian tribes. Further preparation included the learning of songs and the improvisation of speech and action to gain a vocabulary of language and movement to express hunting and dance, which would later be used in the partly organized, partly improvised program, or scenario. In theatreless drama or theatre of participation, actual scenes are presented by the actors in the context of a situation where both actors and audience are part of the imaginary world. In the *Hiawatha* sequence, seven- and eight-year-olds were required to participate as Indians in the imagined life of an Indian village, and also to watch a performance of Indian dances by the actors.

Another program with this age range was based on the familiar folktale structure of tasks to solve, a journey, and the eventual healing of a sick person. The group chose what I call "generic" characters—in this example, a witch, her cat, pirates, giants, and clowns. On entering the performance area, children met two clowns who did various tricks until one became "floppy" and was unable to stand up. The sequence developed as follows:

1. The clown asked the children to help heal the sick clown. The witch was suggested because she could work spells.
2. The witch had forgotten her spells, but she thought the cat might know; unfortunately, she was unable to communicate with the animal because she had also forgotten the language as well as her spells!
3. The children made up the language, communicated with the cat, and discovered that the spell could be found on an island guarded by giants.
4. The pirates were then asked to sail the "crew" to the island, and in this instance, since we were using the school gymnasium, physical education apparatus was imaginatively transformed into the ship with climbing ropes and frames as the rigging.
5. The giants were met on the island and turned out to be friendly and helpful. The spell was found, and everyong returned by the same means they had used in the outward "journey."
6. Various items were collected for the magical potion, one boy claiming he was carrying sheeps' eyes!
7. After making the potion, reciting the spell, and dancing round the sick clown, he came back to life.

Introduced in this theme are familiar folktale elements including the seasonal rhythms preserved in all death and resurrection myths and their rituals. The folktale structure and its perennial fascination of narrative expressing deep-rooted human experiences are fundamental factors in original story-making that, in its turn, forms or should form the base for commedia style playing in theatreless drama or theatre-in-education. Technically, it allows children to express their own feelings at structured times, while they are actually shown events at other prearranged moments. In short, children are involved in the creative process of drama, but are also confronted at certain points by the product of what is, in effect, someone else's process, presented in the organized art of theatre.

Theatre

Theatre as an art form must have some place in education, although its introduction depends largely on the age of the children concerned. A seven-year-old may not be ready for it; an eleven may. Indeed, there is possibly a "theatre readiness" for every individual child, and it is part of the teacher's task to detect it. A hint of theatre readiness appears when children ask if they may perform for others. Another pointer is when they begin to make use of stage or rostrum levels, particularly when, in cooperative play, alternating dominance and submission sequences emerge. As further feeling for theatre grows, children tend to move on and off a stage or level, and group domination by one child appears. But these aspects of drama and theatre-in-education relate more to the older child in the nine-to-eleven range and lie somewhat beyond the limits I set for discussion at the beginning. Nevertheless, it seems to me that it indicates very clearly the distinction between play and nonplay, which is manifest when we recognize the difference between children's total involvement and watching members of a group whom we call actors becoming involved with each other. The original Greek word for actor is *hypocrites* and has two meanings; the first is "one who pretends by wearing a mask," or, as the Romans were to call it, a *persona*, and the second an "explainer." Theatre, then, is concerned with explanation of the pretended role being played at; drama assumes that the role is actually being played by oneself. Thus we arrive at the point where this chapter began: *Play* and *the play* are placed on a spectrum of response, which parallels that of drama and theatre. The phases are related yet distinct and this distinction must be recognized and met by those who work in any form of education. As Peter Slade comments:

> "Theatre" is an ordered occasion of entertainment and shared emotional experience; there are actors and audience—differentiated. But the child, if unspoiled, feels no such differentiation, particularly in the early years—each person is both actor *and* audience.[13]

Though I have been arguing for the equivalence of play and drama in the early years and suggesting that drama is for the under-sevens a form of stimulated play, we cannot totally exclude the experience of theatre from young children. Theatreless drama seems to me to be the most effective means of introducing it, but there is also the possibility of straightforward, conventional theatre by children's theatre companies specializing in this work, which is often excellent providing careful note is taken of the psychology of sound educational practice. Moreover, educational theatre should never "play down" to children in a condescending way and make cheap jokes out of children's lack of life experience, which is the kind of thing one sometimes sees and which makes unthinking and insensitive adults laugh. We laugh *with* children; never *at* them!

One company that meets all the requirements for sound work with children is the American Paper Bag Players, which has toured Britain several times with great success. During one visit, a critic wrote: "The conventions [of the Bags] fall somewhere between A. A. Milne and *Peanuts*;" he went on to say that the company has "a certain kind of knowingly naive stage humour, childlike in its grave and pantomime simplicity but far from childish and never less than charming."[14] Informing the work of the Bags is an implicit recognition of play and nonplay, of directing the respective characteristics of each toward the appropriate age range of children, whose mental and emotional development makes it likely that their responses will be exciting, educative, and aesthetic. A few examples from the program I saw will illustrate my points.

Thus, for scenes directed at the six-plus range, the Bags rely on children's delight in role play. One item, entitled *Red and Checkers*, appealed to a child's pleasure in dressing up. "Red" and "Checkers" merely swap their hats and scarves, but the question is asked: "Can we change names if we've changed clothes?" And the search for the meaning of self-identity is implied if not explicitly stated. The use of scrap or junk material, referred to earlier as a source of imaginative play, underlies the Bags literally appearing with paper bags and cardboard boxes for props. In one item, simply called *Shoes*, the four- or five-year old's delight in wearing a grown-up's shoes was the basis for a scene in which two players wore enormous cardboard boxes while performing a short dance, the sound itself also appealing to a young child's sense of rhythm.

One final reference to the Paper Bags' work shows how a company can capitalize on the psychology of play in aspects of work that verge on actual theatre for the very young. The distinction between fantasy and reality, play and nonplay, or animate and inanimate objects that has been the major theme running through this chapter, and the ease with which young children make the transition from one to the other, were the inspiration for a piece called *S.O.S.* in which a boat assumed a personality and found itself in distress. A charming variation of the fantasy/reality theme inspired *Butterfly*. A postman goes to sleep and dreams of a butterfly, which the audience sees as a paper insect floating over the stage. He wakes up and asks the question: "Am I a postman who dreamed I was a butterfly, or a butterfly pretending to be a postman?" The children spontaneously answered: "A postman." The Paper Bag Players set out to deal unequivocally in "theatre," but with some vocal participation of the order one might guess existed in Elizabethan times if no other, the question posed at the beginning of the chapter, namely, "to play or not to play," is answered by reference to and taking into account the psychological needs and capabilities of very young children.

Conclusion

In education, to clarify and give precision to what has usually been called drama or creative dramatics, we should recognize a spectrum of activities ranging from the self-expressive experience of drama at one end to the communicative art of theatre at the other. In between is theatreless drama, theatre of participation, or the commedia style of theatre-in-education. The terms describing this median phase matter little providing we accept that it draws its form from both drama and theatre and appeals to children's instinctive drive to explore and structure their widening world. With preschool children, however, drama is synonymous with play and as natural part of their learning process. With older children, the stimulated or induced play of drama extends their experience into cooperative activities of learning that may be "social engineering" as well as the gaining of meaningful information. Drama enables a child to feel as well as know, for intellect and emotion are inextricably linked in learning and behavior.

Play and drama are both aspects of life experience, and in these technologically dominated days are more important to the growing child than ever. As Harvey Cox observes in describing the functions of fantasy in contemporary society: Among other things they [machines] cannot really play, pretend, or prevaricate. They cannot frolic or fantasize. These activities are somehow human and if they vanish man loses essential reminders of his singularity."[15]

It is at least part of our task as educators, whose special interest may be in the arts in general and drama in particular, to see that children are given opportunities to play and to participate in dramatic and theatrical events. Failure to appreciate the significance and value of play, especially in the under-sevens, may well lead us all into inhumanity. "To play or not to play" is a question for the world to answer, not just those who are professionally concerned with the education of preschoolers and kindergarten or first-school children. For play, drama, theatre, and life itself can be magic worlds for those who believe in them!

NOTES

1. Benjamin Hunningher, *The Origin of Theater* (New York: Hill & Wang, 1961), p. 11.
2. Peter Brook, *The Empty Space* (London: Pelican, 1972), p. 86.
3. Peter Slade, *An Introduction to Child Drama* (London: University of London Press, 1962), p. 1.
4. Richard Courtney, *Teaching Drama* (London: Cassells, 1965), p. 5.
5. D. W. Winnicott, *Playing and Reality* (London: Pelican, 1974), p. 75.
6. Abraham H. Maslow, *Motivation and Personality* (New York: Harper & Row, 1970).
7. Desmond Morris, *The Human Zoo* (London: Jonathan Cape, 1969), p. 226.
8. C. G. *The Integration of Personality* (New York: Farrar and Rinehart, 1939), p. 96.
9. Courtney, *Teaching Drama*, p. 5.
10. Brian Way, *Development Through Drama* (London: Longmans, 1967), p. 2.
11. Allardyce Nicoll, *Harlequin*, (London: Cambridge University Press, 1963), p. 24.
12. I am indebted to Leslie Williams, former director of the Bournemouth Drama Centre in England, for this phrase and for the example of *Hiawatha* described later.
13. Slade, *Introduction to Child Drama*, p. 2.
14. *Daily Telegraph* (London), 22 December 1967.
15. Harvey Cox, *The Feast of Fools* (Cambridge, Mass.: Harvard University Press, 1969), p. 16.

Drama—At the Core
of the Curriculum

John Hodgson

John Hodgson is chairman of the Drama department at Bretton Hall College of Arts, Yorkshire, England, and tutor in acting at the University of Leeds. His The Uses of Drama *and* Drama in Education: The Annual Survey *are widely known. These volumes reveal the depth and breadth of his knowledge, as well as his skill in selecting material of particular value to the student and teacher of drama. He is co-author with Ernest Richards of the popular text for actors,* Improvisation.

John Hodgson's educational background includes study at Oxford University and extensive training in improvisation, music, dance and stage movement. He has taught at the Old Vic Theatre School in Bristol, and is an External Examiner for Drama Programs.

For the past several summers he has co-directed, with Dr. Nancy Swortzell, a graduate program in educational theatre for New York University on the Bretton Hall campus. This program, designed for teachers, recreation leaders, actors and specialists in the language arts, is unique in that it provides both academic and practical experience in a variety of institutions and communities in Great Britain. John Hodgson is recognized as one of England's foremost proponents of drama as a social and educational force and is one of the few who are able to bridge the gap that so often exists between drama as entertainment and drama as education.

We sometimes speak of the birthrights of young people, and there are several rights that we in Western civilization agree are important. Some of these are given, some have to be worked for, and some require the educational pattern to aid in their development. These days there is much talk of civil liberties and human rights, which suggests that freedoms are handed to us by authorities when in fact they will remain significant only if all citizens take an active role in forging, establishing, and sustaining these fundamentals of our democratic way of life. This presupposes the ability of each individual to take part in the process. It presupposes activity rather than passivity. It assumes a grounding in what has been called the fourth R of education: Relationship. It is surely the right of every person to grow into confidence in meeting, conversing, and relating to other human beings. With this in mind I have formulated what I have called ten tools for learning and living. By the time each person leaves school he or she should be able to

1. Move confidently among people in physical terms
2. Show physical coordination and a sense of rhythm
3. Converse easily with each other on a range of subjects
4. Give instructions clearly
5. Describe a situation vividly
6. Express feelings adequately in words as well as actions
7. Address a small group and hold attention
8. Understand jealousies, anger, stubbornness, irritation, immaturity and the like in themselves and in others
9. Argue effectively
10. See faults in others' arguments and correct these in their own

Some of these learning tools may come easily to us, others may need to be worked at with greater diligence; but there must be a recognition that unless we give priority to *relationship* in structuring the curriculum of our schools we are likely to discover that the rest of the learning is based upon rather doubtful premises and that the young adults who leave our schools and colleges will not have had the start in life necessary to a sense of relationships on personal, social, or political levels.

It is surprising how much of the present school curriculum requires individuals to stay quiet, stay separate, and express ideas on paper or only to the teacher. Drama asks for student involvement in a way no other area demands—to react as people interacting with each other. In the drama lesson it is necessary to aim at involving all the young people most of the time. It is necessary to get them thinking, talking, note making, using imagination, and moving. They have to work with each other; they need to argue and discuss among themselves and realize the best and the worst in themselves and each other. The group process—discovering one another's ideas and problems—is vital. It is through this process that trust, understanding, and awareness are developed. Students learn from their natural interaction and confrontation of issues.

In drama it is not simply a matter of discussion. Learning the kind and quality of interaction comes through the nature of the material we employ, and this is why teachers need to pay special attention to ensure that there is always a strong core to the *matter* of the work. If, as Kenneth Tynan has suggested, good drama is concerned with people in, entering, or leaving a state of desperation, then we begin to see what we ought to be about.

Drama deals with conflict—human conflict within the individual, within the family, within the ccmmunity. But it is also up to the teacher of drama to examine with his students how the conflict arose, what factors led to the conflict, how might it have been prevented, and how that conflict might be resolved. It will not be easy to find good solutions, but it will be important always to analyze the situation so that understanding can result and the insight gained used to alleviate the problem.

What we in drama are creating is a laboratory in which there is control of simulated situation. These can be set up so as to involve certain conditions; they can be interpreted at any point so that examination can be carried out; they can be listened into, repeated, altered, or resynthesized as occasion or aims or exigencies require. More often than not, there are no right or wrong answers but only solutions, which are right in some cases for some people. It is through the laboratory control that students learn to express their ideas and opinions. They learn to test the consequences of different sets of action and reactions. It is not morals we are training so much as awareness of problems and the development of values. Then, too, each discovery can be questioned, challenged, and reexamined. A whole new set of circumstances can be explored when we discover some "truth" to be in the opposite point of view and we process the paradoxical nature of living.

"Acting" remains for some a dubious term. We really should not be afraid of it because it remains the most unified way of studying what after all is a unified existence. We interact with one another with body, mind, and voice and a reconstruction of this that seems an important way of understanding them. Of course there are times when we need to narrow the focus, but it is with the total being that we will generally best gain insight.

There is no need for us to become confused by "acting" just because we recognize that our students may never want to become professional actors. What we are concerned with is the acting phenomenon, the capacity to use imagination to re-create situations or sets of circumstances or other characters, or to develop other aspects of role that enable us both to discover more about ourselves and more about other people.

Because some people associate acting with the false or the showy, they sometimes tend to notice the assumption that all acting must contain these elements. It is up to the teacher to understand the art and his skill as a teacher is needed to exhort and encourage his students to develop, not those skills that are shallow or evasive, but the very acting skills that are as appropriate in life as on the stage—an interesting voice, a capacity to move dexterously, in fact those ten tools we spoke of at the outset.

So it can be seen that because drama affords great opportunities for the student, it presents the teacher with the greatest challenges. Drama must surely remain one of the toughest subjects to attempt to teach, since we *are* asking students to talk, we are asking them to move and interact. Imparting knowledge has its own particular skills, but being in charge of the drama laboratory means knowing how to structure and develop a situation, when to step back or out of it, how and when to intervene, how and when to encourage subjective involvement, and how and when to ask for objective analysis.

Because so many of these aspects of teaching seem to be essential intangibles, it may be helpful to set out some of the areas that can be identified and that may help clarify the needs which ought to be faced.

An environment: First, we need somewhere to work. The drama laboratory needs a space in which about thirty-five people can move about unhindered by conventional school furniture. It doesn't have to be elaborate or expensively equipped, but it does need to give a chance for several groups at once to be able to spread themselves.

It needs to be comparatively noise-free in the sense that the sounds from outside should not easily enter the room and the sounds from inside should not be likely to disturb others. Some people like to have curtains to draw, but my feeling is that we should not associate our work with the secret or the esoteric. If it belongs to life, it needs a sense of openness and honesty; if drawn curtains are needed to establish the initial confidence, we should work rapidly to draw them back again and emerge into the daylight once more.

Next, the drama laboratory *needs an atmosphere:* The atmosphere should be one of order and purposefulness, a sense of freedom that implies that everyone has accepted a personal responsibility. On the discovery level, the class need to know where they are going and have some idea of the problems needing to be solved. There is a recognized feeling of security in which insecurities can be openly explored. Within the overall confidence it has to be possible to take uncertain steps, to make mistakes, and to find negative results. On the teacher this makes heavy demands—the planning has to be detailed and clear enough so that departures from it can be made. The relationship needs to be a reasonable working one, not that based on arbitrary authoritarianism. The class is working for a discovery of the pattern and order within themselves and others, and this will best develop from a knowledge of teacher and class, rising from mutual affection and respect. Martin Graham's advice seems relevant here: Teach every class to make discoveries, have a structure but never dominate!

Drama *needs a purpose:* Many of the problems of discipline and interest are involved with the subject matter of the drama we teach. Stories and themes with human content are central to drama. If the teacher is in tune with the youngsters being taught, it is easier to find the significant theme or the apposite story. But even with a new class it is possible to choose material that will be relevant to the general needs and interests of a particular age group. Some material has the advantage that it can be appropriate on several levels, and this is the kind of subject matter that usually develops most absorbingly.

Because drama is concerned with people, the subject matter there more than anywhere else has to matter, or has to be something about which all can be concerned.

Sometimes to begin with a class, it may be appropriate to let the material arise from the group themselves, to take an issue that comes directly from their experience and turn it into drama. It is here that the teacher's skill will be required to extend and develop the ideas, dialogue, and sense of shape of the class. At the onset the drama may resemble the poorest of television, so it seems important not to leave things at this level for long. Questions designed to encourage thinking about motives and actions will often probe below the surface. I have seen simple bank-robbery action turned into more purposeful drama when the class are asked *why*. Why are these people planning the robbery? Why do they need the money? Why do they choose this way of getting it? Why?

Then other questions can be framed, designed to open up the central action. Who else is involved? What are the repercussions in their families: of the robbers? of the bank clerks? of the police? If successful, how will the robbers use the money? What will be the dangers, what the opportunities? If unsuccessful, what will be the results for the robbers? their families? the other people involved in the plot?

Once the opening-up process has begun it may also be useful to relate the imaginative drama to other sources. Students can be asked to test out their plot line or compare it with life itself. They might begin by talking to the local bank manager or inviting in a local policeman or detective. "What would happen if" questions from the student to this person will add a dimension to their understanding and awareness. Perhaps they are now more ready to observe and listen since they are really testing out their own endeavors and imaginative response against the factual background of the situation.

Similarly, too, the ideas of the students can be compared with reports of actual robberies in the newspapers. The popular press makes a useful start and then the students can be encouraged to seek fuller accounts in other newspapers.

By beginning with their work, it is possible to motivate students more readily in extending their reading and awareness. It seems to me that we need always to be concerned with finding ways of broadening the experience and understanding of the people we teach rather than simply expecting students to draw from themselves and their immediate resources, which is to pitch the drama at the lowest common level. We shall not see improvement in the work unless we, as teachers, deliberately set out to extend students' horizons.

Out of this kind of experience it is possible to broaden the material to other issues. Perhaps it is possible at the next stage to let the subject stimulus come from something similar spotted in one of the newspapers, or we can relate more immediately some topic of general interest to the class to an item reported in some detail in the press. Opportunities arise to make discoveries about different kinds and views of reporting. Students will readily point out how one account differs from another, what is left out of one report and what is included in another. They can at this stage be making discoveries about drama and realizing that it is less about abstract issues and more about individuals who become involved in these issues. On the other hand they can also discover that drama is not only about action but also about the motivations that underline actions, the circumstances that lead up to and the consequences resulting from actions. And so we return to the central issue: Drama deals with people relating to other people in three-dimensional, living situations.

Linked with these purposes is another: to extend the imaginative range of students. It was Caldwell Cook who first made me think seriously about ways of enlarging the points of reference for drama. Once students are beginning to appreciate the nature of drama, we should be looking for other ways of opening up and stimulating imagination. Caldwell Cook points out in his book *The Playway*, that we often ask our students to do what Shakespeare never did: invent the plot. Shakespeare drew his ideas from literature and adapted, modified, and reshaped them in the light of his own experience and the needs of the moment. If we follow his example, we can both find good stories for dramatizing and open up good literature to those we teach. It does seem important that it be *good* literature, for there we have human feelings and failings expressed in language that is generally much richer than that of everyday conversation. Language by and large is caught rather than taught. We absorb it as many other things in life, through imitation, so unless we are constantly introducing our students to these riches, expressions of the human mind that we find in literature, we should not be surprised that we remain frustrated by limited ideas and a narrow vocabulary.

One of our hardest tasks in drama is to develop the dialogue. Good dialogue contains so many qualities. Apart from the words used, the general vocabulary, there is the use of imagery (metaphor and simile), the structure of phrases and sentences, rhyme and pace. Then comes all the skill of relating it to characters and keeping it believable while still making it convey the information we require. Here again we can best help our students by letting them experience good drama. When our students find reading at sight difficult, we can take selected sections, compare different versions, or explore the plot through improvisation *before* looking at the text. We can set up our own recordings and play back the tape at the time of reading or use disc or radio when suitable programs are available.

None of this should ever deflect us from the overall purpose: to explore the human situation. The study of literature is there to help us in this purpose. It helps us in expressing it better, in shaping it more effectively, and in finding ways to stimulate the imagination to communicate it with greater interest.

Drama *needs a method*. It may be said that drama is a method overall. With the youngest children, drama may be hardly distinguishable from play, on the one hand, or a story acted through as it is narrated, on the other. Nor are these approaches mutually exclusive or even confined to the lower age range. Peter Weiss's approach to the persecution and assassination of Marat, as performed by the inmates of the asylum of Charenton under the direction of the Marquis de Sade, show how the simple device of dramatic storytelling may be operating on many levels. In the character of the Herald, there is a good example of the teacher role setting the scene, guiding the players where necessary, using the unexpected moments, and sensitively assisting in shaping the experience. The story is explored in song, movement and mime, and dialogue—everyone takes part—there is no type casting; on the contrary, roles are taken to help the development of the individuals, and there is a growing sense of the team. The story is not developed for listening's sake, but is explored for its relevance today and to those taking part. There is opportunity for sincere, thoughtful, and perceptive acting, but valuable experience is still possible if the response remains at a less skillful level. Rehearsal has taken place, but there is still room for spontaneity and individual response.

The more experience a group gains of the dramatic method, the more they are able to modify and extend their material and approach. In drama it is possible to employ group work so that every person has a chance to think and sift ideas and express them and coordinate with others. So, after the first exploration of a story or part of a story, much small-group work can take place, researching, experimenting, developing ideas and aspects of the drama. Gradually a class can become more aware of characterization, the shaping of a story, and ways of developing and expressing an idea in dramatic terms.

On other levels, other things will be happening: by-products of the method and material. The class will be learning to work together and to modify and use ideas of their own with those of other people. Confidence will be gained in talking and physical presence, and movement skills will develop in oral, kinetic, and emotional aspects of expression. None of this will be obvious at the time; none of this will necessarily be measurable or "objectively" assessable. But the teacher will be aware of the changes taking place, and the pupils will derive the pleasure of growing confidence and satisfaction in rising standards and deepening understanding.

In drama the teacher and the child, though concerned with fundamentals of human growth and understanding, rarely find the conditions desirable within the present framework. Here are three examples of student teachers working under less than ideal situations but still achieving something and discovering for themselves and for others that it is possible to make some impression even within a system that is well out of date and suspicious of the work they are doing.

The first student teacher is working in a boys' secondary school at the outskirts of a small town. The school is winding down and the premises, though newly painted, are antiquated. He is working with a class of school leavers, who some time ago lost interest and whom the rest of the staff consider a difficult form: "If you can make anything of 4A, you can tackle anything," they say. The student teacher chose a scheme on the topic of freedom. The space available is a small classroom with desks and chairs. The topic chosen was a good one in helping to establish the necessary atmosphere because, though the boys resisted much of the early work prepared, the material asked them to consider in a variety of ways the meaning and nature of freedom and responsibility. The lads responded best in groups, and so the student teacher let this aspect of the work develop and within his framework of ideas, after the third week gave them the freedom, in groups, each to choose their own topics, and encouraged them to prepare for short dramatic reports. They chose topics ranging from sailing to fashion, and at last their absorption grew. In the groups they found a capacity to work independently. By the end of the project they had not produced any profound drama, nor even developed the knowledge of their chosen themes very far, but they had learned to work together and to communicate with each other more easily, and they were beginning to learn how to select and shape their ideas in the process of communicating with others.

In another school, not far from the last one, a student teacher was working with a class of twelve-year-old girls, about half of whose parents were from Pakistan or India. The student teacher had chosen to work on the theme of Noah and the Flood, and the class had the curtained-off stage on which to work. There was a Noah from Pakistan attempting to win the cooperation of a very mixed family and neighbors. These girls were attempting to develop the dramatic side of their story and were gaining insight in the process into community organization and the give and take of group life. Several girls were extending their vocabulary range and discovering the value of each other's point of view. There was a growing absorption and a developing desire to achieve something. Two girls had escaped the teacher's notice, and toward the end of the lesson they lost their link with the others and spent the last ten minutes writing all over the blackboard "Miss [the teacher's name] is Fab!" There was a good working atmosphere.

Some distance away, in another school, another teacher was exploring aspects of Lord of the Flies with a group of fourth-year students. The space was small but free of desks. The lesson was clearly structured and began with some discussion in which all were able to remind themselves of the work done in previous lessons. Then the section of the novel reached was divided into short scenes, and the class began to work on these in small groups. Everyone worked purposefully and organized action and dialogue among themselves. The teacher went around to the groups helping over any difficulties and stimulating more perceptive and concentrated involvement. Then the class came together again in order to share the incident they had been working on with others. Out of each scene a host of points were raised, not about the way the scene was done, but about the issues that were underlying the human action of the characters. The class could relate these moments to what they knew of the rest of the story and themselves, and so gain understanding and expression of the novel as a whole.

One might go on with other examples indicating different material, goals, purposes, and circumstances, but these three at least hint at the way that theory moves into practice. Education is in a flux again about how much to give the children and how much to leave it to them. It still seems to be important that the teacher have a clear knowledge of the charted areas of a "subject" so that at least he can point out the chances of surprise, delight, and reward around the corner or over the hill.

Drama used in schools opens up a wide range of opportunities. Still too often thought of as an extra, as the core drama could revitalize and give a great deal of the other school work greater interest and significance. The drama teacher has a chance to work alongside young people in such a way as to contact and get to know them personally—drama demands a total involvement and can draw upon heart and body as well as head. Teaching drama offers incredible opportunities for a structured but open approach because we are working with people in human terms and situations. We cannot measure off progress easily, so we do not formally need to test it. This gives us greater freedom, but it also demands greater skills in the development of teaching approaches.

Using drama in school involves the teacher having a very positive educational philosophy because there is so much feedback and immediacy in the approach. Experience of some of the problems and difficulties can be externalized and sifted. Learning needs to be impressive and vivid if it is to be retained for long, and it needs to be reinforced by practice and rehearsal. Drama is a useful means to both ends. Drama is also useful in setting up situations for language learning. After all, it is in the group that most of us acquire our natural tongue and extend vocabulary. Does it not seem sensible that a second language could be approached in a similar (if perhaps more scientific) way?

In approaching history, geography, myth, religion, or any area of the curriculum where there are human elements, the dramatic method can help both in investigating and researching the material and in unifying it toward an end product—whether that product is thought of as a showing, a presentation, or a production. So many attitudes in education have ground down to a hardened, inflexible routine. Using drama will help sharpen awareness, sympathy, and understanding.

Index

247

Peter
office: 920-1555
restaurant: 925-5466
home: